The Human Costs of Managerialism

The Human Costs of Managerialism

Advocating the Recovery of Humanity

Edited by Stuart Rees
and Gordon Rodley

Pluto Press Australia

First published in October 1995 by
Pluto Press Australia Limited
PO Box 199, Leichhardt, NSW 2040

Copyright © The Contributors 1995

Cover design by Johnny Bruce

Index by Neale Towart

Printed and bound by Southwood Press, 80 Chapel Street,
Marrickville, NSW 2204

Australian Cataloguing in Publication Data

The Human Costs of Managerialism — Advocating the Recovery of Humanity

Bibliography.
Includes index.
ISBN 1 86403 012 7.

1. Management — Social Aspects. 2. Public Administration — Australia.
3. Capitalism — Social Aspects. 4. Organisational Change — Social Aspects.
I. Rees Stuart. II. Rodley, Gordon.

658.408

Contents

List of Poems and Cartoons	vi
List of Figures	vii
Acknowledgments	viii
Introduction	1
I Marks of Managerialism	**9**
1. The Fraud and the Fiction *Stuart Rees*	15
2. The Complicity of Think-Tanks *Ted Wheelwright*	29
3. The Rise of the Generic Manager *Brian Easton*	39
II Means of Asserting Control	**49**
4. Managing Labour in the 1990s *John Buchanan*	55
5. Market Control of the Media *Wendy Bacon*	69
6. Gender Control of Agendas *Meredith Burgmann*	85
7. Contrived Control of Budgets *Michael Muetzelfeldt*	95
III Undermining the Public Sector	**107**
8. Management of Higher Education Policy *Jane Marceau*	111
9. Managerialised Health Care *Alan Davis*	121
10. Managerialising Local Government *Stephen Albin*	137
11. Jeff Kennett's Anti-Government *Mike Salvaris*	145
12. New Mandarins New Zealand Style *Grant Duncan*	159
IV Counting Human Costs	**169**
13. Dismantling Child Welfare *Gary Hough*	173
14. Human Costs: A View From Within *Col Face*	183
15. Greed and Bullying *Stuart Rees*	197
16. The Cost of Efficiency *Karin Solondz*	211
17. Some Health Costs of Managerialism *Susan Britton*	221
Transition	**229**
V Recovering Humanity	**237**
18. Picturing Contemporary Management *Craig Bremner*	243
19. Promoting the Sporting Ethic *Gordon Rodley*	249
20. Reworking Australia *Frank Stilwell*	261
21. Rediscovering the Common Good *Robert Simons*	271
22. Defining and Attaining Humanity *Stuart Rees*	285
Postscript	301
Bibliography	307
Contributors	313
The Poets	317
Index	319

List of Figures

1. Context of Contrasting Themes — 2
2. Context of Managerialism — 5
3. Emphases for Recovery of Humanity — 232
4. Australia's Unemployment Rate — 264

List of Poems and Cartoons

Poems

Spirit of the Age *Michael Brennan*	11
Free Trade *Stuart Rees*	12
Intruder *Susan Bower*	51
News of the Day *Annette Falahey*	52
Crown *Susan Bower*	109
Downward/Onward/Upward *Henry S. Maas*	110
Barking at the Thunder *Les Murray*	171
Humanity *William Wordsworth*	171
All One Race *Oodgeroo Noonucaal*	239
Equanimity *Les Murray*	240
The Welder *Stuart Rees*	241
Delight in Enlightenment *Henry S. Maas*	242
Moon Beams *Vivienne Sinclair*	304

Cartoons

The Economy *Michael Leunig*	13
Level Playing Field *Vicki Saffron*	14
Competition is Good *Cathy Wilcox*	14
All Across the Nation *Michael Leunig*	53
Total Quality Control *Vicki Saffron*	54
Doonesbury *Garry Trudeau*	100
Modern Work Practices *Vicki Saffron*	110
The Economy Says *Michael Leunig*	152
Stakeholder and Team *Vicki Saffron*	172
Continuous Improvement *Vicki Saffron*	191
Greed *Cathy Wilcox*	203
A Fairly Typical Discussion *Michael Leunig*	242

Editor's Preface to the Second Printing

The extensive response to the first edition of this book confirms the institutional and occupational violence being perpetrated by managerialism.

Numerous letters and respondents to radio talk-back shows have revealed the seriousness of the current situation. The obsession with inflicting lean structures on everything is leaving a tide of human destructiveness in its wake. The quality of life of millions of people is being affected by destructive policies and by managers who are encouraging us to think it is a sign of strength to be tough and to promise only more of the same.

But a growing awareness of the level of fraud and deception involved in the 'do more with less' policies is empowering. No longer do individuals have to feel that they are at fault. Collectively we can confront and resist the folly being inflicted on us.

Gratitude expressed in correspondence reflects not only readers feelings that their observations have been confirmed but also that what is at stake and what is required is indeed *the recovery of humanity*.

We thank those who have written and conveyed their experience to us. In contributing to the ongoing debate you have also encouraged us to explore further lines of enquiry.

Acknowledgments

A book which is a compilation of work from different disciplines and various walks of life depends on the support and expertise of many people. At the hub of this project were colleagues from the University of Sydney's Centre for Peace and Conflict Studies and the Department of Social Work and Social Policy. We received generous staff support and other resources from that department, such as the typing and word-processing skills of Nicki Polykarpou and Charlie Reimer. For assistance with organising the initial managerialism forum and subsequent administrative tasks such as maintaining contact with contributors and proofreading we are grateful to Jeanne Leppard and Suzanne Brownhill.

On specific issues including the reproduction of case studies we received valuable advice and information from Liz de Rome, Frances Milne and Cheryl Minx. Michael Howard from the University of New South Wales Public Sector Research Centre was generous in sharing his data on the use of management consultants. From Massey University, Albany, New Zealand, Grant Duncan wishes to acknowledge the help of Shea Nisbet and Lary Mitchell. In our respective homes the support of Ragnhild and Margaret — or rather their patience with our preoccupation with chasing contributors and meeting deadlines — was a very significant contribution to this work. We acknowledge the expertise of our artist friend Johnny Bruce who immediately rejected our ideas for a cover for this book and relied instead on his own judgment and skills.

Every effort has been made to identify the source of quoted material and where necessary we have sought permission to reproduce poems and works of art. We acknowledge Jacaranda Press and Queensland University Press for Oodgeroo Noonucaal's 'All One Race'; *Quadrant* for Stuart Rees's 'The Welder'; *Adelaide Review*, *Sydney Review* and Oxford University Press for extracts from Les Murray's poems 'Barking at the Thunder' and 'Equanimity'; and Henry S. Maas for the reproduction of poems from the anthology *Tide Pools & Swoosh Holes*. Universal Press Syndicate granted us permission to reproduce the Garry Trudeau cartoon. For the use of their previously published cartoons, we also received generous cooperation from Michael Leunig and Cathy Wilcox. The National Aeronautics and Space Administration (NASA) gave us permission to reproduce from their colour slides of 'Earth Rise From the Moon'. We also acknowledge the picture of Uluru from Robert Brennan of Bobby Dazzler Tours, and Vera Wilson's painting, *Warrilyi Dreaming*.

Stuart Rees
Gordon Rodley

Introduction

On 10 November 1994 the University of Sydney's Centre for Peace and Conflict Studies organised an evening's forum to 'identify the human costs of managerialism and to consider the recovery of the principles of humanity'. On the day of the forum several Australia-wide radio stations devoted discussion and phone-in programs to questions about managerialism. In each program a somewhat incredulous compere began by asking: 'What has this issue got to do with peace?'.

Peace implies conviviality, a situation in which people live and work in atmospheres of mutually respectful and creative relationship. By contrast, the suppression of employees' potential within an organisation — even if such suppression is exerted by indirect means — has much in common with more overt forms of violence. On the radio programs listeners responded by saying, 'Yes, we understand what you mean, here is an example'. This book conveys and elaborates this public response.

To focus on the attainment of peace is to identify the direct and indirect means of violence to coerce others, whether the 'others' be children and women at home, citizens on the streets, employees in different work sites, or national and international conflicts which lead to war. In each of those contexts a powerful person or group (usually men) exercises power in a destructive and coercive manner which causes psychological, social or physical harm. These destructive ways of organising and behaving are the common denominators linking violence in apparently different contexts. In this respect the study of management practices, albeit clearly linked to particular economic policies, is as fit a focus for the study of peace with justice as the results of more visible coercive and violent practices.

2　THE HUMAN COSTS OF MANAGERIALISM

Figure 1: Context of Contrasting Themes

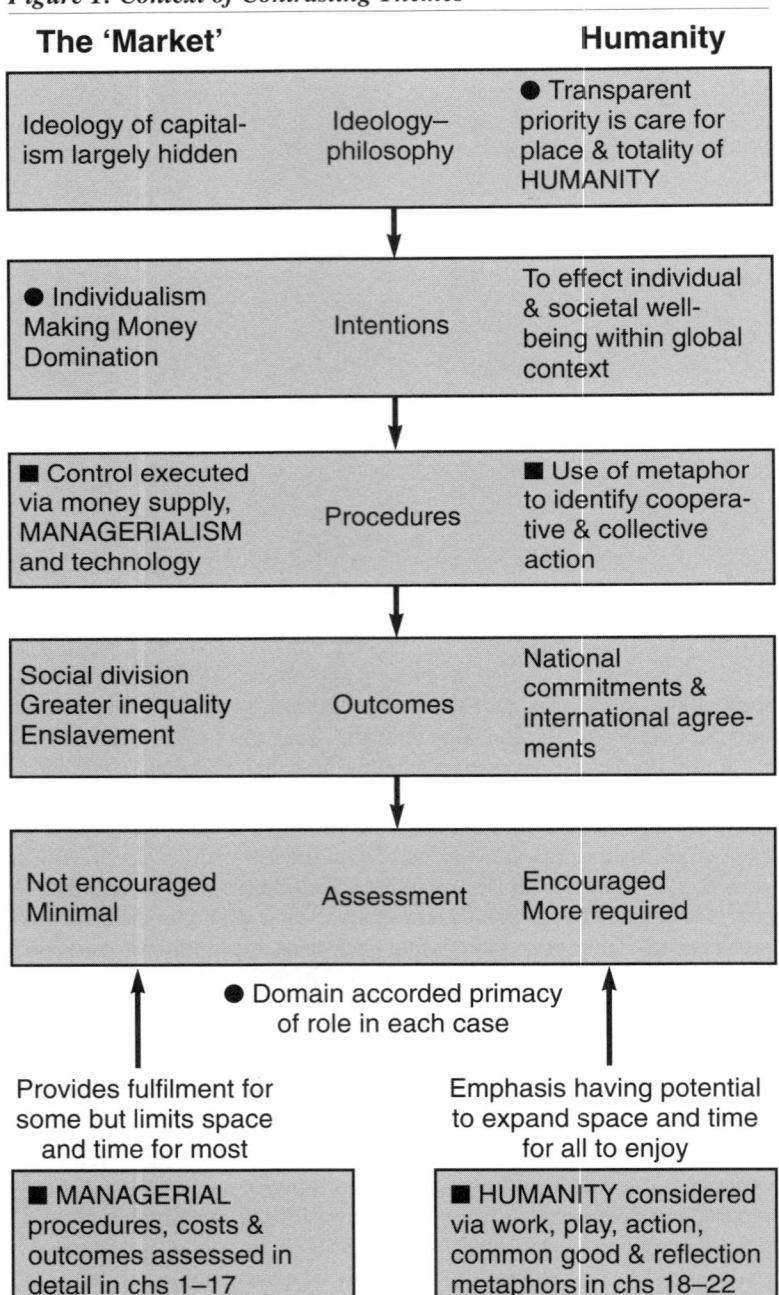

The 'Market'		Humanity
Ideology of capitalism largely hidden	Ideology–philosophy	● Transparent priority is care for place & totality of HUMANITY
● Individualism Making Money Domination	Intentions	To effect individual & societal well-being within global context
■ Control executed via money supply, MANAGERIALISM and technology	Procedures	■ Use of metaphor to identify cooperative & collective action
Social division Greater inequality Enslavement	Outcomes	National commitments & international agreements
Not encouraged Minimal	Assessment	Encouraged More required

● Domain accorded primacy of role in each case

Provides fulfilment for some but limits space and time for most	Emphasis having potential to expand space and time for all to enjoy
■ MANAGERIAL procedures, costs & outcomes assessed in detail in chs 1–17	■ HUMANITY considered via work, play, action, common good & reflection metaphors in chs 18–22

Themes

This book is a sequel to a 1993 Centre for Peace and Conflict Studies publication: *Beyond the Market: Alternatives to Economic Rationalism*. It amplifies this book's concern with the social impact of economic rationalist policies which can be recognised by their deference to deregulation and privatisation and by the immense human costs which they have exacted on disadvantaged communities locally and throughout the world. The spectre of worldwide conflicts and gross violations of human rights derives largely from the disruptive impacts of capitalist exploitation and unconscionable trading in arms.

Managerialism facilitates the destructiveness of market-based economic policies and controls. In different contexts managers have become the means of carrying out the imperatives of financial accountability and cost effectiveness. Our inquiry into 'management', as a means of solving almost anything, provides tangible insights into profound and widespread philosophical changes about the conduct of work and the treatment of human beings. We now find the unsavoury face of capitalism hiding behind the mask of an apparently benign and eminently rational guise of 'efficiency'. Armies of managers are on the march blazing a trail ... but to where? In the euphoria about management, few have paused to ask what is being achieved and where we are heading. This book presents an interim report. It is not reassuring. In collating the chapters on the human costs of managerialism we have been taken aback by the extent of damage being wrought on societies' infrastructures and on individuals' lives.

In searching for a modus operandi which may empower individuals and societies and counter current human and environmental destructiveness we appeal to principles of humanity. This book consequently presents contrasting themes (figure 1).

The managerialist theme, as implied and portrayed in figure 1, is embedded in prescriptive doctrines of the market. This fundamentalist market practice leaves politicians, professionals and the general public in a state of confusion. On the one hand we are to swallow the latest claims that untold benefits will emerge if we participate in a competition to treat everyone and everything as a commodity for sale or purchase. On the other, the increasing evidence of the human and environmental costs of such practices suggests that we should pause, reflect and stick some warning labels on this latest managerial medicine.

In addition to the primary themes contrasted in figure 1, threads of other kinds weave through the chapters of this book. Control and authoritarianism is a theme most evident in the descriptions of how allegedly inefficient workers are identified: in The Cost of Efficiency (ch. 16); in an account of Greed and Bullying (ch. 15); and in numerous references to the intolerance of critics, whether in state welfare agencies in Victoria and in New South Wales (chs 13 and 14), in the management of labour by excluding workers and trade unions from decision-making (ch. 4), or in the avalanche of evidence about Premier Jeff Kennett's authoritarian attitudes and policies in Victoria (ch. 11). Such concern with control is also a distinguishing feature of the generic managers who need to know nothing in detail about that which they are to manage because their mission is to be 'corporate' and ensure the compliance of professionals to a new business ethic (chs 3 and 7). Well-organised forces to marshal and sustain this control are described in a historical overview of the rise of right-wing think-tanks (ch. 2) and in an analysis of advertisers' influence on the media (ch. 5) which shows 'how information, questions and ideas are foreclosed and thus limit the capacity to cover the major issues of the day'.

Deceit and demoralisation are interrelated themes. Deceit is apparent in a series of false claims which management makes about the relevance of the profit motive to the conduct of public sector organisations — the Fraud and the Fiction (ch. 1) and all the issues addressed in the chapters in Part III on Undermining the Public Sector — and in claims about equity even when management leaders seem preoccupied with massive financial gains. Demoralisation occurs because numerous workers — professionals and non-professionals — know of the deceitful claims being made while, all around them, in the media, within government and in public sector bureaucracies, they experience the managerialist fundamentalism being preached and implemented. Demoralisation is almost inevitable when people feel they are powerless to challenge official dogma or they lose their jobs or suffer ill-health. It is also likely if no alternative philosophy and strategies are being articulated.

Readers will find other talking points within the thematic structure adopted in figure 1. Managerialism is identified as the inevitable outcome of capitalist ideologies which have international as well as local consequences. Links between economic policies, managerial practices and the consequences for environmental and human well-being are elaborated in figure 2. The influences and processes depicted in that diagram cover the topics organised into the first four parts (I–IV), under the headings Marks of Managerialism (chs 1–3), Means of Asserting Control (chs 4–7), Undermining the Public Sector (chs 8–12) and Counting Human Costs (chs 13–17).

The contrasting theme of Recovering Humanity (Part V, chs 18–22) is intended to raise hopes and address the sense of powerlessness and demoralisation. It is not presented as an alternative schema but as a series of ideas, examples and principles to confront a range of inhumanities, from massacres in Rwanda to bullying at work, from increasing social and economic inequality to dismissal of workers and management's response that such processes are inevitable.

INTRODUCTION 5

Figure 2: Context of Managerialism

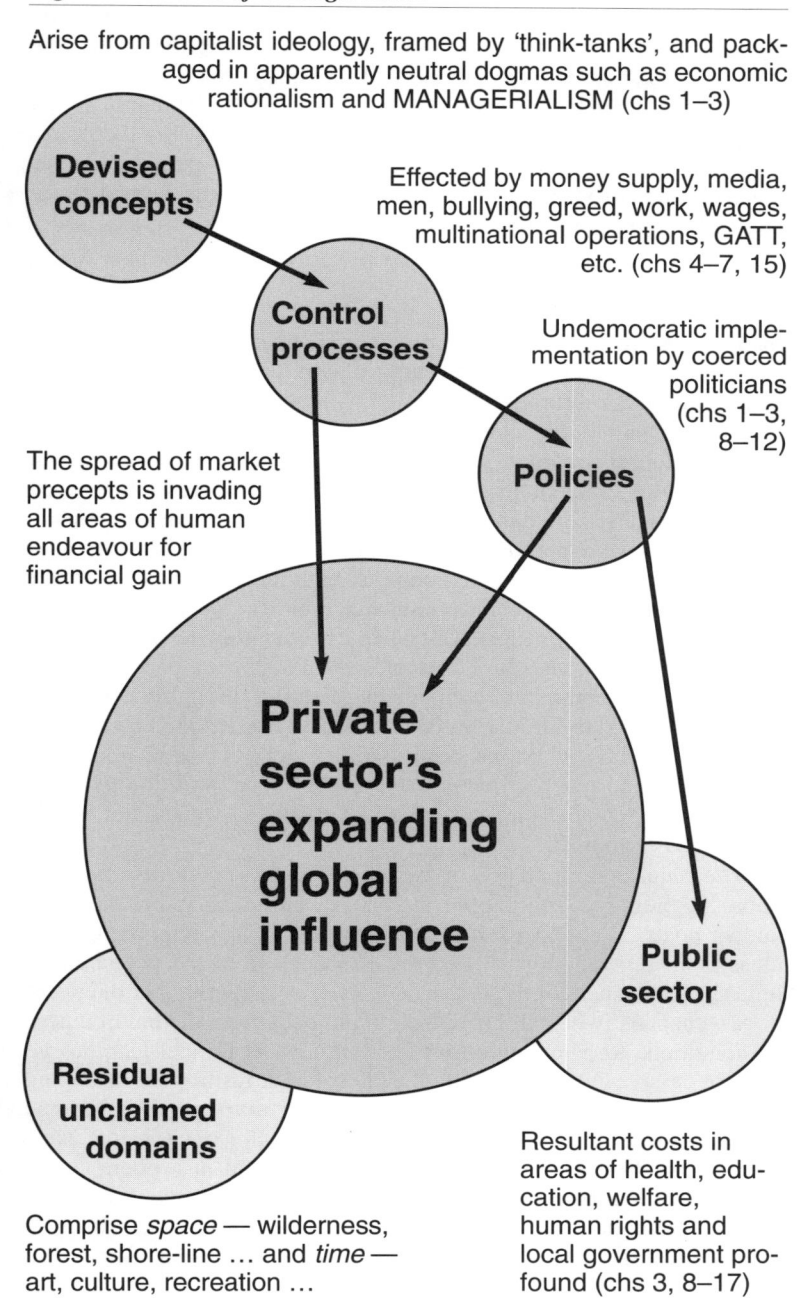

Arise from capitalist ideology, framed by 'think-tanks', and packaged in apparently neutral dogmas such as economic rationalism and MANAGERIALISM (chs 1–3)

Devised concepts

Effected by money supply, media, men, bullying, greed, work, wages, multinational operations, GATT, etc. (chs 4–7, 15)

Control processes

Undemocratic implementation by coerced politicians (chs 1–3, 8–12)

Policies

The spread of market precepts is invading all areas of human endeavour for financial gain

Private sector's expanding global influence

Public sector

Residual unclaimed domains

Comprise *space* — wilderness, forest, shore-line … and *time* — art, culture, recreation …

Resultant costs in areas of health, education, welfare, human rights and local government profound (chs 3, 8–17)

The optimism in this concluding section is derived from an assumption that the sensible use of modern technology — as opposed to managerialism's uncritical introduction of it — together with wisdom from the past and the vibrancy of understanding about the fragile and diminishing riches of the earth could still realise a better world for all. The debate and reflection provoked by this book and the realisation of our embedment in the marvel of space–time existence should also contribute to the attainment of the humanitarian goals of peace with justice.

Poetry and cartoons

Insights into the human costs of managerialism and pictures of alternative aspirations are not the preserve of any one group of critics or commentators, researchers or artists. Successful advocacy of 'the recovery of humanity' requires a searching for sources of inspiration from multiple disciplines, generations and cultures. That is why this book includes cartoons to satirise some of the cruelties and absurdities of managerialism, and poems to convey different connotations of humanity. These added dimensions derive from the creative energies of interdisciplinary insight, and contrast with that uncritical deference to disciplines which have nurtured managerialism.

With humour and insight Australian cartoonists have exposed worship of the market and the effect of such worship on people's lives. Their trenchant comment continues in Australia through the work of artists such as Alan Moir, who contributed to *Beyond the Market*, and those others whose work has been used in this book. As with some of the chapters and poems, we embrace the 'amateur' tradition by using the skilful work of someone — Vicki Saffron — who is not yet an established cartoonist.

The status and reputation of the poets who have contributed to this book, including young people making a beginning and some well-known poets, is not an issue except in so far as it is important to tap ideas from several sources. Figures of speech from the poems highlight the seriousness of the issues addressed by the writers of the twenty-two chapters, who call for reflection on the human and environmental condition. An alternative to reflection is to let critical faculties go rusty in passive compliance with the latest fad or fashion for managing or marketing people, information and entertainment. Les Murray writes that outside of being 'just human, things all slope towards war'. Almost two hundred years before Les's lines and in a poem called 'Humanity', William Wordsworth was warning against uncritical worship of a false idol, 'the Wealth Of Nations'. He mused that in the middle of industrial capitalism's 'dizzy wheels ... The Power least prized is that which thinks and feels'.

Contributors and their evidence

The contributors of the twenty-two chapters come from a variety of disciplines, including sociology and chemistry, social work and social planning, economics and psychology, journalism and medicine, theology and social policy, politics, history, and industrial relations. That range of writers examines managerialism and its human costs from a variety of perspectives and with references to different policies and contexts such as tertiary education, child welfare, health care, local government, finance, the organisation of sport, the management of factories and bureaucracies, science research institutes and the media.

The writers come from two Australian states, New South Wales and Victoria, with two contributors from New Zealand. While the evidence they marshal focuses primarily on regional developments, a wealth of evidence shows the managerialist ideologies and consequences to be worldwide. Particular chapters give detailed illustrations of consequences of managerialist practices in the UK and in North America as well as in the Antipodes.

Some of the writers are reporting on their own research. Others rely on primary sources, on the depth of scholarship from other researchers or on examples culled from journals and newspapers. Most chapters provide detailed references yielding an extensive bibliography by which these issues can be pursued.

A few writers give personal views and take a risk in so doing. One author — who writes on managerialism within the Department of Community Services in New South Wales — has had to use a fictitious name. With good justification the writer fears victimisation if it was discovered who was unmasking practices which have been going unreported for years. While the evidence provided and the need to conceal identity underlines the 'control and authoritarianism' theme, this courageous act of writing restores an element of humanity.

This contribution, in alliance with others, portrays loveless and punitive practices. All the contributors advocate values, strategies and language which address needs for personal security and social recognition, 'nurturing, building and sharing'. The alternative is to accept more of the same economic rationalist and managerialist creed, an approach which may satisfy those who simply find it difficult to identify the monolithic and harmful economic and bureaucratic trends of the last decade of the twentieth century. By contrast, if the humanitarian principles advocated in this book are realised, people will question the official wisdom of the day and will achieve a shared understanding with others to give added purpose and pleasure to their lives. The challenging of managerialist dogma and the recovery of humanity is a global cause.

Part I

Marks of Managerialism

Spirit of the Age

Night lures the lost souls from the closed comfort of sleep,
to this strange meeting place of darkness and solitude.

At the Gap (of tried and true method), the light moves
on the water below with all the strangeness of a human mind.

A horizon, once laid down to distinguish earth and sky,
light and dark, dissolves into the phosphorescent Zeitgeist.

Day is exhumed by the cold neon of the fair lady Sydney,
who, stretched out, pants with the water's soft manipulations.

In an overwrought Punch and Judy show, pallid day laughs sadly.
Pathos no longer remains to redeem these crazed antics

and the only sound to escape the metallic hum, to sound out true,
is the subdued muttering of those estranged by this violent sport.

Within our concrete heaven, we move along the edged lines
of a circuit, rarely allowed to connect with one another

nor to touch the source so long lost to routed spirits.
Touched by the moon aloft, our ghosts play below.

All else has been reduced, all life reproduced in binary,
the child and the saint pour the oceans into a cup

on a foreign shore, and eventually all life fits the formula.

Michael Brennan

Free Trade

In multi-nationals' interests
a game is finalized
by insiders' rules
applauded by savants
whose creed this has always been

I am an African father
pleading for work in a country
choked by two-crops-only conditions
for the repayment of debts
sold by talk of level playing fields

I am an Asian mother,
my possessions swamped
by the world's rivers,
my children dying
in free trade zones

I am your average newspaper reader
with acronym confusion,
the GATT and NAFTA deals
for hamburger chains
to obliterate old skills and tastes

We are Mr. & Mrs. modest mortgage
blinded by balance sheets
mystified by growth
prescribed for our interests
by only a few players

Stuart Rees

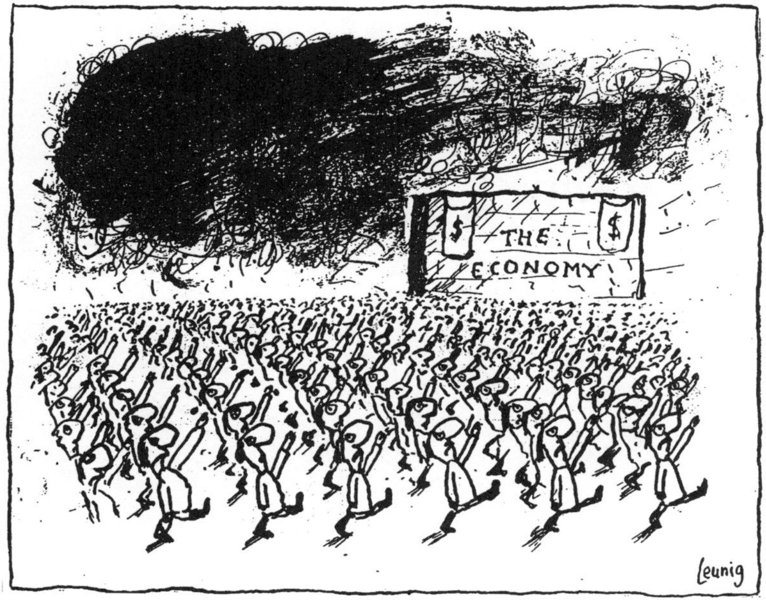
$
THE ECONOMY
$
Leunig

LEVEL PLAYING FIELD

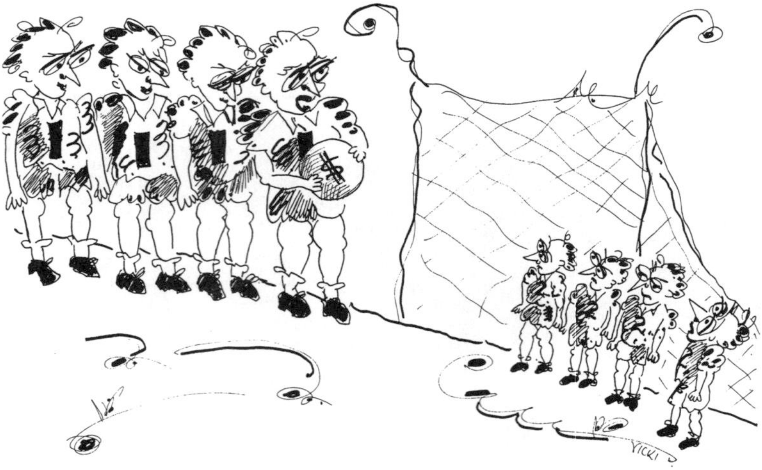

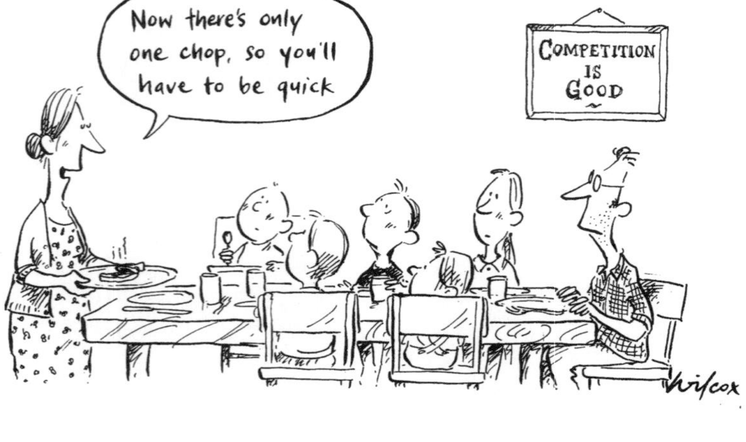

1.
The Fraud and the Fiction

Stuart Rees

Managerialism is an ideology with two distinct claims: a. efficient management can solve almost any problem; b. practices which are appropriate for the conduct of private sector enterprises can also be applied to public sector services.

However dominant, the claims are fraudulent. Managerialism turns out to be a fiction, but a serious and persistent one because of the widespread fascination with theories of management and the status of managers.

This chapter examines the rise of managerialism, examines some of the human costs, makes the case about 'the moral fiction', and anticipates some alternatives to managerialism. A separate chapter (ch. 15) — on bullying and greed — discusses managerialist goals and the means by which they are achieved.

The economic rationalist backdrop

Managerialism is not divorced from social and economic policies nor is it a set of neutral and scientific techniques uncontaminated by politics and struggles for power.

Economic policies have nurtured the ideology of managerialism and the rise of managers who advocate its precepts. More specifically, it is the policies of economic rationalism which the new breeds of managers are employed to implement even if they only comprehend those policies in terms of clichés and prescriptions: cut back on the responsibilities of government and rely on market forces; introduce private competition to public sector services; promote independence as a means of ridiculing the welfare state; and question the existence of 'society' (Pusey 1991; Vintila, Phillimore & Newman 1992; Rees, Rodley & Stilwell 1993).

Details of these economic rationalist policies can be perceived in Anglo–American cultures where governments deregulated finance, privatised public assets, lowered taxes (in particular to business corporations) and made substantial cutbacks on public services (Marquand 1988; Emy 1993; Rees 1994). To achieve these policies a metaphor and a precedent were needed. The image of a strong person taking tough decisions provided the metaphor. An image of lean and mean corporations provided the precedent.

There was no shortage of managers who were willing to give substance to these images. They were being trained in their thousands, or were already waiting in the wings for the call to demonstrate their toughness and efficiency, their willingness to disparage old professional practices and traditions in the interests of a new corporatism. In Australia, support for these policies came from a loose coalition of influential elites, including bureaucrats in the Federal Treasury and Industries Commission, politicians, and representatives of the media and the business world. Each promoted their version of adaptive modernisation to take Australia into the twenty-first century (Pusey 1991; Emy 1993).

Managers are not neutral technocrats. They derive their cues and their scripts from a set of policies which contend that an economy needs to be run like a market with as little interference as possible, that human effort can be counted a commodity, and that in the conduct of organisations financial accountability is the criterion to measure performance. But why would the practice of management be consistent with these economic policies? In terms of size and influence, where did the managerialist dogma come from?

The rise of managerialism

In the management studies section of any academic bookshop there is a range of heavy hardbacks. Titles vary slightly. The contents address twin themes: how to manage people and organisations efficiently. A massive educational and publishing industry presents management efficiency as rational and scientific. It responds to and helps to promote degrees and diplomas in management, as though the English-speaking world can be blanketed by one set of objectives — the maximising of productivity and profit — and one means of obtaining those objectives: efficient management. Associated with this promotion and educational expansion is a corporate language and accompanying attitudes. These are the outcomes of preoccupation with management as the panacea for governments and organisations. How did this happen?

In a careful analysis Pollitt (1993) traces the development of management thought from the beginnings of industrialisation and the need to control large work forces, to the promotion of the managerialist ideology that whatever means are appropriate for commercial activity can be transferred to public sector services. He identifies major texts as reflecting the changing emphases of management thought: from the power of positive thinking (Perrow 1979) and the principles and methods of scientific management (Taylor 1911) to the human relations emphasis on informal as well as formal relationships (Mayo 1933); from the decisions and systems phase after the Second World War (Simon 1947) to the all-inclusive claims of 'culture management' with its emphasis on changing the culture of an organisation by paying attention to language, symbolism and ritual (Peters & Waterman 1982).

If one school of thought has been a thread to link the others, it is Taylorism with its claims that management can be a true science and that such 'science' can be universally applied. Even though other schools appear to humanise the conduct of management, the Taylorist emphasis on control and efficiency in the interests of an organisation and of a country has survived as an essential piece of management wisdom. It is popular with politicians who want to be seen as strong managers, even though Taylorism as such may be regarded as unacceptable.

The claim to moral neutrality and scientific objectivity suits an age in which economy has come to be regarded as more important than society and in which a brand of economics has claimed scientific qualities. If the priority criteria for assessing quality of life and the performance of bureaucracies are economic, a technique which single-mindedly applies such criteria can be seen as indispensible. That technique is management, presented as a symbol of authority, order and control, the powerful means of improving the performance of anything that the energetic manager touches.

As economic policies have changed to complement the competitive attributes and alleged successes of large business corporations, so the national and international fascination with management has gained momentum. Not only has management been defined as a distinct function within organisations, but the values of managerialism have been promoted as universal: management is inherently good, managers are the heroes, managers should be given room and autonomy to manage, and other groups should accept their authority (Pollitt 1993).

In private corporations and in public sector services there are numerous examples of assumptions about the universal value of management. These range from the idea that management is a tool box enabling people to make their way in the world (Alford 1991) to the 1980s Australian policy that public servants should be managers, that a public sector is not about the delivery of public services but about the management of scarce resources (Yeatman 1991).

An example of a belief that management knowledge and skills transcend other areas of expertise occurred in the 1995 search for a new managing director of the Australian Broadcasting Corporation (ABC). Although many commentators said that the ABC needed someone with a record of creativity in broadcasting who would also be a visionary, Phillip Adams (the broadcaster and critic) reported that the managerial headhunters for the director's position told applicants that 'a background in broadcasting is not necessarily a disadvantage'. In Adams's view the phantom in the minds of the headhunters was 'management, management, management'.

Management education and training

Fascination with management has contributed to an education apparently more concerned with profit-based techniques than with ideas and debates. Even if claims about managerial effectiveness turn out to be the cultural confidence trick of the age, corrupted universities are only too pleased to feed into and grow fat on these claims.

Since the Second World War schools of business management have been among the fastest growing divisions in American universities (Locke 1989). The reputation of the qualification Master of Business Administration (MBA) Harvard has produced a worldwide desire to imitate, even though management training is not confined to the MBA degree. Training in commerce, law, accountancy and branches of public administration feed into and from the management stem.

In Australia, between 1981 and 1990, graduates in what the Australian Bureau of Statistics loosely terms 'business administration' more than doubled. The only category of students to show a larger increase was 'health' but that figure was distorted by the training of nurses being transferred from hospitals to universities. Between 1987 and 1991 the average increase in student numbers across all categories of graduates was 35.8 per cent, while the increase in numbers studying business management was 55 per cent.

Enrolment of overseas students in Australia shows an even greater fascination with business management. By 1990, 27.7 per cent of all degrees awarded to overseas students were in that subject area. These outnumbered the next highest categories by 2:1. In 1991 the overseas students enrolled in business constituted 38.5 per cent of all overseas enrolments and outnumbered the next highest category, science, by 2.4:1.

The figures do not indicate whether people in managerial positions have ever been trained in any form of management. But the trends give some idea of the popularity of management education and training. Indications of such popularity include a rise in the number of management courses, including short duration workshops, and an increase in the numbers of students studying various forms of management.

It is one thing to highlight the Harvard MBA as a metaphor which influences the aspirations of hundreds of thousands of politicians, educators and students; it is another to read the newspaper advertisements for part-time training in workshops which offer existing and prospective managers a variety of outcomes: 'total quality', 'leadership success', 'greater personal productivity'. The elixir of management, a cultural phenomenon, is rolling along.

The emergence of management consultants and companies and an almost uncritical reliance on their prescriptions is another indication of the prominence and promotion of managerial precepts within organisations. Management consultant companies are visible not only in the high-rise buildings of central business districts but as evaluators of companies and government departments, of research and welfare agencies, of hospitals and universities.

Representatives of the media — themselves subject to management review or the threat of one — have colluded with the language and values of managerialism. They report clichés about efficiency and productivity, the need to reduce labour costs and to have stronger management. They defer to management prescriptions. In their repetition they become advocates who fail to hear alternative critiques.

Some human costs

If no reference is made to human costs — the loss of morale and jobs and lives at stake — it might be possible to sustain managers' claims that they are effective. But a human costs perspective exposes the fiction that management practices are beneficial. This issue can be examined with reference to the managerial rallying cry of 'doing more with less' and to a brief case study of CSIRO. Other aspects of human costs are detailed in chapter 15 on bullying and greed.

More with less

In Australia the political and cultural context is fertile for the 'more with less' prescription. That context is characterised by unemployment, by the promotion of American corporate values and by an image of successful business corporations. Against a background of unemployment, management can demand the introduction of enterprise bargaining, less security and longer hours for those remaining at work. In those circumstances it is difficult to oppose the view that people should be grateful for a job and accept management demands.

Values which are allegedly good for the conduct of American

business are being promoted with little regard for the consequences, let alone any appraisal of the quality of life of American employees. Privatisation, deregulation, anti-unionism and no minimum wage are regarded as appropriate for any organisation, not least the public sector.

In Australia and in the UK two sets of assumptions influence attitudes to the public sector. On the one hand it has been vilified as hampered by red tape, and on the other it has been depicted as administratively constipated because it has too many staff. If the public sector employee, whether public servant or professional, can be cast as inaccessible or inflexible, bloated not lean, this clears the ground for the managerial hero to establish new values and language. Clients, students and patients can be called customers even if their choices are more imagined than real. In Britain a Hospital Trust chairman, Roy Lilley, advised that doctors' first duty was to the organisations they worked for, secondly to themselves and only then should they discharge their responsibility to patients (Macdonald 1994).

In public transport and health care, deregulation and cutbacks in the interests of productivity have human costs. On some American airlines and in Australian civil aviation there appears to be a direct link between deregulation, and consequent pruning of air safety measures, and the number of fatal accidents. In New South Wales conductors can no longer be afforded on buses, and children caught in the back doors and out of sight of drivers have been killed. Public sector resources, such as nurses in hospitals and teachers in public schools, cannot be afforded.

A chaplain in Britain's National Health Service has bemoaned the diminution in humanitarian attitudes and practices. He reports that nurses and cleaners used to have time for an occasional therapeutic chat with patients and if chaplains put a service on there were porters available to help move those in wheelchairs.

> In a dozen years the essential slack in the system has almost gone. Everywhere three or four people are doing what four or five did a decade ago. Priests are now unemployed in a Church that is short of priests ... The spiritual quality we once knew as 'slack' is now called unemployment. (Radcliffe 1994)

In Australia, Commonwealth public servants' efforts to achieve a shorter working week have been halted and reversed. Since the mid-1980s the National Institute of Labor Studies at Flinders University has discovered that the proportion of full-time workers who work beyond 40 hours has grown from 30 per cent to 40 per cent. Verrender contends that 'Australian workers put in an average working week of 43 hours, ranking them among the hardest working in the world'.

In Britain, when the Tories took office in 1979 there were 732 000 civil servants and by mid-1995 there were 440 000. The treatment of those who remain has been described as both humiliating and stressful. Financial targets and business plans mean that tens of thousands of civil servants must reapply for their jobs, endure a wage freeze and in some cases move home. Elizabeth Jenkins, the secretary of the British Institute of Professionals, Managers and Specialists, says 'Stress is now the major issue for us. There is a new cultural climate that demands longer hours but no longer offers job security' (Hugill 1994).

The CSIRO

Managerialism produces stress and loss of morale. These consequences can be perceived in the atmosphere of organisations and in the experiences of individuals — as in the case of the prestigious Australian scientific research organisation, CSIRO.

In its attitudes to CSIRO the Australian Federal Government and senior managers in that organisation have been influenced by the ethos, 'when in doubt do not try to effect reform internally but bring in outside management consultants'. CSIRO has been subject to several reviews — one report (Dayton 1995) suggests '44 enquiries of various descriptions' — which have produced contradictory conclusions. The Industries Commission, private management consultants and the Federal Senate's Economics Committee have all conducted inquiries. At the end of 1994 a *Sydney Morning Herald* editorial concluded: 'So confused is the organization these days by the relentless probing and reorganizing that no-one has any clear ideas what its job is ... Politicians and bureaucrats love torturing the CSIRO' (*SMH* 16 Dec. 1994).

Scientists from CSIRO's McMaster Laboratory on the campus of the University of Sydney provided their perceptions of the managerial inquiries and the rationalisation of their organisation. Three trends emerged: a. the disempowering role of the management consultants; b. management's preoccupation with control; c. the loss of morale of highly trained professionals who had previously been totally committed to their work and to the organisation.

a. The management consultants

The scientists reflected that when staff hear that management consultants are to be called in, 'that is the first sign of trouble'. In the early 1990s the arrival of consultants signalled an existing CSIRO management belief that there were no resources within the organisation to effect appropriate changes. Large sums of money being spent on accountants called consultants provoked anger as well as anxiety. In retrospect the scientists felt that their anger was justified. Stereotypical views about the role of management consultants emerged. One respondent explained: 'We felt they were bound to recommend cutbacks. We all expected them to say we were inefficient no matter how hard we worked. Their recommendations were that we should become more corporate. We should corporatise.'

Another respondent explained what going corporate had meant for her. 'I now have to raise money for my own research. I have been told I have enough money for six months. This introduces a feeling of panic. You cannot conduct research under duress.' She added: 'In the obsession with consultancies they are about to employ another company to restructure us yet again. They have decided to employ a firm of counsellors to deal with the low morale which they have created.'

b. A preoccupation with control

Two instruments symbolised management's preoccupation with control: the introduction of a performance evaluation system; and the publication of a code of conduct.

Scientists reported that management loved the compliance involved in being able to assess staff as outstanding, very good, satisfactory, fair, unsatisfactory. The system introduced conflict between employees who had previously seen themselves as colleagues. A quota system on promotions meant that only some staff could be given the highest rating and some evaluations were regraded to meet this constraint.

Efforts to discuss the grading system and other grievances were said to have been met with a dictatorial response, though the senior managers concerned, including the chief executive, were perceived as trying to give the impression that they were interested and were listening. One respondent commented on her management superiors in general. 'They do not know how to listen. The humility required for them to suspend their point of view is not there.'

The *Code of Conduct* (CSIRO 1994) combines elements of childishness and authoritarianism. In parts it seems comparable to rules for boy scouts or for induction into the military. The childishness infuriates professionals who resent being reminded of obligations to work to the highest possible standard. 'Staff are expected to perform their duties with professionalism and integrity, and work efficiently to enable CSIRO to meet its research and corporate goals ... Fairness, honesty, equity and all legal requirements are to be observed.'

The code emphasises hierarchy and control and the disciplining of transgressors. It says, 'We are all responsible for doing something about any illegal behaviour or behaviour outside the spirit of the Code of Conduct'. Later in the same document staff are reminded of laws which might subject people to criminal prosecution: 'Staff are bound by various legislative instruments such as the Crimes Act, Privacy Act, and Occupational Health and Safety and Equal Opportunity legislation'.

(c) Loss of morale

Loss of morale, sickness and general disenchantment resulted from the disempowering recommendations of consultants and the management's preoccupation with evaluation and control. The means had become the ends. The human costs were overlooked but were made explicit in the interviewees' accounts.

A scientist with ten years of service to the organisation and ten years of research training at graduate and post-doctoral levels in Australia and overseas said: 'We used to come into this laboratory at weekends, not because we were being paid but because we were not being paid. They do not understand that'.

A colleague agreed:

> I was very committed. Now I have outside interests. They are seeking mediocrity. To show you are accountable you waste time filling in forms and signing on dotted lines. To show you take management seriously you are encouraged to go on management training courses where they play games. You can fall into one another's arms to demonstrate trust. If it was not so serious and harmful you could laugh at the childishness of all this.

If future funding depended on evaluations of individuals or sections of the laboratory, staff said that the high standards of science would be set aside. 'You now have to fudge the presentation of reports in order to avoid the accusation that no worthwhile results are forthcoming.'

The low morale of staff was summed up by a senior researcher who had taken early retirement. 'In the end I could not tolerate it anymore. I rejected the total disaster of these people controlling my life from day to day.'

These accounts could be repeated wherever organisations have been rationalised, staff interests ignored and financial accountability and productivity have replaced professional employees' concerns with research, with education and providing a public service. The costs have been to organisations as well as to individuals, to the general public as well as to governments. Other examples of disempowering experiences, loss of morale and other human costs are a recurring theme of this book.

The moral fiction

The preoccupation of many countries with management panaceas is promoted by the twin forces of an economic policy in which the simple equation is that public sector enterprises should corporatise and by a management education industry which claims to be able to produce cadres of efficient managers. Many of the claims of managerialism are a fiction, but the media colludes. A gullible public is asked to accept more of the same. A dismayed public searches in vain for alternatives.

The moral fiction case needs to be summarised. In previous discussion the claims that managers are neutral and scientific has been rejected. The paradox is that in many circles management is presented as unable to engage in debate about objectives because, by its focus on rationality and efficiency, it stands beyond political and moral controversy. MacIntyre contends that managers, like therapists, see themselves as uncontested figures who restrict themselves to areas in which rational agreement is possible — to realms of facts and measurable effectiveness (MacIntyre 1984).

Inherent in the word 'efficiency' is a value which depicts a view of the world and of order within organisations. This view requires compliance with an image. Human costs are not allowed to cloud the efficiency equation. MacIntyre concludes that claims about effectiveness and efficiency are about means of control, 'the manipulation of human beings into compliant patterns of behaviour'. 'Managerial expertise', he says, 'turns out to be one more moral fiction because the kind of knowledge that would be required to sustain it does not exist' (MacIntyre 1984).

The rise of managerialism has coincided with increasing social and economic inequality in many countries (Raskall 1993; Stillwell 1993). An example of that inequality can be seen in the very high salary packages and other rewards given to senior managers, in particular in privatised public utilities. Those salaries are awarded at the same time as large numbers of a work force are discarded. It is not the cruelty of this which is of concern at this point but the justification of these salaries and rewards. The senior managers and their patrons apparently believe they are a breed apart, that the public and shareholders should be grateful for their existence. In exercises of self-promotion and self-delusion they can be heard justifying their rewards. Sometimes they even have the nerve to do so with references to equity as well as efficiency.

Whether or not the relationship between equity and managerial efficiency is addressed in management education, what is certain is that there is no shortage of management courses around the globe. Institutions which do not have schools of business management have deluded themselves into believing that their educational status will be undermined if they do not have one. In search of income from high-fee-paying students, at home and overseas, almost every educational institution seeks to produce an MBA program. Even Australia's apostle of competition at all costs, Professor Fred Hilmer, says that there are so many management programs that the value of an MBA has been eroded.

Perhaps the worst piece of managerialist fiction is the rejoinder that if the prescriptions of management do not work, it is because the organisations or the employees have not taken their medicine or have not fully understood the prescription. Offices can be closed and staff dismissed but the remaining staff are expected to produce the same level of service or better. Politicians and their managerial servants claim that service to the public will be enhanced by more efficient organisations. In ten years of financial cuts to the New South Wales Department of Community Services there was no acknowledgment by managerialist reformers that their remedies had been ineffective, disempowering and often cruel. They continue to argue that efficiency can be restored if only the organisation would employ staff with the right corporate attitude.

Managerial fundamentalism is apparent in its dogma, intolerance of critics and gratitude for compliant staff. The very connotation of the word 'manage' means that managers must have all the answers. To expose such fiction requires energy, courage and a willingness to swim against the tide. In November 1994, in a radio phone-in program on the ABC's 2BL Sydney, a caller described managerialism as 'the new fundamentalism'. 'It is popular because you are simply asked to accept what they say. No-one has to think.'

Even as claims are made about democracy in organisations, the style of decision-making is towards secrecy and control. Even as the rhetoric about greater devolution is heard, the tendency is to control decisions from the centre, to set managers apart, to develop their own cultures, language, symbols and networks.

Anticipating alternatives

There have been attempts — as in reference to competencies and a new 'public service orientation' — to establish alternative systems to managerialism. Those alternatives have discussed replacement of 'the equity of the market' with 'the equity of need', 'the search for market satisfaction' with a 'search for justice' (Stewart & Ransom 1988).

That begins to sound attractive but it seems premature and inappropriate to replace one system with another. The very concept of another 'system' is open to the same tendency to develop dogma and self-justification (Hames 1994). For a time there may be nothing inherently unjust or wrong in a new system. But in foreshadowing the alternatives to managerialism it is the revival of attitudes and values which needs to be addressed; values which place human considerations over economic ones, values which demonstrate the interdependence of environmental and human well-being and which resist automatic acceptance of the alleged benefits of efficiency.

Advocacy of the revival of respect for humanitarian principles in the conduct of human relations is the alternative. Details of that case will be spelled out in part V of this book.

References

Alford, J. 1991, 'The concept of the public production process: beyond managerialism and its critics', Working Paper No. 10, Graduate School of Management, University of Melbourne.
CSIRO 1994, *Code of Conduct*, CSIRO Australia, Information Services, Canberra.
Dayton, L. 1995, 'Review of CSIRO has a corporate thrust', *Sydney Morning Herald*, 5 April, p. 8.
Emy, H. 1993, *Remaking Australia: The State, the Market and Australia's Future*, Allen & Unwin, Sydney.
'Give CSIRO a break' 1994, *Sydney Morning Herald* (editorial), 16 December.
Hames, R. 1994, *The Management Myth: Exploring the Essence of Future Organizations*, Business & Professional Publishing, Chatswood, NSW.
Hugill, B. 1994, 'A civil service on its last legs', *Observer*, Focus, 29 May, p. 22.
Locke, R. 1989, *Management and Higher Education Since 1940*, Cambridge University Press, Cambridge.
Macdonald, V. 1994, 'Put patients last, NHS manager tells doctors', *Sunday Telegraph*, 13 November, p. 1.
MacIntyre, A. 1984, *After Virtue: A Study in Moral Theory*, 2nd edn, University of Notre Dame Press, Notre Dame, Indiana.
Marquand, D. 1988, *The Unprincipled Society*, Fontana Press, London.
Mayo, E. 1933, *The Human Problems of An Industrial Civilization*, Macmillan, New York.
Perrow, C. 1979, *Complex Organizations*, 2nd edn, Scott Foresman & Co., London.
Peters, J. & Waterman, R. 1982, *In Search of Excellence: Lessons From America's Best Run Companies*, Harper & Row, New York.
Pollitt, C. 1993, *Managerialism and the Public Services*, 2nd edn, Blackwell, Oxford.
Pusey, M. 1991, *Economic Rationalism in Canberra*, Cambridge University Press, Melbourne.
Radcliffe, A. 1994, 'The Church manages to get itself into a fix', *Guardian*, 2 May.
Raskall P. 1993, 'Widening income disparities in Australia', in S. Rees, G. Rodley and F. Stilwell (eds), *Beyond the Market*, Pluto Press, Sydney, ch. 3.
Rees, S. 1994, 'Economic rationalism, an ideology of exclusion', *Australian Journal of Social Issues*, vol. 29, no. 2, May.
Rees, S., Rodley, G. & Stilwell, F. (eds) 1993, *Beyond the Market, Alternatives to Economic Rationalism*, Pluto Press, Sydney.
Simon, H. 1947, *Administrative Behaviour*, Macmillan, New York.
Stewart, J. & Ransom, S. 1988, 'Management in the public domain', *Public Money and Management*, vol. 8, no. 2, pp. 13–19.
Stilwell, F. 1993, *Economic Inequality: Who Gets What in Australia*, Pluto Press, Sydney.

Taylor, F. 1911, *The Principles of Scientific Management*, Harper Brothers, New York.

Verrender, I. 1994, 'Bludgers no more', *Sydney Morning Herald*, Spectrum, 1 October.

Vintilla, P., Phillimore, J. & Newman, P. 1992, *Markets, Morals and Manifestos*, Institute for Science and Technology Policy, Murdoch University, Perth.

Yeatman, A. 1991, Corporate managerialism: an overview, paper presented to NSW Teachers' Federation Conference, 'The management of public education: a question of balance', 8–9 March, Sydney.

2.
The Complicity of Think-Tanks

Ted Wheelwright

> A self-selecting elite of super-corporations and their managements dominate the decision-making process, with union and university leaders co-opted through a variety of economic and political mechanisms. The economic and political power of the United States has been used ... in the interest of the managers of the corporate state. (Fusfield 1979)

Much of the literature on managerialism is American, for obvious reasons. One of the earliest contributions was about universities (Veblen 1918); the author was an academic inveighing against the way that American universities were being modelled on the big corporations, competing in the market for a 'vendible commodity', that is, knowledge. He thought this was a salutary example of the way the capitalist system reduced everything to a commodity to be bought and sold in the marketplace.

Veblen coined some memorable phrases which are applicable today: university presidents were described as 'captains of erudition ... itinerary dispensers of salutary verbiage'. When academics become administrators 'they take on the characteristics of an administrator, ie ambiguity and evasiveness'. The outcome of university courses for managers would be that 'they would be able to secure ... a larger portion of the aggregate wealth of the community'. This was a remarkable prophecy for our generation, which has seen an enormous increase, both absolutely and relatively, in the income of corporate executives, including those running universities in Australia.

For industry, the decisive work (Berle & Means 1932) was the first to describe the 'euthanasia' of stockholder power, and the rise to dominance of managerial power. In the 1940s the phrase 'the managerial revolution' was coined (Burnham 1942), suggesting that capitalism was not being overthrown by the proletariat as Marx had thought, but by a new class of managers: 'The instruments of production are the seat of social domination; who controls them, in fact if not in name, controls society'. In the 1950s the term 'managerial demiurge' was used to mean that 'at the top society becomes an uneasy interlocking of private and public hierarchies, and at the bottom, more and more areas become objects of management and manipulation' (Wright Mills 1956). Enterprise comes to have a motive of its own, to manipulate the world to make a profit:

> In a world dominated by a vast system of abstractions, managers may become cold with principle and do what local and immediate masters of men could never do. Their social insulation results in deadened feelings in the face of the impoverishment of life in the lower orders and its stultification in the upper circles ... the social control of the system is such that *irresponsibility is organised into it*. (Wright Mills 1956, pp. 110–11, emphasis added)

However, managers need an ideology to justify their actions, and this is provided by economists (Galbraith 1992). 'One of the most distinguished accomplishments of economics is its ability to accommodate its view ... to specific economic and political interests.' Galbraith emphasises that the subject has been doing that for 'some centuries'. For several decades now it has been called 'economic rationalism', but, as a 1994 book shows, it did not simply 'evolve', but had generous helping hands along the way (Cockett 1994).

Cockett describes these in great detail, showing how, over half a century or more, what can only be described as a kind of 'economic mafia' turned the profession into little more than the *apparatchiks* of capitalism, although he does not use that terminology. In the inter-war period, John Maynard Keynes, a Cambridge don and scion of the British establishment, was the world's pre-eminent economist. He denied the central tenet of economic 'liberalism', which was that the capitalist system worked best if left alone and not interfered with by governments; market forces would ensure this if there were worldwide competition. He believed the evidence showed that free trade, the international mobility of capitalism and foreign ownership of national assets were more likely to promote war than peace (Keynes 1933).

On the contrary, Keynes thought that all the evidence of the capitalist system indicated that full employment was a rare and short-lived occurrence. Investment for the long term was being crowded out by short-term speculative investment, consequently there should be a tax on speculative activity. Monetary policy did not work, hence the state should take increasing responsibility for organising investment. There could be great benefits from the gradual disappearance of a rate of return on accumulated wealth, what he called 'the euthanasia of the rentier' (Keynes 1936).

During the war years Keynes was a negotiator for the British government on post-war trade arrangements, and was in favour of state trading for commodities and international cartels for non-essential manufactures. He saw these as 'future instruments for orderly economic life', which the Americans saw as 'economic planning' and wanted to outlaw. To the capitalist establishments in the western world, especially the American and the British, and the orthodox economists in their universities — the high priests of laissez-faire — these thoughts were subversive of the economic order to which they wished to return, and hence had to be eliminated.

To do this, a counter revolution to the 'Keynesian revolution' had to be orchestrated. This is what Cockett documents in excruciating detail. A key role was played by the London School of Economics (LSE), which ironically was established by British Fabians to facilitate the discussion of social and economic reform. At the LSE in the early inter-war period, two radical professors of history and politics — Tawney and Laski — were having an impact, as was Keynes in Cambridge. To counteract these it is believed that the doyen of the Austrian school of economic liberalism, F. A. Hayek, was brought to the LSE in 1931.

The resulting debate between Hayek and his supporters, and Keynes and his, paved the way, Cockett considers, for an international movement of economic liberals against Keynesian economics. This in turn led to anti-Keynesian think-tanks financed by business, and later to Thatcherism and Reaganism, and eventually their spin-offs in Australia: Fraserism, Hawkism and Keatingism.

Hayek's *Road to Serfdom* (1944) became the Bible of the Right. It was published in abbreviated form in the *Reader's Digest* in 1945, the year he was invited by the University of Chicago to tour the USA. A Swiss businessman invited him to address students at the University of Zurich, and afterwards to dinner with a group of industrialists and bankers. Some of them offered financial support for Hayek's plan to found a society for converting the next generation of intellectuals to the creed of economic liberalism.

British and American financial support followed, and the inaugural conference of the society was held at Mont Pelérin, Switzerland, in April 1947. Thirty-nine people attended it, mostly academics, Cockett records, including Hayek, Robbins and Popper from the LSE, Friedman and Knight from the University of Chicago, some high-level public servants, and three journalists, one each from the *Reader's Digest, Fortune* and *Time and Tide*. It became known as the Mont Pelérin Society

(MPS) and originally was very much an Anglo-American affair, twenty-four of the thirty-nine being from the USA or the UK, the rest being from Western Europe. None was from the Third World. Hayek was elected president, and foreshadowed an attack on trade unions:

> If there is to be any hope of a return to a free economy the question of how the powers of unions can be appropriately delimited in law, as well as in fact is one of the most important of all the questions to which we must give our attention. (Cockett 1994, p. 114)

The MPS initially met about every two years, and remained secret until its growing size made this difficult; by 1980 its conference at the Hoover Institute at Stanford University was attended by 600 people. In August 1985 it met in Sydney under the auspices of the Centre for Independent Studies (CIS), probably Australia's most influential think-tank. This was reported in the *Weekend Australian* (24 August 1985, p. 17) by Greg Sheridan who said 180 people attended, and it was 'arguably one of the most high powered intellectual groups to assemble in Australia'. He added that the ideas underlying the analysis on which the Reagan and Thatcher governments were based came from economists and political philosophers associated with the MPS. It now had a meeting every year, he said, and half its members were economists; from the late 1960s many of the think-tanks and lobbying institutions were formed by people with connections with MPS.

Probably the most influential think-tank is the Institute of Economic Affairs (IEA) founded in London in 1955 by Anthony Fisher, a businessman who made a fortune out of broiler-chicken farming, and used some of it to finance the IEA, as well as fostering many of the world's other think-tanks later. Another industrialist put in half the working capital of the IEA, whose objective was 'to propagate sound economic thought in the universities and all other educational establishments'. Margaret Thatcher must have thought it most successful, for she knighted Fisher in 1988.

In 1956 a former economics lecturer at St Andrews University, Ralph Harris, who had previously worked for the Conservative Central Office, was appointed director. Under him the IEA published an array of pamphlets and papers in the 1960s and 1970s on many topics, from privatising communications systems to closing down coalmines. Many big names in economics contributed. After her first election to office as prime minister, Margaret Thatcher wrote Harris a note, saying: 'The debt we owe you is immense'. She then helped to repay it by making him Lord Harris of High Cross. She also wrote to Hayek on his ninetieth birthday, thanking him for his leadership and inspiration. There is no wonder that Milton Friedman remarked: 'Without the IEA I doubt very much whether there would have been a Thatcherite revolution' (Cockett 1994, p. 158).

The role of the press in propagating the ideology of the IEA was crucial, with Conrad Black's *Daily Telegraph* and Rupert Murdoch's *Times* both giving it access and publicity.

Student papers were also produced by the IEA, which had strong links with student Conservative associations in various universities. Other think-tanks were also created in the UK, such as the Centre for Policy Studies (1974) and the Adam Smith Institute (1976). In North America, the Heritage Foundation was formed in 1973 by a former student of the LSE; in 1980 this foundation published *Mandate for Leadership*, which served as a blueprint for the Reagan government. As Cockett notes, this illustrates how closely the British and American movements were interwoven, guided as both were 'by the same economists and publicists of the Mont Pelérin Society' (Cockett 1994, p. 282).

Anthony Fisher, the founding father of the first British free-market think-tank, was instrumental in setting them up in many parts of the western world. There were so many that he established the Atlas Economic Research Foundation, which in 1991 claimed to have helped, created, financed or advised in some way seventy-eight institutes, and had a relationship with eighty-one others in fifty-one countries. The mission of the Atlas Foundation was said to be 'to litter the world with free-market think-tanks'. In Australia, Fisher was involved in developing the CIS, directed by Greg Lindsay, which 'became an important contributor of free market ideas to Australian politics in the 1980s' (Cockett 1994, pp. 306–7).

Significant research has been done on think-tanks in Australia by David Kemp, Marian Sawer, Tim Duncan, Jeffrey Babb, Paul Kelly and Tom Dusevic, which is drawn on here. The oldest think-tank is the Institute of Public Affairs (IPA), formed during the Second World War by C. D. Kemp, whose son Rod greatly expanded its operations in the 1980s. It has attracted some important people to its ranks, such as Dame Leonie Kramer, former ABC supremo and professor of Australian literature at the University of Sydney, now its chancellor. Also included were former UNESCO ambassador Owen Harries, originally a lecturer at the University of Sydney, former Treasury officer Des Moore, and Gerard Henderson, former adviser to John Howard. (In 1989 Henderson broke away to form the Sydney Institute, another think-tank.)

The decade of the 1970s was the crucible for think-tanks in Australia, and the cradle of the 'free market counter-revolution'. Both Hayek and Friedman, Nobel Prize winners for economics, visited Australia in the mid-1970s. Friedmanite views began to appear in *Quadrant*, and in January 1975 the Worker's Party was formed to promote them. The Society for Austrian Economics emerged, and so did the Adam Smith Club. But the most important by far was the CIS founded in 1976 by Greg Lindsay in conjunction with Anthony Fisher after Hayek's tour.

By 1979 the CIS had sufficient financial support to set up a full-time secretariat at St Leonards in Sydney. Its Council of Advisers included 'overseas figures such as F. A. Hayek and Murray Rothbarth; Australian economics professors such as W. Hogan, C. G. F. Simkin, and H. W. Arndt; the sociologists T. H. Kewley and John J. Ray; the journalist Peter Samuels, and the philosopher Lachlan Chipman. The chairman of the board was John Bonython' (Sawer 1982). In 1981 it organised a seminar addressed by Milton Friedman which was attended by 700 people. In October 1994 Rupert Murdoch was the star guest at the CIS $100-a-head dinner held at the Grand Hyatt Hotel in Melbourne (*Sydney Morning Herald*, 20 October 1994).

In 1979 the Centre for Policy Studies was founded at Monash University by Professor Michael Porter, and attracted $600 000 in its first year. By 1981 it had a staff of twenty-one; bodies which contributed funds include the Australian Mining Industry, Alcoa, and the Australian Research Grants Council. In Perth, the Australian Institute for Public Policy (AIPP) was founded in the early 1980s by John Hyde, former leader of the dries in the Federal Parliament, to whom is attributed the statement: 'We do not mind at all that the politicians who have so far done most to implement our ideas ... call themselves socialists' (Babb 1989). Hyde was also the leading activist in the Society of Modest Members, formed in 1981 to commemorate the work of Bert Kelly, the MP for Wakefield for many years, who was a staunch opponent of tariffs and wrote a newspaper column espousing free trade under the pseudonym 'a Modest Member'. Members included Malcolm Fraser, Andrew Peacock, J. J. Carlton, Peter Shack and Murray Sainsbury.

Other think-tanks included the Institute of Labor Studies at Flinders University, headed by Professor Richard Blandy, and the H. R. Nicholls Society founded by John Stone, Peter Costello, Ray Evans (adviser to Hugh Morgan of Western Mining), and Barrie Purvis of the Wool Brokers Employers Federation. The Flinders Institute began with a free-trade outlook on tariff matters and began to apply it to the protection of the labour market. The Nicholls Society is concerned with 'overturning' the arbitration system in the sense of abolishing arbitration and reducing union power.

At the end of the 1970s an organisation was formed which was not exactly in the think-tank mould, but very influential nevertheless. It was called Crossroads and, according to Paul Kelly, was in effect:

> a counter-establishment to the prevailing Fraser establishment. The name derived from the first comprehensive statement of the free market position articulated in a 1980 book, *Australia at the Crossroads*. It was jointly conceived by the professor of

economics at the University of New South Wales, Wolfgang Kasper, and the management of Shell Australia Ltd, in particular its chief economist, Douglas Hocking. (Kelly 1992)

Shell financed the study, which argued the need for a new long-term strategy aimed at moving Australia away from mercantilist policies towards a market economy, by means of which new export markets would be won in minerals, energy, food and raw materials processing. A conference was held in February 1981, most of whose participants became the nucleus of the 'free market' counter-establishment of the 1980s. 'Within the decade, the Crossroads core group and its ideas had taken control of non-Labor politics in Australia' (Kelly 1992).

The group included politicians, academics, bureaucrats, think-tank directors, and company economists and directors from Western Mining, CRA, Amatil, BHP, and Bain & Co. It met 'twice a year for about six years, well into the Hawke era. It was a network, a political cell for market policies, a talkfest, a lobby group on the Fraser government ... and later a pressure point against Hawke' (Kelly 1992).

There may have been similar connections between think-tanks, politicians, business leaders and the press, but few are documented. However, there seems to be some agreement on the key roles played by Malcolm Fraser, prime minister from 1975 to 1983. Sawer notes that he acknowledged Ayn Rand as a favourite author, drew heavily on Hayek *via* David Kemp, professor of political science at Monash University, who was a major speech writer, and had Professor W. P. Hogan of Sydney University as an adviser (Sawer 1982). Kemp considers that a central role was played by Fraser, who supported the *Quadrant* group in Sydney and entertained at the Lodge 'intellectuals such as Hayek, Friedman, and Kissinger' (Kemp 1988).

The role of the Labor government has yet to be fully assessed, but there is little doubt that it will be shown to have been far more influential in establishing 'market forces policies' than the Fraser government ever was. It will be seen as a classical case of 1984 Orwellian 'newspeak and double-think'. Paul Kelly writes that the floating of the dollar and the abolition of exchange controls transformed the economics and politics of Australia:

> It harnessed the Australian economy to the international marketplace ... The decision transformed the financial sector ... This move was an irresistible catalyst to further de-regulation of Australian society — its markets for goods, labour and services. That meant, in effect, an economic and political revolution ... Hawke and Keating ... chose to elevate belief in market forces to an article of faith for their government and the ALP — an historic step ... [The float] sealed a de facto alliance between the government

and the financial markets ... it brought the former Fraser government into disrepute among its own kind because the socialists had shown more faith in market forces than Malcolm Fraser! (Kelly 1992)

Dusevic suggests that by the early 1990s there were seven privately funded think-tanks dedicated to the social sciences. He calls them idea factories, but notes that they have not been content with ideas alone, but have sought to 'set the agenda, and influence government policies'. To do this, he believes that they have waged: '*what has amounted to the greatest propaganda exercise outside wartime.* Their targets are the intellectual elites in politics, the bureaucracy, business and the media' (emphasis added). He cites Ian Marsh, former research director for the federal Liberal Party, now an academic at the Australian Graduate School of Management, who considers that the IPA, CIS, AIPP and the Sydney Institute constitute 'the springboard for the new right in Australia ... this group has influenced the thinking of both major political parties as well as setting the frame of discourse for key public servants and media commentators' (Dusevic 1990).

Control by think-tanks has bolstered support for managerialist attitudes and values, which include the notion that American corporate practices should be promoted universally as a dogma for a new generation of true believers. To the new cohorts of managerialist mullahs it does not seem to matter that their values and practices have had cruel consequences for hundreds of thousands of employees, past and present, and have made a significant contribution to the growth of unemployment. A new slogan may yet emerge: 'Workers of the world unite; you have nothing to lose but your managers'.

References

Babb, Jeffrey 1989, ' "New Right" dedicated to the principles of freedom', *Australian Financial Review*, 3 March.
Berle, A. A. & Means, G. C. 1932, *The Modern Corporation and Private Property*, Commercial Clearing House, New York.
Burnham, James 1942, *The Managerial Revolution*, Penguin, London, p. 99.
Cockett, Richard 1994, *Thinking the Unthinkable: Think-Tanks and the Economic Counter-Revolution*, HarperCollins, London.
Duncan, Tim 1984, 'New Right crusaders challenge the Labor line', *Bulletin*, 2 October.
Dusevic, Tom 1990, 'The idea factories: Australia's think-tanks are waging a propaganda war', *Australian Financial Review*, 25 May.
Fusfield, Daniel 1979, 'The rise of the corporate state in America', in Warren J. Samuels (ed.), *The Economy as a System of Power*, vol. I, Transaction Books, New Brunswick, p.121.
Galbraith, J. K. 1992, *The Culture of Contentment*, Houghton Mifflin, Boston, p. 78.

Hayek, F. A. 1944, *The Road to Serfdom*, Routledge, London.
Kelly, Paul 1992, *The End of Certainty: The Story of the 1980s*, Allen & Unwin, Sydney, pp. 40–2 and 76–7.
Kemp, David 1988, 'Liberalism and conservatism in Australia since 1944', in Brian Head & James Walter (eds), *Intellectual Movements and Australian Society*, Oxford University Press, Melbourne.
Keynes, J. M. 1933, cited in Robert Skidelski 1992, *John Maynard Keynes*, vol. II, Macmillan, London, p. 476.
——1936, *General Theory of Employment, Interest & Money*, Macmillan, London, p. 376.
Sawer, Marian (ed.) 1982, *Australia and the New Right*, Allen & Unwin, Sydney, p. 8.
Veblen, Thorstein 1918, *The Higher Learning in America*, Sentry Press, New York.
Wright Mills, C. 1956, *White Collar*, Oxford University Press, New York, p. 77.

3.
The Rise of the Generic Manager

Brian Easton

A central notion of the New Zealand reforms of the 1980s and early 1990s was that an able manager was capable of managing any agency in the private or public sector.[1] This has two crucial implications. First, it suggests that all economic activities are broadly the same, or may be treated so for policy purposes, since the required management skills and approaches are not sector specific. Second, it encourages the replacement of specialist managers, who had typically developed in the sector, with generalists who had not, but who would be loyal to the managerialist philosophy and eager to impose it on the institution.

It might seem that this issue is marginal, except perhaps to those who were promoted or made redundant as a result. However, the consequences are widespread, and potentially destructive. For example, the theory says that the same skills are needed to run a hospital as to manage a brewery, and that ultimately the production of health services is not fundamentally different from the production of beer. Put so bluntly, the theory now seems laughable, even absurd, but it is a matter of record that the chief executive officer (CEO) of New Zealand's largest hospital system was previously involved in managing New Zealand's largest brewer.

Indeed, the experience of the health reforms in New Zealand shows the fallacy of the notion of the generic manager, and the consequential costs of the implementation of the fallacy. The fallacy could be illustrated with parallel changes in other sectors, but focusing on this one example can illustrate the issue in greater detail, and give some indication of the human and other costs which resulted.

The fallacy of generic managers

Arguing the fallacy of generic managers is not to argue an uncritical case for specialised managers. It is certainly not an argument for inbred management where senior managers enter the firm at the bottom level and work their way up, without any other sectoral or firm experience. A successful senior manager is likely to have had a range of experiences in a variety of agencies. Neither does rejection of the fallacy mean that a senior executive should never come from outside the industry. Rather, it suggests that if a new manager comes from a sufficiently different industry, he or she will take considerable time to settle in.

Nor does the fallacy deny the existence of generic management skills which the Master of Business Administration (MBA), for instance, provides to students. A good MBA graduate should be able to go into almost any junior management position. As the manager progresses, industry specific skills add to the generic ones. The fallacy of generic managers applies to senior managers.

Like most such misconceptions there is just sufficient truth in the fallacy of generic managers to deceive the unwary. A senior manager may be able to move successfully between what appear to be quite different products or firms. The chief executive officer of a car maker may be recruited from the pulp and paper industry. The successful seller of an aerated drink may move on to men's toiletries. As an aside, we should not make too much of these shifts. A misunderstanding of their nature led in the 1980s to mergers between firms of very unlike characteristics in the name of 'synergies'. Typically these mergers came unstuck, and the firms, if they survived, later sold the disparate activities. The fallacy, however, is concerned with a broader issue. While some products or services have sufficient similarities for the same skills to be broadly applicable for a senior manager, many do not. That a foodstuff CEO may make an admirable hardware CEO, does not mean that inevitably he or she will make as competent a health services CEO.

Moreover, there will always be managers, generic or otherwise, who have the talent to rise above the limitations of their training and background when placed in a new situation. Undoubtedly some of the new managers in the health services have done well. The concern is with the average level of performance, not a few isolated peaks.

The rise of generic managers

There are a number of economic products and services whose characteristics are so different from the general run of commodities that they have typically been treated quite differently from those conventionally supplied by private enterprise. Indeed it could be argued that the raison d'être of the public service was that its 'outputs', to use the current jargon, were so different from those of the market that they required different management styles. These public services not only include the core activities of advising on and administering government policies, but also education, science, state-supplied housing, health services, cultural services, and so on.

By the 1980s this view was under attack. Although the paper does not explicitly use the expression 'generic manager', Pollitt (1994), describing the rise of managerialism, includes the reminder that the phenomenon is not peculiar to New Zealand, although that country may well have experienced one of the most intense applications of the theory.

The origins, as for so much of the New Zealand reforms, occurred within the Treasury. The process of market liberalisation, and especially the corporatisation of state-owned enterprises, shifted Treasury towards a commercialisation strategy which is underpinned by the motto 'business is best' (Easton 1989). When faced with a problem of institutional reform the Treasury tended to solve it by converting the institution as much as possible to a private enterprise firm. While this may make sense for public enterprises which are functioning in a competitive market with (at least nominally) profit objectives, the extension of the model to traditional social services is problematical. Why the Treasury was captured by the policy is puzzling. Certainly the underpinning managerialism and private sector ethic was flavour of the decade. No doubt the success of the first corporatisation program of market-driven state-owned enterprises was important. The linkages between the government and business that this program generated, as consultants were hired and businessmen (and the occasional woman) were appointed to corporate boards, reinforced the attraction.

Obviously the Treasury despaired of the old public service ways, but the selection of the business alternative was a little like awarding the prize to the second singer in a competition after having only heard the first. Few Treasury officials had real private business experience (if any it was in the finance sector), so they were attracted to an idea with which they had little familiarity.[2] This equally applied to the Labour Party cabinet, and to some of the key theologians in the succeeding National Party cabinet.

There is an evident process in the application of business management procedures, starting in those public activities where they were most applicable and moving out to steadily less applicable areas. Thus, the main corporatisation program was in the first three years of the Labour government, from 1984 to 1987. Following the Treasury 1987 post-election briefing, *Government Management*, commercial principles became increasingly applied to the core public service during the second Labour term to 1990. In particular, the State Sector Act (1988) established government departments more like businesses, and switched their industrial relations to a private sector basis. Meanwhile the Public Finance Act (1989) placed the government accounting systems, and the funding of government activities, as close to private business parallels as was practicable. The return of a National Party government in 1990, following Labour's loss of power by the largest election swing on record, led to managerial reforms in the social services sectors, of which the health reforms are a good example.

The health reforms

The debacle of the health reforms is described elsewhere (Bowie & Shirley 1994; Easton 1994). By way of background, the National government published a 'green and white' paper, *Your Health and the Public Health*, setting out its proposals for a radical transformation of the health sector in July 1991 (Upton 1991). With astonishing rapidity the plans were implemented, in an incomplete form, by July 1993. The original proposals seem to have had an overt and covert intention.

The overt intention was to separate funding from provision, and put the government providers of health services (mainly Area Health boards) on a business-like basis, while integrating public and private provision (so that they would, for instance, compete for funds).

The covert intention appeared to be to move to an even greater degree of privatisation of the health sector, with perhaps the government providers (called Crown Health Enterprises or CHEs) to be sold off, and private funding of health to be increased. Whether any of the politicians contemplated such a move remains open to speculation, but it is clear that some of the advisers had this objective in mind, and that the proposed structure would have facilitated further steps towards privatisation (Easton 1994).

This may seem unduly conspiratorial, until the actual record of the corporatisation process of five years earlier is examined and the parallels observed (Easton 1989). It is clear with hindsight, and from leaks at the time, that government advisers saw the corporatisation of state trading enterprises as a step on the way to an ultimate destination of privatisation, an objective which was broadly attained a few years later. Moreover, it is not at all clear that the politicians who agreed to the corporatisation process appreciated the steps that were being undertaken, nor the ultimate destination. At the time they hotly denied it was privatisation.

However, the health reforms have been so chaotic that any covert objective is probably not as practicable as was envisaged. In any case the public objected strongly to any privatisation (and indeed to many of the reforms). Even the prime minister who presided over the reforms, Jim Bolger, has publicly stated that they were a major factor in the National government's loss of voter share in the 1993 elections, comparable in magnitude to the Labour government's loss in 1990, but due to the peculiarities of a first-past-the-post electoral system, this did not lead to a comparable loss of seats.

What is instructive is how the reforms illustrate the fallacy of generic managers. From the beginning, the underlying premise was that health services were just like any other economic commodity and could be supplied in the same way, and ideally should also be funded privately. In fact the provision of health services is very different from the standard commodity, because the person who decides on the health care service to be provided is rarely the user (i.e. patient) and frequently the provider (i.e. doctor), while the funder is rarely either the user or provider but someone else (in the private sector the funder is usually a private insurer). Thus the main strengths of normal market transactions simply do not apply to the standard health service exchange.

Generic reformers

This elementary point, which is at the heart of why a specialised subject of health economics exists, was simply ignored by the reformers. None of the New Zealand economists hired by the agencies supervising the reforms were experienced health economists. Rather, generic economists with little health economics experience were employed.

The reform units did hire some overseas health economists, carefully selected for their ideological sympathies (while some of the world's top health economists, most notably Bob Evans of Canada and Alan Maynard of Britain, who were visiting New Zealand on other business, were ignored). Even so, the overseas consultants did not have enough local knowledge to be useful, while the local ones with whom they interacted did not know enough to give them key information. For instance, New Zealand has the peculiarity that litigation for medical malpractice is all but prohibited (by accident compensation legislation). Thus, one of the key mechanisms for quality control of a privatised medical system is missing. Yet at no stage did the reformers address the question of quality control in a system becoming more exposed to commercial pressures.

Illustrating the effects of generic professionals by the example of economists is apt because the modern economist is often given the role of the ideologist, even high priest, of the managerialist revolution. The debate occurs in terms set by them. But the economists were not the only generic professionals who made elementary mistakes.

The most obvious example was Peter Troughton, the man appointed to head the National Provider Board, who had been chief executive of Telecom New Zealand, and then became involved in the electricity distribution reorganisation in the state of Victoria. Telecom and electricity are both network industries, so there may be sufficient overlap for a good manager to move easily between the two. But by no stretch of the imagination are health service providers. Trained as an engineer, the man exuded a charming confidence which soon betrayed a not surprising ignorance. For instance, he confused an intensive care unit with a post-operative recovery unit. Such a misunderstanding could be fatal for a person suffering a cardiac arrest, but it was also potentially disastrous for reforming a health system.

Troughton claimed that under the reforms there would be early productivity gains of 20–30 per cent. Challenged, he said that whenever he had been involved in industry rationalisation he had attained such gains.[3] The generic manager failed to observe that labour productivity gains in a capital intensive network industry are a very different matter from those in a labour intensive service industry.

Pressed further, Troughton cited the example of a particular hospital which he claimed was already making such gains. The logical flaw is that a hospital already making such gains under the old regime hardly suggests that a new regime was needed. In any case there was no such systematic measure of productivity gains to support the claim.

Some of this hospital's gains as a result of improvements were cited. For instance, the introduction of a preferred medicines list had the effect of cutting the hospital's drug bill by the equivalent of a productivity gain of 1 per cent.[4] The advocates from the non-specialist background were unaware that preferred medicine lists had been introduced into leading hospitals a decade earlier. Another marker was the substantial reduction in waiting lists at the hospital. True, except that this was the result of a special grant from the central government which enabled the purchase of more inputs. The non-specialists had no institutional memory.

Generic managers

The generic reformers appointed non-specialists to the boards of directors who would govern the CHEs according to commercial criteria. The government's own list identifies less than 5 per cent of the board members as having medical health services experience. In turn, the non-specialist directors usually appointed generic managers to be chief executives, who in their turn appointed generic managers to other senior management positions. Many managers who were professionally skilled and trained in the area of health services management lost their jobs. Some were appointed to managerial positions in Australia, Britain, and North America, suggesting that it was not incompetence that led to career failure in New Zealand. The general perception was that the system of reform was so committed to generic management that it was a disadvantage to have health sector experience.

There is only anecdote to report on the new managers for, despite their claims to emphasise systematic management and to monitor worker performance, there is surprisingly little effort by the managers to monitor themselves. Anecdote has medical personnel reporting that some of the new management teams did not understand the medical issues with which they were grappling, and were wasting resources as a result. It seems almost certain that ongoing efficiency improvements were delayed because the generic managers had to get up to speed in the specialities of their new industries. Sometimes the new managers were taken in by latest fashions, having no criteria by which to judge feasibility. At one stage the enthusiasm favoured heavy investment in information technology, a perception encouraged by the not-so-generic managers of the information technology industry.

An instructive anecdote comes from a meeting which involved presentations by three new CHE chief executives. Anxious to impress the mainly health service audience, each insisted that they had quality staff with whom they would be working to obtain performance gains. One chief executive officer enthusiastically announced that his task was to get his staff 'to own the problem'. He was promptly asked what he meant by that, since if someone went into a hospital with a medical condition the staff already worked extremely hard to resolve it. The new CEO responded by saying 'the problem' was his profit line, and then his voice trailed off for even he realised that his staff would not be overly impressed by the profit outcome, nor that his salary package included a bonus if he met it.

To be clear, the issue of the effective use of resources by clinicians has been one of the persistent problems for at least a quarter of a century and possibly before then, throughout the world.[5] Slowly clinicians have accepted that they have a responsibility to be efficient in their resource use, and that this need not compromise their medical ethics. Clinicians have been even more hesitant about the notion of not providing effective resources to one patient in order to make them available to another (who perhaps is not even a patient of the clinician). Their reluctance reflects deep, and not easily resolved, ethical questions. The overall profitability of a hospital may have some connection with these questions, but in practice they are tangential and even irrelevant. In the end there is a clash of culture between generic managers focused on profit and clinicians focused on patients, with the reformers ineffectually claiming the objectives are much the same thing.

The outcome

Evaluation of the reforms is complicated by the fact that there would have been changes, including productivity increases, even had the old regime continued. However, in terms of three key elements of the original conception, the reforms have failed miserably. First, the ministers of health have not been able to distance themselves from day-to-day issues. They may be even more involved than they were in the past, because the reforms have either increased the number of problems or so raised public expectations that small cases loom larger. (Possibly the reforms reduced staff loyalty to the system, increasing the willingness to leak and whistle blow.)

Second, there have not been the promised productivity gains. The official estimate of the gains has been revised to an increment of 1–2 per cent a year, probably about the rate that was occurring before the reforms.

Third, and consequentially, there have not been the hoped-for fiscal gains. Instead, the government has found itself having to pour public monies into a system which had performed tolerably well in the past with small annual reductions in real per capita funding (Bowie 1992; Easton & Bowie 1993). Of course, it is possible that some, or all, of that amount would have had to be spent under the old regime. The point is there is no evidence that the new regime is performing better, and some suspicion that its implementation delayed ongoing improvements. Moreover, the new structure may have added to costs by putting at least one additional management tier into the system. Generic managers and their associated requirements are not cheaply acquired.

This does not prove that the generic managers failed. It could be argued that the reforms were so ill-conceived that no class of managers could succeed. Even so, there is no evidence of these managers contributing to resolving a difficult situation. (It needs to be remembered that the theory of generic managers and the related theory of the management of generic industries was central to the justifications of the reforms.) If the generic reformers had not been so certain that health services were just like any other economic activity, they would not have been so committed to appointing generic managers.

But the final word should go to the generic managers themselves. Within six months of taking over the running of the health public provider system, the chairman of Crown Health Enterprises Chair's Consultative Committee (i.e. the committee of the chairpeople of CHE boards) wrote to the ministers of Health, Crown Health Enterprises, and Finance that 'the CHE group is of the view that the business of providing [health care] is not a genuine commercial mode' (Wilson 1993). If that had been the conventional wisdom earlier, those men (and the occasional woman) would never have been appointed to their boards.

Conclusion

The story told here about the health reforms could be told with similar detail about the changes in a variety of other activities, including education, housing, science, social services, and even the core public service itself. Generic managerialism did not lead to marked improvements in the ability of agencies to carry out their tasks. In many cases there is now a return to older management forms, in so far as the reversal can be undertaken without appearing to be an admission of failure. However, the language of the new managerialism dominates the public discourse, even if its practice is in retreat in some places.

All public sector agencies have a positive impact on the welfare and prospects of New Zealanders. The turmoil of reform, without any evident gains, has meant that those who benefit from the agencies have suffered, as has the public purse and the future. Undoubtedly the health of some New Zealanders has suffered. Yet less than might have been expected. For despite the insecurity and demoralisation the reforms have caused staff, they have continued to maintain their high standards of performance in health care. Fortunately for the patients, the culture of the health professionals has triumphed, despite the attempt by the new managerialism to override it.

Notes

1. Throughout this chapter the term 'reform' is used in its dictionary meaning of 'form again'. It is not intended to imply that the changes were necessarily progressive.
2. Ironically, the Treasury is one of the few public sector organisations which has not been affected by generic managers. All its senior executives had experience as junior Treasury officials, and few have outside public sector experience, other than perhaps graduate school.
3. Systematic measurement might find that the gains were somewhat less than claimed, since the conventional measures have tended to look at output per person employed, and failed to incorporate the redundant labour force which often became self-employed subcontractors.
4. A preferred medicine list usually involves the hospital doctor being able to prescribe from a limited list. Where it is necessary to go outside the list (to more expensive drugs) agreement is required from a senior clinician or a panel.
5. Here the term 'clinician' is used to refer to the person making a decision at the personal or clinical level. Traditionally the clinician was a doctor, but today such decisions can be made — explicitly or implicitly — by nurses and technicians.

References

Bowie, R. D. 1992, 'Health expenditure and health reforms: a comment', *New Zealand Medical Journal*, 11 November, no. 105, p. 458.

Bowie, R. & Shirley, I. 1994, 'Political and economic perspectives on recent health policy', in J. Spicer, A. Trlin & J. Walton (eds), *Social Dimensions of Health and Disease: New Zealand Perspectives*, Dunmore Press, Palmerston North, pp. 298–322.

Easton, B. H. 1989, 'The commercialisation of the New Zealand economy: from think big to privatisation', in B. H. Easton (ed.), *The Making of Rogernomics*, Auckland University Press, pp. 114–31.
―― 1994, 'How did the health reforms blitzkrieg fail?', *Political Science*, vol. 46, no. 2, December, pp.214–33.
Easton, B. H. & Bowie, R. D. 1993, Some aggregate health statistics: through time and between countries, paper presented to the 1993 Public Health Association Conference, Wellington.
New Zealand Treasury 1987, *Government Management: Post Election Briefing to the Incoming Government*, Wellington.
Pollit, C. 1994, *Managerialism and the Public Services: Cuts or Cultural Change in the 1990s?*, 2nd edn, Blackwell, London.
Upton, S. 1991, *Your Health and the Public Health*, GP Print, Wellington.
Wilson, P. D. 1993, Letter to the Ministers of Health, Crown Enterprises, and Finance, 17 December.

Part II

Means of Asserting Control

Intruder

I know I should not be here
there are factory
signs and dogs
that say so.

Afraid that my curves
will protrude across
some edge
I seek the dark and moist
parts of the place.
The parts that are
useless for industry

where even the moon
is not.

Susan Bower

News of the Day

Asserting control but only remotely
through channels one to ten
moves me across a non-information spectrum
of news
filtered to produce
manageable comment
by snappy, made-up crews.

Diluted by products
which sandwich programs
for an exchange of futures
which I cannot control,
this mass
bolsters my isolation,
crosses wires of distraction
and has a soothsayer effect
which beguiles vulnerable publics.

Annette Falahey

ALL ACROSS THE NATION – COAST TO COAST – LIVE
LAUGH
BE ANGRY
FEEL GOOD
BE HORRIFIED AND ANXIOUS
WELL DONE. THIS IS ALL PART OF THE NEW FASCISM. YOU'RE IN IT UP TO YOUR NECK
ONLY JOKING. YOU'RE A FREE MAN. EVERYTHING IS O.K. STAY TUNED.
Leunig

TOTAL QUALITY CONTROL
TQC
CONTINUOUS IMPROVEMENT
TOTAL QUALITY MANAGMENT
TQM
QUALITY ASSURANCE
MANAGEMENT
WORKER
VICKI

4.
Managing Labour in the 1990s

John Buchanan

> The most powerful instrument of political authority is the power to give names and to enforce definitions. (Thomas Hobbes, cited in Chorover 1979, p. 182)

One of the hallmarks of contemporary managerialist discourse is its tendency to define social, economic or political issues as management problems. In the field of labour management (i.e. managing people at work) the 'problem' no longer involves addressing the complexities of 'personnel' or 'industrial relations' issues. Rather, labour-related issues are seen as a special case of managing resources to achieve particular outcomes, the only difference being that the resources are human. Unsurprisingly, this branch of managerialism is commonly referred to as 'human resource management'.

This chapter addresses three issues. First: what are the key characteristics of managerialist ideology as applied to labour-related issues? This section examines the rhetoric of the 'new' ideology of human resource management. Consideration is then given to the reality: how extensively is this rhetoric applied in practice? It is argued that while elements of the rhetoric sound attractive, the reality is that unilateral control on the basis of the management prerogative is the prevailing norm in most Australian workplaces. The chapter concludes by considering more appropriate ways of understanding and addressing problems associated with organising labour at work in the 1990s.

Key characteristics of managerialist ideology as applied to managing people at work

Managerialist ideology places managers at the centre of Australia's current and future economic development. The report of the Federal Government's Industry Task Force on Leadership and Management Skills (the Karpin Report) provides a useful statement of this sentiment:

> The adaptive capacity of the economy depends on managers. Seizing opportunities offered in the changing global economy is a formidable challenge ... The adaptive capacity of our economy therefore depends on the flexibility of our managers ...
>
> Without appropriately skilled managers who can adapt themselves and their organisations to change, it will continue to be difficult for Australian enterprises to maintain their competitiveness. (Industry Task Force on Leadership and Management Skills 1995, p. 8)

Having established the centrality of management to future prosperity, managerialist discourse typically devotes most attention to identifying the 'rigidities' and 'inflexibilities' that constrain effective management performance. Inefficiencies in the field of labour management are commonly held to be:

a. personnel and industrial relations functions that are not integrated with the mainstream management of the enterprise;
b. approaches to personnel management that are too centralised within the enterprise;
c. neglect of workers as individuals arising from 'collectivist' approaches to labour management such as industrial relations; and
d. worker estrangement and alienation arising from all these 'inefficiencies' (Storey 1989).

Having identified these 'problems', human resource management theorists have developed a range of 'solutions'. The literature on this subject is enormous. For the sake of convenience the critical synthesis prepared by Storey (1989) will be considered. Other useful summaries and critiques have been prepared by Rose (1989), Blyton and Turnbull (1994) and Wright (1994, 1995).

Storey argues that the essential features of human resource management ideology can be summarised as follows:

1. *A commitment to making human resource management strategic* One of the major tenets of modern labour management ideology is that 'people management' issues should be integrated with mainstream management thinking and practice. Traditionally, labour management has been secondary to financial, marketing or production management.

Modern advocates of human resource management believe human resources should be recognised as just as central to business success as other resources. This objective is regularly contrasted with the allegedly 'strategic' personnel and industrial relations management practices of the past where labour issues were treated as problems of a different order compared with other areas of management.

2. *Devolution and decentralisation of authority — letting go of the chains* Better integration of human resources in production will occur if responsibility for labour issues lies with line managers instead of personnel or industrial relations specialists. Line managers, it is argued, are better placed to integrate the management of labour with the other functions of the enterprise. If a central human resource department is to remain, it should act as a facilitator and adviser to line management and not be directive or prescriptive. This type of change is often referred to as devolution or decentralisation of the labour management function.

3. *Increasing the focus on the individual* Human resource management ideology has had a major impact on the policy and practice of industrial relations. Advocates of the new approach argue that there is an urgent need to have the concerns of labour management shift from management–trade union relations, to management–employee relations. The profoundly political nature of modern labour management ideology is most apparent in this context. It is especially clear in the preference for employee relations based on individualist philosophies (e.g. individual contracts of employment) and its desire to undermine more socially based approaches to managing employment issues such as collective bargaining with unions. This aspect of the new managerialist ideology has been most strongly supported by peak employer bodies such as the Business Council of Australia (BCA) and the Australian Chamber of Commerce and Industry (ACCI). These forces have had a profound impact on industrial relations policy. Indeed, most recent industrial law reform has resulted from the agenda set by groups such as these.

4. *Empowering workers* Allied to this individualism is a commitment to empowering workers. Human resource management advocates believe that employees should be encouraged to exercise initiative and increase their commitment to work as a result. In this context it is argued that managers should now see themselves as 'enablers' or 'facilitators' and not as supervisors controlling the work force. The popularity of team-based forms of work organisation is a manifestation of this sentiment.

It is important to note that these elements of modern labour management ideology are not part of a tightly formulated program with which all adherents agree. Like any political movement there are different tendencies. For example, some advocates are keen on the individualist aspect, as is evident among New Right managers supporting individual contracts of employment. Others prefer to emphasise the 'team' concept and the need to empower workers. Despite differences such as these, most supporters subscribe to the key tenets outlined earlier.

The benefits purported to be associated with this new approach to labour management are considerable. These include greater flexibility and hence competitiveness for firms in the marketplace, and more challenging and interesting jobs for employees. The BCA has gone so far as to assert that if changes inspired by this agenda are introduced, labour productivity should increase by over 25 per cent (BCA 1989, pp. 25, 60).

The reality of labour management in the 1980s and early 1990s

The ideology of human resource management has become very influential in management education and public policy circles. For example, the old Institute for Personnel Management, the professional association for labour management specialists in Australia, has changed its name to the Australian Human Resource Institute. Most labour-related courses in management schools are based on a human resource management approach. Even in departments teaching industrial relations, units in human resource management are on the increase. The human resource management push has been most influential in the area of industrial relations policy, with the attack on the award system and rise of enterprise bargaining (Buchanan & Callus 1993; O'Brien 1994). As noted earlier, this approach has also been very popular with both peak representatives of employers: the BCA and the ACCI. While support for this ideology is widespread in leading management circles, it is important to consider what impact it is having on the day-to-day practice of managing labour in the workplace.

Fortunately, major data sources are now available on approaches to labour management in both Australia and overseas. These range from large-scale surveys of workplace industrial relations through to the conduct of quite detailed case studies of labour management on the job. The most comprehensive study of this nature has been the Australian Workplace Industrial Relations Survey or AWIRS (Callus, Morehead, Cully & Buchanan 1992). This involved face-to-face interviews with 2004 managers at workplaces with five or more employees in all industries other than agriculture and defence. Although the survey field work was conducted in late 1989 and early 1990, the findings of the survey have been confirmed in a range of later studies (e.g. Callus 1993; Peetz, Short & Preston 1993; Watts, Rimmer, Buchanan & Callus 1993; Short, Romeyn & Callus 1994). The AWIRS is of most interest because it provides insight into both management philosophy and practice prevailing at workplace level.

When asked about their approaches to organising people at work, most workplace managers involved in the AWIRS tend to use the rhetoric of human resource management. Table 4.1 reports on their responses to the open-ended question: How would you describe management's approach or philosophy to managing employees at this workplace?

Table 4.1: Management approach or philosophy to managing employees

Type of approach	Workplace managers (%)
Open communication	11
Teamwork–consultation	33
Personal approach	35
Open-door approach	17
Committees	2
Confrontation	1
Pragmatic	6
Other	24

Source: Callus, Morehead, Cully & Buchanan 1992, p. 269.

It is apparent that most managers believe they are open and consultative. If these sentiments were followed in practice a large number of managers would be 'empowering workers' and 'sensitive to their individual needs'.

Responses to attitudinal questions can, however, be misleading. What people say and what they do are often quite different. A good indicator of how managers treat their employees is revealed in the way they manage change. Managers involved in the AWIRS were asked about the nature of changes affecting employees at their workplaces. The survey found a vast amount of restructuring occurring with the introduction of new products or services, major redesigning of jobs, and particularly the introduction of new technology. Managers were then asked who was involved in the key decisions concerning these changes. The results are summarised in table 4.2.

Table 4.2: Involvement of employees and unions in decisions about significant workplace change

Level of involvement in decision-making	Employees at the workplace (%)	Unions at the workplace (%)
Made the decision	–	–
Were consulted	32	28
Were informed	45	26
Were not informed	23	46

Source: Callus, Morehead, Cully & Buchanan 1992, p. 190.

This table clearly shows that employees and their unions rarely, if ever, make decisions about workplace change and are only consulted in a minority of cases. In many instances they are not even informed of the key decisions affecting their working lives. Trends similar to these were identified in the 1992 workplace bargaining survey. This showed that while the level of change had increased, very few of these changes involved negotiations with employees or their representatives (see Callus 1993; Short, Romeyn & Callus 1994).

How management makes decisions within its own ranks is another good indicator of how human resource management philosophy is applied. Table 4.3 provides information on which levels of management decide particular industrial relations issues.

Table 4.3: Who decides on labour management issues at the workplace

	Line management (%)	Specialist workplace management (%)	Senior workplace management (%)	Manager beyond the workplace (%)
Levels of overtime	35	14	34	5
Recruiting non-managerial employees	23	22	32	13
Deciding changes in non-managerial pay	8	17	35	33
Employment levels for workplace	6	15	41	31
Purchase of major capital equipment	4	8	36	44

Source: Callus, Morehead, Cully & Buchanan 1992, p. 78.

It is very clear that the less important decisions are settled 'down the line', while the critical issues affecting workplace performance are settled by senior workplace or head office management. Far from 'letting go of the chains', most organisations still appear to be quite centralised and controlled from above. The rhetoric of devolution and decentralisation is yet to make a real impact in practice at most workplaces.

Much of the impetus for reducing the rigidities and inflexibilities allegedly imposed on workplaces by external factors such as unions and awards has come from human resource management advocates. Management, it is said, needs more room to manage. What, however, do workplace managers report as the major barriers to improving efficiency in their workplaces? The responses from those involved in the AWIRS are summarised in table 4.4.

Table 4.4: Major reasons why management cannot make changes at the workplace

Issues	Managers afflicted by this constraint (%)
Lack of money or resources	29
Management or organisation policy	20
Unions	14
Government rules and regulations	12
Awards	7
Other	24

Source: Callus, Morehead, Cully & Buchanan 1992, p. 340.

It is apparent that problems within management structures, as well as access to resources, are a far more significant hindrance to effective day-to-day management than problems arising from unions, governments and awards.

In the arena of labour management, it appears that the new managerialism suffers from a number of serious problems. First, its rhetoric on the need for employee involvement and focusing on the individual is hardly matched in practice. Instead, it appears that unilateral decision-making is still very much the mainstream management practice. Second, its rhetoric concerning the organisation of management itself is empty. Decision-making within management is highly centralised on key issues such as setting overall staffing levels and deciding on new capital investments. Third, the alleged need to reduce the role and influence of unions and 'allow management to manage' is poorly informed. The key issues retarding management performance arise from problems within management itself and not from external labour market institutions.

If the rhetoric of human resource management provides few insights into what is actually occurring in day-to-day labour management at the workplace, what role is it performing? The widespread support for this new ideology implies it performs some kind of function. Arguably its attractiveness lies in the central role it allocates to managers for improving organisational (and ultimately national economic) performance. In this sense it provides a modern version of the old doctrine of the management prerogative. Previously this doctrine linked management's right to control the workplace with ownership of the means of production. The evolution of different corporate forms and the emergence of professional managers as agents responsible for running organisations has generated a need for more sophisticated discourses of control. Human resource management is best understood in this context. At its most basic it represents a modified version of this very old doctrine of management's right to run the workplace as it sees fit. While some of the rhetoric may be about participation and devolution, these practices will only be adopted if senior management maintains ultimate control.

This development in management discourse has an important political dimension. Human resource management ideology marks an explicit break with earlier industrial relations notions of management which recognised differences between managers and employees and the right of unions to share in the regulation of some workplace issues (Flanders 1966; Fox 1974, pp. 251–73). Human resource management ideology leaves no space for such a pluralist approach to workplace operations. People can participate on management terms or not at all. Far from contributing to the development of an exciting new world of increased opportunities at work, what is actually occurring is the restoration and legitimation of managerial prerogatives under the guise of an allegedly new approach to labour management (see Wright 1995; McInnes 1987 and Gospel 1992 develop similar lines of argument concerning UK experiences.)

Promoting a basis for organising labour at work

There are no universal labour management problems which can be remedied by some universal set of management solutions. To begin with there is no such thing as the typical enterprise. On the contrary, there is a diverse range of employment situations. The nature of this diversity can be appreciated by considering the variety of Australian workplaces according to their industry and scale of operation. In terms of industry differences, for example, a quarter of the work force is employed in retail and a quarter in blue-collar-dominated industries such as manufacturing, mining and construction. Labour management structures and practices that prevail in the former are unlikely to work in the latter, let alone in other sectors such as banking, communications, transport and community services. It is also important to remember the segmentation of the work force in terms of enterprise size: about a third are employed in businesses with fewer than twenty employees and an equal proportion are engaged in enterprises with more than 1000 workers (ABS 1992). Labour management strategies designed for the former will, generally speaking, be totally irrelevant in the latter.

In addition, when thinking about the issue of organising labour at work it is important to define it as something other than a 'management problem'. No workplace is an island and often the problems that afflict one workplace are shared by others. The challenge is to identify these and address them on a coordinated basis. The most important labour market problems are unemployment, arbitrary inequalities in pay (especially for women), inadequate skill formation arrangements and limited opportunities for career advancement. Simply letting 'management manage' will do little, if anything, to address these issues. Labour market problems are not primarily managerial in nature; they arise from major structural inequalities.

Addressing these problems will require creative solutions. Historically, labourist and social democratic initiatives have relied on legislative interventions to maintain certain standards in the labour market. Since the Second World War, limited reliance has also been placed on monetary and fiscal policy to manage demand to maximise employment growth. In more recent times attempts have been made to increase democracy at the workplace. These initiatives have helped alleviate many labour market problems. Together, however, they have not eradicated the problems of unemployment, inadequate skill formation arrangements and gender-based segregation in the labour market.

It is therefore essential to consider developing additional measures to address these long-standing problems in the labour market. Indeed, many employment-related problems will require reforms that go beyond the workplace and the labour market. Redirecting investment flows, for example, will be essential if a capital stock capable of maintaining full employment is to be established (see, for example, Pasinetti 1981, pp. 148–50; Pontusson 1992, pp. 29–31). A range of labour-market-related initiatives could, however, contribute to a wider strategy of social, economic and cultural renewal. Maurice Glasman (1994) has argued that the agenda for progressive reform should be broadened to include promotion of what he calls 'vocational democracy' (Glasman 1994; p. 73). For him, one of the pressing priorities is to increase citizens' skills and capacities to both reduce their reliance on the state for protection and to enhance their labour market position relative to management. He believes this is best achieved by them acquiring transferable skills which minimise the need for close supervision on the job. Drawing on the experiences and the 1981 reform program of the Polish trade union movement, Solidarity, Glasman argues there is a strong link between levels of vocational competence and the role of management. According to Glasman, Solidarity held that efficiency would not be improved through granting greater power to management but rather by giving enterprise-based works councils the power 'to nominate and dismiss managers (Glasman 1994, p. 73). Glasman notes that this was justified because management was seen as the responsibility of all employees. He continues:

> The meaning of this is not that there should be no management, but that self-discipline and efficient organisation does not require

an external enforcer with scientific techniques and abstract power. Self management is the responsibility of each member of the enterprise, and as the people most affected by the decisions and who know their job and industry best, workers should exercise the responsibility of decision making. [Solidarity's policies were] a justification for vocational democracy based on the principles of efficiency and not only on ethical principles or class power. (Glasman 1994; p. 73)

The nexus between levels of vocational competence and managerial authority has long been recognised in the literature on how skill formation contributes to international competitiveness. One of the most extensive projects on this subject involved an examination of why German manufacturing appeared to be superior to French manufacturing in the 1970s and 1980s (Maurice et al. 1984; see also related studies by Prais et al. 1989). Twelve detailed case studies of matched plants in similar industries using similar technologies in the two countries formed the core of the analysis. The researchers identified how firms' practices were intimately related to the environment in which they operated, especially the education, training and wage determination systems. In particular the strong vocational training system in Germany ensured that a steady supply of technically competent workers requiring minimal supervision were available to employers. France's generalist education system meant employers there had to rely on internal labour markets and close supervision to ensure work was performed efficiently. The study clearly highlighted the direct relationship between general levels of vocational competence and management; the higher the level of vocational competence the lower the need for close supervision (Maurice, Sellier & Silvestre 1984, 1986; Marsden 1990).

The importance of this underlying approach to labour market operations has been borne out by the relative success of key elements of the German labour movement in the 1980s and 1990s. Despite facing anti-union governments at federal and regional levels, key sectors of the German labour movement, especially in metal and engineering, have made major gains in reducing working hours, defending employment conditions and increasing labour productivity (Swenson 1989; Thelen 1992). Building reform strategies on the basis of coherent and widely recognised notions of skill gives all those interested in progressive social change at the workplace and in the labour market a key point of reference when struggling in a hostile political environment. The insights from the early Solidarity movement and the German metal industry provide important lessons for all those seeking an alternative to the free market, managerialist rhetoric (see Buchanan, forthcoming, for more details). It should be noted that key elements of these experiences have inspired many of the reforms under way in Australia's vocational training system, many of which were initiated by the union movement (see e.g. Carmichael 1992; Evatt 1995).

Conclusion

Despite the claims of its supporters, the emergence of human resource management as the dominant ideology for labour management in the 1990s does not represent anything particularly new. In many ways it is simply the reworking of old concepts dressed up in contemporary jargon. The chasm between the rhetoric and actual labour management practices highlights this fact. It is the underlying structure of the ideology with its assumptions about the central importance of management control at enterprise level and not its specific concerns with things like decentralisation of decision-making and 'empowering' workers that are the key to its popularity.

In devising alternatives it is important to break with the key features of the human resource management ideology. The problems concerning the organisation and deployment of labour are not those that reside at the enterprise level. No one set of solutions can be applied irrespective of the industry and size of a workplace. Most labour-related problems arise from the structure of the labour market. When devising strategies to address these it is important to recognise the limitations of reforms inspired by social and industrial democrats in the past. New institutions that go beyond the market and the state need to be established to enhance the power and dignity of ordinary workers. The issue is not how to create 'progressive' managers, but rather how to create social conditions in which the management function is shared more equitably and efficiently among all concerned. In this respect, institutions and practices that raise the general level of competence of employees appear to be essential. Lessons in how such institutions can be established have been provided by labour movements overseas and in parts of Australia's own union movement. It is important that we build on these insights and begin to undermine the ascendancy of human resource management as an ideology and the resurgence of the managerial prerogative as a practice.

References

Australian Bureau of Statistics (ABS) 1992, *Profiles of Australian Business*, Cat. no. 1306.0 AGPS, Canberra.

Blyton, P. & Turnbull, P. 1994, *The Dynamics of Employee Relations*, Macmillan, London.

Buchanan, J. (forthcoming), 'Industrial relations, enterprise bargaining and the continuing relevance of socialist principles', in G. Maddox & T. Battin (eds), *Socialism in Contemporary Australia*, Longman, South Melbourne.

Buchanan, J. & Callus, R. 1993, 'Equity and efficiency at work: the need for labour market regulation in Australia', *Journal of Industrial Relations*, vol. 35, no. 4, December, pp. 515–37.

Business Council of Australia 1989, *Enterprise Based Bargaining Units: A Better Way of Working*, Melbourne.

Callus, R. 1993, *Change and Bargaining in Australian Workplaces: A Report on the 1992 Workplace Bargaining Survey*, Mimo, Australian Centre for Industrial Relations Research and Teaching, University of Sydney.

Callus, R., Morehead, A., Cully, M. & Buchanan, J. 1992, *Industrial Relations at Work: The Australian Workplace Industrial Relations Survey*, AGPS, Canberra.

Carmichael, L. (Council Chair) 1992, *The Australian Vocational Certificate Training System*, Report of the Employment and Skills Formation Council, National Board of Employment, Education and Training, Canberra.

Chorover, S. L. 1979, *From Genesis to Genocide: The Meaning of Human Nature and the Power of Behaviour Control*, MIT Press, Massachusetts.

Dawkins, J. 1994, 'Business Council set the government's agenda', *Australian Financial Review*, July.

Evatt Foundation 1995, *Unions 2001: A Blueprint for Union Activism*, Evatt Foundation, Sydney.

Flanders, A. 1966, *Industrial Relations: What's Wrong With the System?*, Faber & Faber, London.

Fox, A. 1974, *Beyond Contract: Work Relations, Power and Trust Relations*, Faber & Faber, London.

Glasman, M. 1994, 'The great deformation: Polanyi, Poland and the terrors of planned spontaneity', *New Left Review*, no. 205, May–June.

Gospel, H. 1992, *Markets, Firms and Management of Labour in Modern Britain*, Cambridge University Press, Cambridge.

Industry Task Force on Leadership and Management Skills 1995, *Enterprising Nation: Renewing Australia's Managers to Meet the Challenges of the Asia–Pacific Century*, Executive Summary, Canberra.

MacInnes, J. 1987, *Thatcherism at Work*, Open University Press, Milton Keynes.

Marsden, D. 1990, 'Institutions and labour mobility: occupational and internal labour markets in Britain, France, Italy and West Germany', in R. Brunetta & C. Dell'Aringa (eds), *Labour Relations and Economic Performance*, Macmillan, London.

Maurice, M., Sellier, F. & Silvestre, J. J. 1984, 'The search for a societal effect in the production of company hierarchy: a comparison of France and Germany', in P. Osterman (ed.), *Internal Labour Markets*, MIT Press, Massachusetts.

——1986, *The Social Foundations of Industrial Power*, MIT Press, Massachusetts.

O'Brien, J. 1994, 'McKinsey, Hilmer and the BCA: the "New Management" model of labour market reform', *Journal of Industrial Relations*, vol. 36, no. 4, December, pp. 468–90.

Pasinetti, L. 1981, *Structural Change and Economic Growth — A Theoretical Essay on the Dynamics of the Wealth of Nations*, Cambridge University Press, Cambridge.

Peetz, D., Short, M. & Preston, A. 1993, *Enterprise Bargaining and Workplace Change: Evidence from the Workplace Bargaining Research Project*, Department of Industrial Relations, Canberra.

Pontusson, J. 1992, *The Limits of Social Democracy — Investment Politics and Sweden*, Cornell University Press, Ithaca, New York.

Prais, J., Jarvie, V. & Wagner, K. 1989, 'Productivity and vocational skills in Britain and Germany: hotels', *National Institute Economic Review*, November, pp. 52–69.

Rose, N. 1989, *Governing the Soul: The Shaping of the Private Self*, RKP, London.

Short, M., Romeyn, J. & Callus, R. 1994, *Reform and Bargaining at the Workplace and Enterprise: Evidence from Two Surveys*, Department of Industrial Relations, Canberra.

Storey, J. 1989, *New Perspectives in Human Resource Management*, RKP, London.

Swenson, P. 1989, *Fair Shares — Unions, Pay and Politics in Sweden and West Germany*, Cornell University Press, Ithaca, New York.

Thelen, K. 1992, 'The politics of flexibility in the German metalworking industries', in M. Golden & J. Pontusson (eds), *Bargaining for Change — Union Politics in North America and Europe*, Cornell University Press, Ithaca, New York.

Watts, L., Rimmer, M., Buchanan, J. & Callus, R. 1993, The enterprise bargaining project: cross case analysis, unpublished manuscript, National Key Centre for Industrial Relations, Monash University & Australian Centre for Industrial Relations Research and Teaching, University of Sydney.

Wright, C. 1994, *New Production Concepts in Australian Industry: A Re-evaluation of the 1970s and 1980s,* Working Paper No 32, Australian Centre for Industrial Relations Research and Teaching, Sydney.

——1995, *The Management of Labour — An Historical Analysis of Labour Management in Australian Industry*, Cambridge University Press, Melbourne.

5.
Market Control of the Media

Wendy Bacon

According to a 1994 survey, the great majority of Australian journalists see themselves as professionals who must strive to be as 'objective' as possible. Objectivity for most of them is associated with fairness, and presenting both sides of a dispute (Schultz 1994). They see themselves as professionals applying independent judgment to the selection of news stories. The paradox which needs to be explained is why, if this is the case, news agendas are so closely mirrored across news organisations, stories are based on common underlying and unstated assumptions, and the stories produced seem to follow a set formula.

A short news report on the Ok Tedi mine in Papua New Guinea in an April 1995 business section of the *Australian* (Caruana 1995) is an example. The good news reported was that the mining companies had nearly settled their dispute with the local landowners. Only half way down the item is it stated that a tailings dam will be built to stop river-system pollution. What was the dispute about? Are the landowners satisfied? Is the compensation deal on which the settlement is based a good one from their point of view? Will the tailings dam work? What will be the human cost if it does not? These questions are not raised. They do not need to be because there is a shared unstated understanding between publisher and assumed reader that getting on with mining is the key objective. This does not mean that the odd reader might not react with horror at the mention of pollution and go hunting for more information, or that a reader might not even find a feature published elsewhere by News Ltd backgrounding the issue, but the preferred message is crystal clear — what matters most is that business continues as usual.

As Australia's only national newspaper, News Ltd's the *Australian* likes to remind its readers and advertisers that they are more likely than others to be highly educated people who eat in restaurants, drink bottled wine, own computers and travel overseas. In this case they are also businesspeople. The journalist does not need to be reminded of these matters. They are underlying assumptions which infuse the selection of the story, its leading paragraph and the decisions about what readers need to know.

Daily there is a blow-by-blow description of the battle to decide *who* will own Australia's media. The question of ownership is an important one although readers and audiences are rarely told why that is the case. Those capital cities in which the only daily newspaper is owned by News Ltd are unlikely to read a critical perspective about one of the world's largest entertainment and media companies, nor are they likely to be fully informed about debates about Australia's aviation industry, in which News Ltd through Ansett is a major player. Those who read magazines owned by Kerry Packer's Consolidated Press will not read exposés of Australia's richest man.

The even more important question of *how* the media is controlled and what impact that control has on society is missing altogether.

An explanation of why whole slices of everyday life and the voices and perspectives of whole sections of the community are missing or unrepresented in the most popular media is one of the biggest untold stories. There have been many studies demonstrating that this is the case (Australian Centre for Independent Journalism 1992; National Report on Women 1993; Jakubowitz et al. 1994). Women, especially poor women, citizens from non-Anglo-Celtic backgrounds, and young people are all unrepresented. Deregulation is good, industrial disputes are bad, cuts to government spending are good are all underlying assumptions behind much economic and political reporting.

It is the commercial nature of the ownership rather than the identity of the particular owner which provides at least part of the answer for why the public sphere created by the media fails to meet the interests of so many citizens. The point is a simple one: control over the most popular media is exercised by combinations of huge media companies whose main objective is to make money out of informing and entertaining. A large proportion of that money is made from attracting advertisers who need to reach audiences with their marketing messages.

The journalists who produce the stories which inform and entertain are just one group of players in the media production line. Just down the passage are the advertising executives whose job it is to attract the advertisers who need to reach audiences, and marketers whose job it is to maximise those audiences.

The press gallery promotes 1980s 'economic rationalism'

The Ok Tedi example could be repeated hundreds of times from around Australia each day. Brian Toohey has written of how the media promoted 'economic rationalist' policies in the 1980s. Counter-arguments and policies were ignored or dismissed as 'irrational' (Toohey 1994). He interviewed twenty press gallery journalists who all agreed that the Australian Parliament's press gallery uniformly adopted an economic rationalist point of view. Explanations varied from those who agreed with the Editor in Chief of the *Australian*, Paul Kelly, that the 1980s provided an opportunity for 'crusading zeal and idealism' in support of economic rationalists, to those who preferred to believe that they were simply reporting the prevailing government orthodoxy.

According to Toohey, the most influential source of all during that period was the Federal Treasurer, Paul Keating, who gave those who conformed closely to the official line of the government and top economic bureaucrats the journalistic privilege of being placed on the 'high grade drip'.

> The 'high grade drip' is a favourite Keating phrase referring to the mix of information, opinion, gossip and outright distortion which flows via non-attributable briefings from himself, his staff, and senior members of the official family.
>
> Being put on the drip certainly makes for an easier journalistic life. There is no shortage of stories, regardless of how self-serving the sources. Nor is there likely to be trouble with head office. No journalist was ever sacked for excessive obsequiousness during Keating's heyday as Treasurer, nor likely to be so during his more abrasive term as Prime Minister. (Toohey 1994, p. 22)

Those who did not conform were not only denied the supply of information but say they received angry calls, even threats that friendly media executives would be persuaded to remove them. Meanwhile back in Sydney and Melbourne, John Fairfax and Sons and News Ltd launched new glossy business magazines, *Business Review Weekly* and *Australian Business*. These magazines, fuelled by business advertising and news designed to be useful to readers, were openly celebratory of the worst excesses of the 1980s entrepreneurs.

Although Toohey's book, which is a broad analysis of economic policy formation in the 1980s, was widely reviewed when it was published, there was almost no discussion of the section of it which dealt with the media. Many journalists do recognise that the uncritical economic stance of the press betrayed Australian society in the 1980s and declare that it must not be allowed to happen again. But there has been little discussion of the more general questions which Toohey's analysis raises: the reliance by journalists on official sources, the methods by which journalists who do not conform to the 'party line' are controlled, and why certain underlying beliefs and views underpin news coverage.

History

A historical glimpse at the development of Australia's media shows that it is no accident that notions of objective journalism and a free press prevail in a media dominated by commercial values. Indeed the beginnings of the media in European history can be traced back to the development of commercialism in the sixteenth century.

The drive to discover new trade possibilities and to accumulate capital was accompanied by the development of what the German social theorist Jurgen Habermas has called the 'public sphere', an arena in which political debate could occur between citizens. Face-to-face discussions between merchants through messengers and later in public places such as coffee houses were soon followed by the circulation of literary tracts, newsletters and finally newspapers. Over several centuries 'liberty of the press' became a slogan in the tussle for power between the new economic class of the bourgeoisie and royal authority.

The development of notions of a free press and its relationship to the rise of the middle class can be traced in a variety of cultural settings. But the American War of Independence and the Bill of Rights provides one of the strongest statements of the free press as a vehicle to protect the interest of citizens against the government. The American Constitution and its First Amendment guaranteeing free speech was an expression of the importance of a free press.

As Chris Nash (1995) put it in an Australian Centre for Independent Journalism seminar on media accountability in 1993:

> What it [the First Amendment] amounts to is that people need to be empowered against their governments, against the judiciary, against the legislature and against the executive. In other words the right to freedom of speech and hence freedom of the press is a political right that restricts the power of government and in that respect also restricts the power of the courts. It presupposes that the media is on the side of the people against the power of the government.
>
> The First Amendment was framed towards the end of the eighteenth century when the media as we know it did not exist. The publishers that it set out to protect were, by and large, individuals writing seditious tracts against the government of the day and perhaps passing it amongst their very small circle. The media as we know it, large corporations with many employees, financial resources and

enormous reach in terms of the number of people who read, watch or listen to what they publish is quite a different kettle of fish. These days the media are giant corporations with a global reach and the power to topple governments. The professional relationship between journalists and their publishers is complex and very ambivalent. So is the relationship between journalists and governments.

Similarly, during the nineteenth century in Britain, commentators characterised the press as a Fourth Estate which would provide a check on the power of three other estates — the monarchy, the clergy and the Parliament. The role of the press was to inform the public and represent those with grievances. The public, of course, did not include those who were yet to get the vote — everyone but middle-class men. Most of the relevant work which has been done on the economic history of the press has addressed British experience. O'Malley (1971) described how during the period from 1800 to 1850 the printing establishments which produced newspapers grew from what was virtually a backyard industry to become heavily capitalised enterprises characterised by large-scale investment and potential profits. This was as a result of technological developments which radically increased both the potential circulation and the potential capital growth of the press.

> As the century progressed, it increasingly became the case that only wealthy interests could afford to establish or maintain a competitive daily newspaper ... On top of the costs of establishment, there were the tremendous expenses involved in the continuing production of a large-scale newspaper. (Curran 1977)

As James Curran has pointed out, 'The escalation in printing costs in the meantime did not just affect individuals' access to the public sphere: it debarred access to large sections of the community' (Curran 1977).

The market for the expanding press was the prosperous middle class, the market for the manufactured goods. The trend was for advertising to provide an increasing proportion of revenue from the press, a trend which accelerated with the advent of commercial broadcasting.

While the origin of the press lies in the economic developments which gave rise to a middle class, a vibrant and outspoken radical press developed which was popular with working-class readers. Curran (1981) has described how the British radical working-class press survived a century of government opposition before it was finally threatened by this increase in production costs and the intrusion of advertising in the second half of the nineteenth century. He cites an advertising manual which warned in 1851 that 'character is of more importance than number. A journal that circulates thousands among the upper or middle classes is a better medium than would be one circulating a hundred thousand among the lower classes' (Curran 1981).

Curran says that one of four things happened to radical papers that failed to meet the requirements of advertisers: 'They either closed down, accommodated to advertising pressure by moving up-market, stayed in a small audience ghetto with manageable losses, or accepted an alternative source of institutional patronage'.

The contradictions of professionalism

Much has been written about whether or not journalism is a profession. It is much more important to look at what meaning professionalism has for those who would claim it. It was partly in the context of increased advertising that notions of professionalism developed in the early twentieth century among journalists.

An important part of professional values which developed among journalists embodied the idea that editorial should be separate from advertising. The idea was that news should have a legitimacy and a representative nature beyond the interests of the advertising base which drives the paper. Professionalism ensured that the focus remained on a supposedly autonomous individual carrying out a series of reporting tasks. A focus on balance and accuracy left few opportunities to think about the questions that were not being asked, or the stories that were never run.

Soloski (1989) argues that journalism, accountancy and engineering are three professions which depend on large organisations for employment. In fact, management relies on news professionalism which cuts across organisations, along with internal editorial news policies (which also may be widely shared across organisations) to control the work of journalists. Editorial meetings play an important role in deciding which stories will be pursued. What is valued will be demonstrated by the stories given a 'good run', and which journalists receive rewards. Journalists learn that good reporters quickly develop a sense of what their editor or producer regards as a good story; that it is just as important to be able to 'pitch' a story as to produce it; that it pays to develop good relationships with those higher up the editorial hierarchy; and that some sources will get a run no matter what they say while others lack any credibility. Professionalism means knowing which 'facts' can be taken for granted and which facts need to be carefully checked. It involves taking rejection on the chin and recognising that there will always be another story.

But it would be a mistake to suggest that news production works smoothly. A minority of journalists remain critical of the news agendas of their media organisations. They see their role as pushing to extend the boundaries in an effort to make sure that stories of injustice or of the lives of the disadvantaged or other stories do get a run. They flourish at times when someone sympathetic to their view is in a position of influence or when the stories they see as news are also seen to be ones that will sell to readers. (For example, if there is a drive on to acquire women readers, more stories will be run on social issues in which market research has suggested women have an interest.) There are also many high-quality journalists in Australia who have been marginalised into advertising-driven supplements, banished to minor outlets or programs, or otherwise sidelined onto the backbench.

Toohey himself is a good example of how control and resistance works in the media. As editor of the now defunct weekly *National Times*, he fought to run what he regarded as one of the biggest stories of the 1980s: links between certain entrepreneurs and leading political figures. Eventually he was replaced as editor and later resigned from John Fairfax and Sons where he had been highly regarded by peers for his 'professionalism' for more than a decade. He started a small magazine of his own which was pursued in court by the Federal Government and lasted only several years. He now writes books and has become a regular contributor, but not a fully employed journalist, in the radio and print media.

The irony is that the same 'professionalism' which assists a normally smooth production process can also be used as a means of resisting management control. Editorial charters of independence, which became popular among journalists concerned about the possible damaging effects in shifting ownership during the late 1980s, are an example of this (Chadwick 1991). They are mostly intended to provide a bulwark against direct attempts by management to stop certain stories being run. On occasions John Fairfax and Sons' journalists have been prepared to stop work to resist such interference. But as time has shown, charters of independence do not help when the policies of editors are the problem. Recognising that charters do not challenge day-to-day control or the right of the owner to select the editor, media managers and owners have mostly been prepared to live with them.

Journalists working for Eastern Suburbs Newspapers (partly owned by the Hannan Group and Fairfax Community Newspapers), which publishes three of Sydney's largest suburban newspapers, also appealed to notions of professional ethics during an industrial dispute in which they campaigned for a modicum of editorial independence. At the beginning of their 1994 campaign these journalists did not have an editorial fax or the right to open mail addressed to the newspaper. Features were written by the advertising staff. On several occasions a manager directly interfered with copy which might offend advertisers. While the journalists were successful in gaining a fax and a little more independence in the news department, they adopted the 'realistic' stance of offering to assist in the writing of 'more professional' features to promote the activities of advertisers rather than resisting the idea that the articles should be run at all. But two young journalists left demoralised to work in other places. When interviewed, one said:

> I had the feeling we [journalists] were just there to fill in space. There were so many issues to cover and it was such a big catchment area — it was frighteningly hard to get stories in. You might get the story in and then it would be taken out if an advertisement came in at the last minute ... It made me really angry because suburban newspapers are the breeding ground for top newspaper people. The suburban newspaper is the only media outlet where you can find out what is happening in your community.

The other was concerned that the constant emphasis on advertising can have a 'destructive effect on journalism to the point where you might not recognise a good story if you saw one'. These journalists battle to find a niche in the industry where they can tell the stories they believe are significant.

Media ethics

There is a widespread view among journalists and the public that media ethics are a problem. Many journalists are aware of the contradiction between the ideas which legitimate their work and the daily practices in industry. Some respond with cynicism, others keep moving or quietly lobbying within their organisation to achieve a situation which fits more comfortably with their notion of what journalism could be in society.

Most of the debate about professional journalists' ethics focuses on issues of privacy, confidentiality of sources, cheque-book journalism, and in what circumstances journalists might hide their identity. There is surprisingly little discussion of the section of the journalists' Code of Ethics which says 'no journalist must be subject in their work to commercial influences'.

Yet the line between editorial and advertising which was part of the basis of professionalism and of this section of the code is collapsing. Many journalists work for sections of the media where the line between journalism, public relations and advertising is blurred. This is more obviously so in the magazine trade, in the suburban press and in info-tainment programs, but it is increasingly so in newspapers as well.

It was scarcely a surprise when, in May 1995, the *Australian*'s massive headline 'WE DID IT!' turned out to be a supplement of articles written to celebrate Australia's win in the West Indies cricket packaged as part of a wrap-around advertisement for News Ltd's Superleague. The entire back page of the supplement was occupied by a photograph of the 'Best of the Best', footballer Allan Langer, who said, 'With Superleague, I'm getting a chance to test myself against the best in the world. It's going to be a great challenge'. Global sport, News Ltd self-promotion, nationalism all neatly rolled into one.

More newspaper reporters have now been redirected to supplements while those left to report news complain that space is shrinking, giant headlines on the front page which were supposed to be reserved for the biggest news story may be just another advertisement, the availability of advertising and a niche market of readers drives the development of the magazine market, and the 1995 inquiry into sponsorship of ABC features are all indications that even the *appearance* of a separation between editorial and advertising is breaking down. The implications of these developments for either journalism as an occupation or for what is published have been glossed over in the recent Media, Arts and Entertainment Alliance review of the journalists' Code of Ethics. Yet they go to the very heart of the perception by many groups in society that the media coverage of many social issues is inadequate.

Women's magazines and advertising

There has been little research examining the relationship between advertising and editorial in the media. Curran first described how his historical analysis can be applied to the women's magazine market. Because cover prices do not meet production costs, the magazines had to attract advertising and so they are increasingly oriented towards the middle class. 'Much of [this] consumer journalism is sycophantic and uncritical. Consumer protection, even straight monitoring and evaluation of rival products, has tended to be avoided', he writes. Earnshaw took Curran's work on women's magazines further to examine the effects of advertising on the editorial content of British women's magazines. She identified two key areas of influence. These were that:

> a magazine must be pitched at a specific group of women in their capacity as consumers and not at a potentially new group of readers not yet provided with a section of the media to reflect their non-consumer interests. This may not be achieved by a conscious effort on the part of the journalists working for the magazine, rather the limited field in which creative activity is to take place has already been defined.

The second influence takes the form of a more overt pressure on 'journalists to provide a suitable editorial environment for the use and consumption of advertisers' products' (Black 1992).

When Julie Black (then a postgraduate journalist at the University of Technology Sydney, now working at the British Broadcasting

Corporation) interviewed Australian editors and advertisers working on women's magazines for a radio documentary, she found a more complex picture. For a start, while ex-editors said that the pressure to meet the demand of accompanying editorial by advertisers had increased, current editors wanted to assert that editorial independence as a value was still protected. Advertising managers were much more likely to talk openly of their success in getting special features for their advertising clients.

Julie Black asked *Mode* editor, Diana Chiccio, what influence advertising had on editorial considerations:

> CHICCIO: We don't go out and slander anyone or act irresponsibly in an editorial sense towards an advertiser, which I think is foolish in any magazine anyway. Well, I think we've got pretty much a free hand. Certainly that's my experience since I've been here.
>
> JB: Do you think it's important to have a clear distinction between advertising and editorial?
>
> CHICCIO: Oh absolutely ... yes.
>
> JB: Do you think there's quite a clear distinction in *Mode* between advertising and editorial?
>
> CHICCIO: I feel there is, I do. Yes.
>
> PATRICK CONNELLY (ADVERTISING MANAGER): We don't make any guarantees, but it is important that editorial is aware of advertisers. There's no reason why the two can't work together in most instances.
>
> JB: Do you think in any case the compromise is too much?
>
> CONNELLY: In our editorial department they certainly say so if they feel that way, though most of the time they can be resolved and we have a really nice group of advertisers and fortunately they are companies that are difficult to support, which I think makes a big difference. You know most fashion advertisers have something that we can incorporate in their range — we pass on beauty news, we do *Mode Maison*, which is home decorating twice a year, so there's always things happening in the magazine that if they have a product and it's suited to what they are doing, they certainly include them.

A different perspective emerged from ex-*Mode* editor Sandra Symons :

> Well, it was all very nicely done and very subtle. It would be, even not putting it in so many words, but always the idea was seeking to remind us not to forget the advertisers. And there would be a real fuss made down the chain of command if you prepared a

major story and published it and you neglected to include one of your key advertisers. It would certainly be made known to you that you had been remiss or negligent in not making sure that they feature prominently in the story.

The picture that emerged from Black's research on women's magazines is that while there is a close working relationship between editors and advertisers, there is still a recognition and appeal to a professional journalistic separation between advertising and editorial (most often shown by a reluctance to talk about examples of where editorial was in fact *advertorial* editorial copy which had been paid for by an advertiser). There was a variety of practices within the women's magazine trade, and even within the same company.

Because of the role of women's magazines in selling notions of femininity and beauty to women, there has been some attention paid to advertising in that area by feminist and cultural studies researchers. But little attention has been paid to the same questions in the rest of the media. The identification of markets and audiences with potential buying power shapes new developments and the content of all Australian media with the exception of the public Australian Broadcasting Corporation (ABC), the Special Broadcasting Service (SBS) and public radio. But even with the ABC and SBS, the years since 1985 have seen moves towards advertising, sponsorship, joint ventures with commercial organisations and a static public budget. The scarcity of airwaves once provided an argument for regulation, but with far more stations available in radio and television and computer communication, the old argument that a free marketplace leaves openings for all threatens whatever public subsidies exist. As publicly funded media respond to these pressures by building up the business side of operations, opportunities presented by the development of new media are accelerating the merging of public with private media and the development of 'value added' services.

Delivering the Olympic bid

According to liberal democratic theory and more specifically to the High Court of Australia, Australians have a constitutional right to a media which can provide an arena where important political decisions can be debated. The coverage of the Sydney 2000 Olympic bid provides a useful litmus test of the extent to which people are able to exercise that right. It also provides a glimpse at how powerful interests in the public relations, advertising and media industries can work together to achieve a result.

There is no doubt that the decision was a significant one, in terms of its cost in economic and human resources. Initially the Sydney media, especially the *Sydney Morning Herald,* adopted a somewhat critical editorial stance based on its concerns about public costs. The then New South Wales premier, Nick Greiner, was also unconvinced at first but finally climbed aboard a Sydney bid.

Greiner approached three big media companies: Kerry Packer's Consolidated Press, Rupert Murdoch's News Ltd and John Fairfax and Sons. John Alexander, who was then the editor in chief of the *Sydney Morning Herald* and also a member of the board agreed, together with representatives of the other two media companies, to sit on the committee which would drive the bid. When questioned about this decision, Alexander said it was part of the company's obligation as a 'corporate citizen'. The media companies also agreed to supply some free advertising space to the Olympic Bid Committee. Also on the board were representatives of major companies and industries which would commercially benefit from a Sydney Olympic Games. On the committee and chairperson of its media subcommittee was Greg Daniel, managing director of Clemengers advertising agency; Clemengers was also the advertising agency used by a number of Liberal government departments.

Alexander's position on the committee would not itself have guaranteed favourable coverage, although it did indicate that the entire company was backing the bid. More important was the editorial decision that the Olympic bid story was big enough to have its own 'round' and the choice of Sam North, a sports reporter, rather than a general or economics reporter, to cover the round. This meant it was difficult, although not impossible, for others to do the bid stories. North soon became convinced by the Olympic Bid Committee's public relations team that the bid was an excellent idea, and many of his news stories followed press releases from the committee. In running these stories without further investigation he was merely performing his role as the 'professional reporter'. Indeed, in an interview (Bacon 1993) he expressed pride in his 'balanced' and 'accurate' coverage. He might have run critical press releases, but there were very few, as Greenpeace, one of the leading environmental groups, was campaigning for a green bid. There were certainly no editorial directions suggesting he go out and independently report on the merits of the bid.

Over 1993, the year preceding the final bid selection, there were a few articles and columns which raised the difficulties with the bid, especially from economic columnist Max Walsh. But even Walsh found himself in the unusual position of being criticised by the Olympic Bid Committee on the news pages without even being given a chance to comment.

When Sam North was interviewed (Bacon 1993) shortly before the result of the bid was announced, he was in his office preparing the copy for a $40 000 advertising supplement prepared in advance for the victory edition. In between snatches of interview he negotiated with the supplement layout people, senior journalists, and the Prime Minister's office who were supplying advance copy. If the bid had been lost, the supplement was to be pulped. As it turned out it was a winner for the company and was followed during the following weekend by a bonanza of nearly half a million dollars worth of 'Congratulations Sydney!' advertisements from government departments and companies.

The Australian Centre for Independent Journalism had been aware that two articles with much fresh information about the commercial interests driving the bid and its environmental and social aspects had been offered to a number of media outlets but rejected in the months leading up to the bid announcement. So in the week before the announcement of Sydney's success, the Australian Centre for Independent Journalism announced at a press conference that it would publish these articles, along with information showing that the coverage of the bid had been one-sided. Senior staff at the *Sydney Morning Herald* were offended at what they saw as an attack on their professionalism. 'Why aren't you criticising the real baddies — News Ltd?', they argued, pointing to the *Daily Telegraph* which had openly campaigned for the bid. They referred to a tiny minority of articles raising difficulties with the bid and argued that these proved the coverage had been fair. The editor, Milton Cockburn, undoubtedly a most respected political journalist, argued that he was not in a position to direct the economic editor to do an analysis of the bid. (The notion of *independence* is being used here to explain questions not asked.) When asked why the paper had failed to report that the fare of senior journalist Peter Bowers to Monaco had been paid for by the Australian Olympic Bid Committee, Cockburn asked whether I was actually questioning the integrity of this eminent Australian journalist.

Conclusion

The same survey which found that most journalists still believe in a notion of objectivity also found that 90 per cent of journalists still believe in the liberal democratic notion that the media has a watchdog role to play in a democracy (Schultz 1994). This notion has been strongly supported by the High Court of Australia which has found that a crucial part of any democracy is a media which provides an arena for political debate for all its citizens. While such idealistic statements can be used to extend the boundaries of news agendas and promote a more critical journalistic culture, the structure of the media guarantees that it cannot meet this ideal. New technologies are developed to meet the needs of global communications companies; the same rhetoric is heard about new democratic media utopias that accompanied the development of the newspaper industry in the eighteenth and nineteenth centuries.

Confronted with the contradiction between the way they see their role in a democracy and the evidence of that role which the media provides, some journalists assert the intrinsic worth of prevailing news values and treat critics as outsiders who simply do not understand. Others resort to the notion of the market — that the media simply provides the public with what it wants — an appropriate approach for a free media to adopt. To assess the role of the media by whether its heavily promoted products, which are carefully crafted to match advertisers with consumers of the right demographics, are popular is to remove any wider role for the media in promoting debate and circulating information and ideas in a democracy. It reduces the public to many overlapping groups of consumers. Audiences, especially those whose needs are not fulfilled by existing media, have very limited ways of expressing what they do want. When pushed to explain how they know what the audience wants, that audience often turns out to be little more than an imaginary group who happen to agree with the judgment of the professionals themselves.

It will always be worthwhile supporting journalists who use notions of professionalism to resist conformity. But diatribes about bad journalism and a rejection of 'popular' in favour of the 'quality' media do not come to grips with black holes left by a media dominated by commercial values. To come to grips with why these black holes exist, we need to move to a prior question: what sort of media and what sort of society might more adequately express the views and perspectives of all citizens?

Addendum

I chose the example of the coverage of the Ok Tedi mine before, late in 1995, the conflict between some of the PNG landowners and BHP became a major news story.

The daily dumping by Australia's largest multinational of 80 000 tons of waste into the Fly River system near the mine until recently received only spasmodic coverage in the Australian press. Despite its potential international legal implications, even a lawsuit for damages filed in the Victorian Supreme Court by some landowners against BHP initially received only limited news coverage. The only program to examine the issues in depth was Radio National's documentary program *Background Briefing*. (Despite its very limited resources, *Background Briefing* was mentioned several times at an Australian Centre for Independent Journalism 1994 Hidden Stories seminar as the only media outlet to cover a number of significant stories.)

What catapulted the story into the headlines were accusations by an Australian legal firm, Slater and Gordon, that BHP had conspired with the PNG government to deny landowners basic civil rights by assisting in the drafting of a PNG law making legal action against BHP unlawful. A Victorian Supreme Court contempt finding against BHP received further blanket coverage, and led to a few features focusing attention on the environmental damage caused by the mine.

The question to ask is would BHP's critics in PNG have received much coverage in the news media of the Asia-Pacific region without the public statements by white Australian lawyers and a judgment against BHP by an Australian judge?

References

Australian Centre for Independent Journalism 1993, *Youth and the Media*, March, University of Technology, Sydney.
Bacon, W. 1993, Interviews with Sam North, unpublished, September, University of Technology, Sydney.
Black, J. 1992, 'What the ads add', unpublished thesis, Australian Centre for Independent Journalism, University of Technology, Sydney.
Caruana, L. 1995, 'PNG villagers move to drop part of $4bn Ok Tedi suit', *Weekend Australian*, 8–9 April, p. 45.
Chadwick, P. 1991, Charters of editorial independence: an information paper, Communications Law Centre, July, Sydney and Melbourne.
Curran, J. 1977, 'Capitalism and control of the press, 1800–1975', in J. Curran, M. Gurivitch & J. Wollacott (eds), *Mass Communication and Society*, Edward Arnold, London.
Jakubowicz, A., Goodall, H., Martin, J., Mitchell, T., Seneviratne, K. & Kendall, L. 1994, *Racism, Ethnicity and the Media*, Allen & Unwin, London.
Nash, C. 1995, 'Journalists, confidential sources and the public interest', in W. Bacon, *Media and Accountability*, Australian Centre for Independent Journalism, University of Technology, Sydney.
National Report on Women 1993, *Representing Women in the Media*, Australian Senate, AGPS, Canberra.
O'Malley, P. 1981, 'Capitalist accumulation and press freedom' *Media, Culture and Society*, vol. 3, no. 1, p. 72.
Schultz, J. 1994, 'The paradox of professionalism', in J. Schulz (ed.), *Not Just Another Business*, Pluto Press, Sydney.
Soloski, J. 1989, 'News reporting and professionalism: some constraints in reporting the news', *Media, Culture and Society*, vol. 11, no. 2.
Toohey, B. 1994, *Tumbling Dice*, Heineman, Melbourne, pp. 214–39.

6.
Gender Control of Agendas

Meredith Burgmann

It is a truism that organisations only work to their peak potential when all the talent in an organisation is utilised, and it is quite clear this is not happening. No matter what the institution — a university, a water board, a trade union, or Parliament — 50 per cent of the population is being properly utilised and only a very small proportion of the other 50 per cent of the population is. What I am talking about, therefore, is how male-dominated organisations operate against women and how women can fight back to make that different and better for the entire organisation, and also for the good of the women.

Involvement in organisations

My interest in organisations is twofold. As an academic I studied organisations; my PhD was on a trade union and that was where my interest in organisation theory arose. But more importantly, for the past thirty years I have been struggling in political organisations — not just party political organisations like the Labor Party, but in trade unions and in other voluntary organisations. So most of what I say stems from my practical experience, but I like to think that there is also a sophisticated overlay of theory which came to me from my years as an academic.

What I became interested in when I was looking at the Builders' Labourers Federation was 'where are the decisions actually made?'. It became clear that decisions are not made in the places where they are meant to be made. They are not made in meetings. They are often not made by the people who are meant to make them. I became very interested in the informal aspects of decision-making and I was helped in this endeavour by the work of Richard Hyman and, further back still, by the seminal work of Robert Michels and his work on political parties in 1911.

But looking at my own experience I became increasingly intrigued by three questions: Where are the decisions made? Who makes them? And why are women not there?

When I talk about informal aspects of decision-making, I mean the really important decisions that you know have been made before you even enter the room. When I eventually got onto the executive of the Labor Council I thought this was terrific, because all my life I had been searching for where the decisions were made and I thought, 'At last, I'm on the executive. This is where decisions are made'. I went to my first meeting, which was pretty horrifying. I was the only woman and there were twenty blokes in grey suits. John Ducker entered the room, followed by Barrie Unsworth (Ducker was secretary and Unsworth was assistant secretary). They walked in and sat down and ran the meeting and it became clear that every single decision had been made, presumably in Ducker's office, before they walked into the room. I think my entire political life has been spent in that quest of finding where the decisions are actually made, and I am never there when they are made.

Male arenas

I have come to the conclusion that decisions are made in very male areas. They are made in Ducker's office, surrounded by his mates; all male, because decision-makers at the moment are still all males. They are made in very male areas like pubs. People laugh at me when I say decisions are made in pubs. They are. It is not that men decide to leave the women and go off and have a conspiracy in a pub. It is just that decisions are made where decision-makers hang out and decision-makers at the moment are male and males hang out in pubs. So that is where decisions are made, such as, 'Who should we put on as a temporary organiser?'. 'Oh, you know, that bright young bloke, you met him, what was his name?' That is the sort of decision-making that goes on in pubs.

It also goes on in male toilets. How do we know this? We know this because for many years in the Star Hotel after Labor Council meetings, the women discovered that you could hear everything that was going on in the men's toilet from the women's toilet, and for thirteen years not one woman told her male partner. It was a very fruitful area for academic research. We also found out a lot. I have always said to women who doubt this, 'You know yourself what conversations go on in women's toilets, so exactly the same goes on in men's toilets'.

Decision-making goes on at football matches. Once again the men are not sneaking away from women to conspire against them but, as Adam Smith said about the merchant class, when the merchant class get together they will conspire to make decisions that operate against the working class.

Decisions are made in the general secretary's office after hours. The blokes come round and he opens his little bar fridge and pulls out a few tinnies and they sit around and have a discussion about the day's work. Once again, a very male area.

Not only were women not at the places where the informal decision-making was occurring, but when they did get to those places where the formal decision-making was meant to occur, that is at the meetings, they often did not believe that they should be there. Their disbelief was affected by the ways that meetings were arranged.

Twenty-five years ago a group of women wrote a seminal work called *The Tyranny of Structurelessness*. The collective was known by the name Joreen. It is ironic that a work which was attacking the idea of structurelessness was actually written by an anonymous collective, but the point they made was very important. If there are only unwritten rules (which you have in an unstructured meeting situation) it is a sure bet that only the men will know them. The women certainly will not.

It is often a good idea for women to fight for fairly formal structures, because if rights are written down (for example, you can now speak for three minutes), at least the participants know their rights. Whereas in a totally unstructured situation, women sometimes wonder 'should I be here?'. I spent my life in the union movement wondering if I should be there. Male union officials at that time had a way of looking straight through you and making you wonder, 'Gosh, was I really meant to be invited to this meeting?'. Whereas if there had been clear criteria as to who had the right to be there, it would have been much easier for women.

All women know of course about the invisible woman syndrome. Not only do men stare right through you, but they actually do not hear what you are saying. A woman makes an important point and it goes over everyone's head, but ten minutes later a man says the same thing and they all say, 'Oh, good idea Joe!'.

Establishing women's confidence

The next point I want to make is that the real problem for women in organisations is the problem of confidence. It is an old one, but the more I think about it the more I think this is the one that really matters.

When women in surveys were asked why they did not take more interest and have a more active part in their trade union, they always ticked the square that said 'Don't know enough to get involved'. Men never ticked the square that said 'Don't know enough'. They probably ticked the square which said 'Doesn't leave enough time for golf'. But it is interesting that in the same surveys men and women knew the same amount about their union and about industrial relations. It was just that the men did not perceive that what they knew 'wasn't enough', whereas the women did perceive it as not knowing enough, a shorthand way of the women saying they did not have enough confidence.

Women are used to sitting in public meetings and hearing men get up and speak confidently, and with silver tongues. They fill space with words. By contrast, women seldom speak for long. Women rarely speak longer than they are meant to (after I have said this I am always really careful to finish within my allotted time). Women tend to speak when they believe that if they do not intervene in the debate then something terrible will happen, or if they feel very, very strongly about an issue. This situation means that men get lots of practice in speaking. We all know the sort of speaker who says at a meeting, 'Well, I agree with Joe and I agree with Bill, but don't quite agree with Fred'. In fact they did not need to speak in order to change the debate.

I know there is a lot of academic work being done on why women's confidence disappears. I know *when* it disappears, I just want to know why. Their confidence disappears at about the age of eight. Until eight they are bright, confident, mature, amazingly well-rounded individuals. From eight or nine onwards, something happens and they become the timid little things that boys boss around and start beating at school work; I have just seen it happen in my child's class at school.

I have noticed over the years that women are more at home with a structure where they can apply for a job in a fairly civilised fashion, that is, a job is advertised, you apply, and you may or may not get the job. Reasonably civilised human beings, we hope, interview you and you either get it or you do not.

However, we are trying to encourage women into becoming real decision-makers in Australia. We are encouraging them to go into Parliament. That is the hardest thing of all for women to do because women see elections as very aggressive things — and they are not wrong. Elections, especially preselections, are absolute bloodbaths and women do not like it. They find it very difficult to stand up and say, 'Not only am I terrific, but Joe Bloggs is a dunce', which is really what you have to say in a preselection to get elected. Women find that whole process very difficult.

Women are very bad at blowing their own trumpet, which is why I have great concerns about enterprise bargaining, especially pure enterprise bargaining at the workplace level. The system expects women to go in to the boss and say, 'I'm terrific, give me a pay rise'. That simply will not happen in a lot of areas.

Four machismo rules

Next I want to mention the four great factors which are almost indescribable, but which are absolutely crucial to the way men operate in organisations and the way they rise and women sink. The indescribables are: mentoring, networking, 'pea' for the job, and use of the telephone. They are the four things which women are hopeless at.

'Pea' for the job is a labour movement expression. I have since discovered it is a New South Wales labour movement expression because they do not understand it in Melbourne. 'Pea' for the job means the obvious candidate. Men are very good at setting themselves up as the obvious candidate. Women are not only bad at it, they are hopeless at it. They have not a clue. For example, everyone knew that Joe Bloggs was going to be president of the ACTU two years before he was made president, so he was 'pea' for the job. If anyone else had decided that they might want to do it too, they would have been seen as the troublemaker or the splitter, because they had not set themselves up as 'pea' for the job.

How do you go about setting yourself up as 'pea' for the job? I have absolutely no idea. I am not a boy. I did not come up in that network of mentors who presumably tell you how you become 'pea' for the job. I suspect it is something to do with working out where the nodes of power are in an organisation, ringing them up, and telling them that you are interested in the job. Not so much that you are interested, but rather that the job is yours and you are just letting them know. I presume it is that sort of operation, but it is the sort of thing that women are sociologically incapable of.

Another point which is to do with networking and mentoring is that leaderships replicate themselves. Male middle-class leaderships replicate themselves. It is very unusual if there is a jousting for position and another leadership emerges. Mostly a transformation of the present leadership occurs.

The way this replication would normally operate, say in a union, is that there is a dispute on a job site; an organiser is sent down from head office to deal with it; a bright young thing makes a speech from the shop floor; the male organiser thinks, 'Oh, I'll take them over to the pub, give them a bit of a chat, see what their politics are like and maybe suggest that they go on the Branch Executive and then later the State Executive'. Then if the bright young thing keeps voting correctly they are put on as a temporary organiser and then if they still keep voting right, maybe they are allowed to stand as organiser next time round. That system breaks down immediately when the bright young thing from the shop floor is a woman, because as soon as the male organiser says to her, 'Come over to the pub', it becomes a totally different relationship than if it had been a male that he was asking to the pub for a discussion. A film, *Norma Rae*, about a female unionist, made the point beautifully.

I had a problem about how to do my job when I became the first female president of the Academics Union of New South Wales. I did not have a mentor, although the previous president had suggested I do it. I resigned when my child was born, because I realised I could not go on being a full-time academic, being a mum and trying to be an honorary union official in my spare time. I recognised later of course that a male would never have resigned when his child was born, but I did. Because I was the first woman president, I had no (I hate the use of the term) role model. I did not really know how to do it.

Very soon after I became president I had to do some informal negotiations with a vice-chancellor about superannuation and I did not have a clue how to go about an informal negotiation. I rang up Neil, the previous president, and said, 'I've got to have a chat to Joe Bloggs. How should I do it? How did you do it?'. And he said, 'Oh, I used to invite him down to the Staff Club for a beer'. I just thought, 'Imagine me ringing up Joe Bloggs and saying "Come down to the Staff Club for a beer, Joe" '. He would have died of fright.

So I realised that I had to work out a whole different way of negotiating with elderly men who were not very comfortable with younger women. We used to have our negotiations at 11 o'clock in the morning, with a table between us, cups of tea, and I would have someone with me because that made him feel happier, and he had someone with him too. So it was not terribly informal, but it was really the only way we could go about it.

I think that having a chat about important issues over the bar is very, very difficult for women because they just find that way of operating very alien. I am not opposed to chatting over the bar at all, it is just that it is hard to do work that way if you are female.

I do not like the word 'mentor' but because the issue keeps cropping up and because I feel that I have never had a mentor I keep thinking, 'Who is my mentor?'. In politics you are meant to have a mentor and I cannot think of one. The closest thing I have to a mentor is a bloke who is twenty years younger than me. I know you are not meant to have mentors younger than you. However, he is the only person who has ever come to me and said, 'Meredith, you've got to stand for Parliament'. I was very surprised because I was an academic and I had never thought of myself in that way. I think mentoring is important, but I do not quite know how to do it, because I have never seen it work woman to woman. I just grab all young women quite hysterically and say, 'You've got to stand for Parliament!', whether they want to or not!

I hate the word 'networking' too; I prefer to think of it as partying. Men network naturally, women forget to. I know I am very bad at the actual 'work' part of networking. I am good at the 'partying' part.

Recently a preselection was called. I knew a woman was standing against a man and a few days after the preselection was called I thought, 'I wonder if she knows'? So I rang her up and told her about the preselection and of course she did not know. The bloke had known the minute the decision was made, so he was out there getting his numbers and the woman did not even know the preselection had been called. Probably I should have remembered to tell her straight away, but I just forgot.

Information is power. The longer I spend time in organisations the more I realise it. You see people who bottle up information because it gives them power. People have to come as supplicants and get the information out of them. So one of my bits of advice to women is always, 'spread the information around, tell all the other women everything you know, because eventually people will end up with enough information to be able to make properly informed decisions'.

Of course that comes to the use of the telephone, which I still find very strange. I have not quite worked out how to pick up the telephone and change events by just ringing up. I know male politicians and male union officials ('Tiberius with a telephone' is an accurate description of a lot of males in political organisations) can sit there on the phone and change events. I really do not know how to do it. I do not know how to ring up men and say, 'Don't do that Roger' or whatever, because I am not certain how they would respond.

Exhaustion

I think there is one more crucial male strategy which keeps women ineffectual in organisations and that is simply keeping them exhausted. I want to look at unions, academia and Parliament for the strategies used to exhaust them.

In unions it was simple. Women who wanted to be active in their union did not have two jobs, they had three jobs. To be active in their union to start with meant they had to be in the waged work force, and even if they did not have children to look after they had a husband or a partner or they had to look after themselves. Whereas mostly the men had a nice little unit at home called a wife who looked after their every need. So the three-job burden for women was always the problem. When we were looking at why women did not come to more union meetings we discovered that even at lunchtime (of course they could not come at five o'clock, they had to pick up the kids) they had another chore. They had to pop out and get the meat, or get the car registered, or something. When we instituted union meetings in paid time, women flocked to them. They were interested in their union, they had just never had the time to get to union meetings before. I was once at what is called a women's consultation at the University of New South

Wales where women staff get paid time off to come and talk to the vice-chancellor and there were 300 women there. So it really works.

My view is that women in academia are now totally exhausted because they have to sit on so many committees. There has to be at least one woman on every committee and because there are not enough senior women in universities to go round, they end up completely exhausted.

I have calculated that I probably have three hours less in every day than the average male politician. Not only do I have the primary care responsibility for a child, I also do not have a wife. I do have to get the car registered, get the meat, go to the bank and all those things which keep the household going which male politicians have wives to do for them.

Ten commandments

I am going to finish with my ten commandments, which are aimed directly at women, but men might find useful too, because this is how women are going to fight back against them.
1. Help each other. There is absolutely no point in more women getting into decision-making positions if they are going to do nothing about helping other women along the way. I am not one of those people who believe we must have more women in Parliament. I want more *good* women in Parliament. I do not want to be part of any organisation that helps Bronwyn Bishop into Parliament. To me, they have got to be feminists and preferably socialists.
2. Find out where decisions are really made and make certain women are there. We all know that decisions are not made in meetings.
3. Information is power. Spread it around. Tell other women what you know. I am sometimes referred to (I think not all that nicely) as Radio 2MB. It is seen as gossip, and I say, 'No, it is not gossip; it is telling women what is going on so that they do not make mistakes or put their foot in it'.
4. Fight for formal structures. If there are only unwritten rules, the men will know what they are and the women will not.
5. Be the way you are with women. Do not be intimidated by having men in the room. I know a lot of women who get up and make great speeches when it is just all women, but as soon as men are there they feel intimidated. See yourself as a worthwhile actor in the proceedings, because men always do.
6. Be aware of body space and the way men take it over. I am becoming increasingly aware of this at meetings, but it is true that the way space is used by men and women is very different.
7. Learn to say 'no' when appropriate. Women are always allotted the low-status, time-consuming tasks and continue to say 'yes'. As

my researcher was helping me with this she laughed because she reckons that I never say 'no'. This became clear to me when, just after I had had my baby, I went back to full-time work when he was three months old. He was not a good sleeper and I was just keeping my head above water. The Head of School rang up and asked me to run the school Christmas party for 150 people and when I found myself saying 'no' I was very proud of myself, but he never forgave me. I said, 'No, ask Sam, he is good at that sort of thing'. He thought that was an appalling thing for me to say.

8. This is another one which as I get older is more important to me. Be cranky if men are displaying inappropriate behaviour. Now I am not saying what some people think I am saying, which is that if men throw tantrums to get their own way, you throw tantrums too. I am just saying that when they are behaving absolutely terribly and are frustrating you beyond belief, it is all right to be cranky. People are really surprised when this happens because they are so used to women being accommodating and pleasant.

9. Do not destroy yourself with self-doubt. That is, do not lock yourself in the toilet and cry because you think you made a fool of yourself at some public event. Do not forget, men in a similar situation think it was the audience's fault and not theirs.

10. Never apologise when it rains. My friend, Ann Symonds, says she finally realised that she was totally hopeless when she took her family on a picnic and it rained — so she apologised. I said, 'Don't be silly Ann, you just thought you were God'.

7.
Contrived Control of Budgets

Michael Muetzelfeldt

Managerialism has been described by Mike Codd, the secretary to the Department of Prime Minister and Cabinet, as 'a management revolution' in the Commonwealth public sector (Codd 1991, p. 1). The motivation for this revolution was increased efficiency. Codd points to 'a natural focus on the part of ministers on how to improve effectiveness and efficiency in the public sector ... [and provide] a higher quality service to the community at minimum cost to the taxpayer' (1991, p. 3). He says that as well as politicians, public servants shared the motivation and commitment to efficiency, and that is why many managerialist changes were generated and able to be implemented. This is neatly summed up in the slogan of the Commonwealth Department of Finance: 'value for money'.

The Commonwealth's management revolution centred on a shift from the traditional bureaucratic emphasis on following rules to a more entrepreneurial emphasis on getting results. This shift from process to output was mostly implemented by increasing flexibility and devolving some responsibilities within what was still a basically hierarchical and public sector organisational structure. These changes have been made to look quite tame compared with the radical restructuring introduced in Victoria by the Kennett government.

Victoria has adopted a contract model (Alford et al. 1994), which gives preference to market mechanisms and competition. The relationships between different organisational units, between employees and employers, and between organisations and the people who use their services, are based on a series of specific negotiated contracts rather than on a shared commitment to following the general rules of bureaucratic organisation, industrial awards, and established ideas of citizens' relations with government. Under this model, government concentrates on governing through making and overseeing policy, which Osborne and Gaebler (1993) call 'steering', and it contracts with others to do the 'rowing' work of implementing and delivering policy and services for it. Most of the rowing could be, and over time will be, done in the private sector, and the public sector will become small, specialised and focused on governing for results without being distracted by the details of how those results will be achieved.

There is debate over whether the contract model should be seen as a development of managerialism, or as a radical departure from it (Alford et al. 1994, p. 12; Alford & Considine 1994, p. 47). The Commonwealth's managerialism, and similar changes in the public sectors in the states and territories, have retained a basically hierarchical organisational structure. The shift to an output orientation has been moderated by a continuing emphasis on the rules of due process, equity and accountability that have been basic to the idea of public service. There has been some privatisation and contracting out of apparently marginal activities such as cleaning services, and some reduction in staff levels; however there has been no push for wholesale privatisation and massive staff reductions. Despite these important differences, the contract model shares with managerialism the core motivation of efficiency (Alford et al. 1994, p. 5). The two are grouped together because they share the problems that this motivation produces, although because of the contract model's emphasis on market mechanisms, these problems tend to be worse than they are under managerialism.

Technical efficiency

The idea of efficiency is taken for granted, and generally assumed to be a good thing. People talk about being efficient without giving too much thought to what that actually means or how they might assess how efficient they actually are: usually people probably mean not being obviously wasteful, and being fairly purposeful in their activities. In contrast to this taken-for-granted notion, technical efficiency is a measure of the ratio of input costs to output benefits. Efficiency increases if outputs can be maintained at the same level while input costs go down, or if outputs can be increased without increasing input costs.

So any measure of efficiency assumes that input costs and output benefits can be accurately measured. This means that when there is a choice between alternative outputs, they can be compared and assessed. Is it more efficient for a surgical ward to spend a certain amount of money on many tonsillectomies or one heart transplant? One approach to answering questions such as this is to devise useful statistical measures such as quality-of-life years, but this still leaves important value questions unanswered. For example, how could the benefits of a tonsillectomy and cosmetic plastic surgery on protruding ears be compared? Another approach is to leave the answer entirely up to the market, and refuse to even consider the value questions. That way it would be efficient for each patient to be treated by the medical practitioner, who will give them what they consider will be the best treatment they can get (regardless of how necessary it might be) for the lowest price. Both approaches involve assumptions that are usually hidden and that remain untestable. And when the questions become truly complex — such as a choice between spending public money on preserving a forest, reducing inequality or improving schooling — the answers from statistical indicators or the market's bottom line can become quite detached from the ideas of public value that lie behind talk of efficiency.

The technical measure of efficiency also means that there is a clear link between inputs and outputs. In any real organisation people are involved in several overlapping projects, and it may not be clear which project is being advanced by any particular activity. As well, the organisation has human costs and human outputs as well as financially costed inputs and technically measured outputs. There are generalised processes of communication through which people share information, learn, support each other, build trust, and find the knowledge, inspiration and courage to innovate (Considine 1988). So it is not possible to keep track of exactly which costs go into producing each particular output, and so it is not possible to measure efficiency accurately.

A heavy emphasis on efficiency leads to a tendency to minimise or ignore these other complex, subtle and important issues, because they get in the way of clean, unambiguous efficiency measures. Managing for results has, in fact, required people to establish for each program exactly what it is they should be trying to achieve, including the nature of any equality objectives, and then to ensure that their efforts are productively directed to that purpose (Keating 1990, p. 387).

Michael Keating acknowledges the problems involved in adopting a technical and quantifying approach to assessing outputs in the name of efficiency, but concludes that the benefits outweigh the problems, provided people remember that 'performance *indicators* are precisely that, an *aid* to judgement' (1990, p. 393). Despite this optimism, it is debatable that the use of easily measured quantitative measures will always be tempered by qualitative indicators or social justice outcomes. As Weller and Lewis observe, the Commonwealth public sector reform program 'encourages the inclusion of objectives such as social equity in calculations, but it does not suggest how this calculation, always so intractable, will be completed' (1989, p. 15).

It is not worthwhile to follow the by now well-trodden path of debating whether it is organisationally and politically feasible to expect Michael Keating's caution to be regularly and routinely taken into account — although in the press of real pressures and interests managers will at times use indicators mechanistically and at other times use them as aids to judgment, with unpredictable results (e.g. Parker & Guthrie 1990). Rather, there is a somewhat different point to be made. Despite the assumptions of precision and certainty in the technical notion of efficiency, in practice any discussion based on implementing efficient management involves much ambiguity. This ambiguity, particularly when it arises in the middle of what purports to be a precise and technical system, provides opportunities for concealment, displacement and distraction. The rest of this chapter examines ways in which managerialist practice conceals and displaces costs, while at the same time distracting people's attention so that they tend not to notice what is happening.

Managerialism claims to increase efficiency by doing things more cheaply through new forms of organisation and new technologies. Politicians have used the rhetoric of an inefficient public service for at least twenty years. Malcolm Fraser spoke this way in the mid-1970s. Bob Carr said at his first press conference as premier of New South Wales that he was going to 'cut waste and mismanagement' in New South Wales to free up resources to implement Labor's education and health priorities. To do this he had recruited Ken Baxter, who as director-general of the Victorian Department of Premier and Cabinet had used the contractual model for the restructuring of the Victorian public sector (*PM*, ABC Radio, 4 March 1995).

Politicians might be expected to use this rhetoric to justify cutting costs and reallocating resources, but public servants and management academics also speak the same way. A range of new management techniques have been introduced, such as focused strategic and corporate planning: reducing duplication, replacing bureaucratic rule-following with output-oriented multiskilled work teams, and using information technology and management information systems to re-engineer work practices. These practices can result in substantial financial savings: for example, the Evatt Research Centre has found some cases of efficiency gains (1989; 1990), and a survey in New South Wales found average direct cost savings of nearly 20 per cent as a result of contracting out (Messiter 1993, p.55). How are these savings achieved, at what costs and for whom?

Technical efficiency and cost displacement

Efficiency can be increased by doing things more cheaply through new forms of organisation and new technologies, as is proposed by these managerialists. However technical efficiency can also be increased by displacing costs 'off budget', so that they are not taken into account in the cost–benefit calculations through which they are measured. An example of this is the practice of state public hospital systems shifting costs from themselves to the Commonwealth by bulk billing public patients for medical and diagnostic services so that the costs are paid by Medicare, instead of the hospital's budget. This costs the Federal Government at least $300 million per year (Ferrari 1995), while making state hospitals 'more efficient' by reducing their costs as measured by their own budgets. This practice apparently increases the total national health bill (because bulk billing costs more than providing the same services through salaried hospital medical staff), so that increasing the efficiency of state public hospitals may actually decrease the efficiency of the total national health system.

In a more subtle form of displacing costs 'off budget', costs are not merely transferred from the budget of one agency to that of another. Instead, they are shifted into areas where there is not a clear budget through which they can be measured; this typically involves imposing social or personal costs on people, and not compensating them within the financial cost structure. This does not just shift costs: it also hides them because they are dispersed among many people and do not show up in any budget.

There are several ways of displacing costs into areas where they become hidden, for example costs may be displaced from the budget of the service-providing organisation either onto its beneficiaries (or, as they are now called, its clients) or other people, or onto its labour force. As well, costs can be displaced by producing generalised public 'bads' instead of public goods. For example, costs may be imposed on the environment, or on the society as a whole by increasing inequality. Other chapters in this book discuss these effects, and here only cost displacement onto clients and the community, and onto employees is considered.

Displacing costs onto clients and their communities

Costs can be displaced onto clients and other people in a variety of ways. The process is illustrated by the examples of childhood education and health care.

In Victoria, early childhood education services were restructured in 1993, with kindergarten teachers and committees of management carrying more responsibilities and with funding based on enrolments rather than on salary and associated costs. As a result, costs to government were reduced by 20–30 per cent. A survey of teachers found that there were reductions in the six major quality indicators of: curriculum, staff–child ratios, staff–child relationships, staff–parent interaction, physical environment, and administration (Hammer 1994).

Doonesbury

BY GARRY TRUDEAU

Courtesy DOONESBURY © 1995 G. B. Trudeau. Dist. by UNIVERSAL PRESS SYNDICATE. All rights reserved

Hammer reports evidence that 'for every dollar invested in high-quality pre-school programs there is an eventual saving of $7.16 to the public purse' (1994, p. 1), so even in measurable financial terms the immediate cost saving and increase in short-term efficiency can be expected to be inefficient in the long term. And of course if the unquantified social and personal benefits of quality education are taken into account, the overall costs will be even greater.

In health care, case mix funding and associated cost-cutting management practices are designed to increase the efficiency of hospitals by paying them an agreed price for the completed treatment of patients in particular diagnostic groups, rather than paying them for whatever services they provide regardless of how necessary or efficiently delivered those services may be. This gives hospitals an incentive to discharge patients as soon as possible, and early discharge can in turn increase the financial, practical and emotional burdens on discharged patients and their carers. There is considerable evidence available on the consequences. A survey by the Victorian Office of the Public Advocate found that efficiency-seeking policies in agencies providing services for people with disabilities imposed new costs and stresses on these people and their carers (Montague 1993). The Commonwealth has a policy of encouraging the frail elderly to stay at home rather than live in nursing homes, while at the same time not providing adequate support services for them and their carers. On the basis of a survey of carers, the Carers Association of Australia has argued that the Commonwealth's policy 'hinges on reducing its costs and passing the burden of care to relatives often almost as ill as those they care for' (Birnbauer 1995).

The costs are still there. Indeed, as each household works to deal with the extra demands placed on it the overall costs may even increase. That is, the overall efficiency of the formal and informal health care systems may decrease as a result of the cost-cutting of formal agencies. The carers are more often than not women, so there is in effect an increase in hidden costs for women (Gerrand 1993), and a corresponding reduction in direct monetary costs that are funded through the taxation system. As men contribute more to the public purse through taxation, there is an overall transfer of costs from men to women when costs to the public purse are reduced and costs to carers increased. There may also be similar transfers of cost from more affluent to less affluent people.

The most general case of 'the client' is of course all those who stand to gain (or lose) if the public interest is not adequately protected. This general case tends to be overlooked, because 'the client' is often thought of as an individual, or as a collection of similar individuals. However, the public interest can have an impact on people who are not directly involved in the relationship between service provider and the direct recipient of that service. For example, a 'client focus' approach in the Taxation Office may concentrate on potential and actual taxpayers as the clients, even though the whole population — including those who pay no tax — benefit from the direct and indirect government benefits, from the public goods and services, and from the economic stability achieved through fiscal management that are all made possible through the work of the Taxation Office. A technical measure of efficiency, with its concern for direct outputs, tends to ignore these wider public interests. And so the 'efficient' redesign of work risks disregarding them.

For example, in New South Wales the Roads and Traffic Authority (RTA) contracted out the manufacture of photo-licences, and in 1990 the Independent Commission Against Corruption (ICAC) and the RTA Internal Audit found that the contractor's procedures made it possible for bogus photo-licences to be produced (Beauris 1993, pp. 8–10). There is a sense in which all Australians (and not only those in New South Wales) share in the public interest of ostensibly genuine identification documents such as photo-licences being reliable and dependable. Yet in this case the push for technical efficiency, expressed through the competitive tendering process, diminished this public interest, and in effect displaced onto all, the cost (in the form of a reduced public interest) of achieving increased technical efficiency.

Cost displacement and accountability

Some areas of the general public interest, particularly those concerned with financial probity and all forms of corruption, are subject to systematic scrutiny by public bodies. For example, ICAC's brief to detect actual and potential corruption in the New South Wales public sector made it possible for it to identify the problems in the photo-licensing case. Similarly, the Victorian auditor-general has exercised his authority to inquire into the risk analysis undertaken in the Victorian government as part of its planning to privatise major public utilities.

However, other areas of the public interest are less open to formal systematic examination, and they depend on the vagaries of political campaigns for what protection they can get. For example, there has been debate over the adequacy of safety standards under the control of the efficiency-oriented Air Safety Authority, but this debate has been driven by the prospect of party political advantage, and it is not obvious that it would have taken place if politicians had not seen an advantage in pushing it. So there may be areas of public interest that are diminished without scrutiny or debate as part of the cost-displacing processes of the pursuit of technical efficiency.

There is a clear democratic public interest in making sure that activities that are funded, sponsored or initiated by public sector agencies are subject to the scrutiny and ultimate control of Parliament. However, the Australian National Audit Office (ANAO) has found examples where '[Commonwealth] Public Sector agencies have established subsidiaries, or entered into joint venture arrangements, for the *express* purpose of placing certain operations outside or beyond the reach of review agencies such as the ANAO, and even the Parliament' (Coleman 1993, p. 18, original emphasis). These attacks on the public interest are hardly ever taken up in political debate. Indeed, hiding behind the claims that contracting out and similar commercial-like arrangements increase efficiency, they are more likely to be praised than questioned by politicians from all parties, who use the rhetoric of cutting waste and mismanagement.

Such reductions in public accountability are unlikely to be brought to political attention without first being identified by public interest watchdogs such as ICAC and the various public sector internal and external auditors. ANAO clearly sees part of its role as protecting public accountability, and believes that it can contract out some of its own audit work in ways that still ensure that this role is not compromised (Coleman 1993). However, when public agencies such as the Commercial Services Group in New South Wales contract out 75 per cent of its internal auditing to a private company (Messiter 1993, p. 61), there must be a real risk that the protection of the public interest will not be part of that company's values or culture, or a high priority for it when it audits the public agency. A basic issue here is this: what are the core functions — or, as they are called in managerialist discourse, the core businesses — of the public sector? 'What is, and is not, "core" depends on Government policy and Government policy changes over time' (Jones 1993, p. 45). The more governments and the media subscribe to technical efficiency above social objectives, the more government policies are likely to lead to public agencies treating public accountability and other public interest matters as non-core, and the less chance there is that reductions of public interest will be noticed by public watchdogs or politicians, or taken up in the media.

Displacing costs onto employees

Efficiency may be increased within an organisation by moving costs off budget and imposing them onto its employees. The Victorian Commission of Audit (VCA), set up by the incoming Kennett government to examine the state's financial position and propose ways of improving it, advocated the use of contracts and similar arrangements to increase efficiency. It identified several 'threats' to efficiency increases. These threats refer to those who were being targeted to pay the costs that were no longer going to appear in formal budgets. The cost saving was to be achieved at the expense of 'providers of inputs, particularly labour inputs ... lobby groups seeking funding for narrow sectional interests, to the detriment of the general community ... [and] direct interference and therefore undue lobbying ... from lobbyists (including unions)' (VCA 1993, p. 3). With the benefit of hindsight, 'narrow sectional interests' can now be seen to include the clients and their immediate communities who have shouldered displaced costs. But it takes no hindsight to see that the work force is being directly identified as an area of cost saving, and employees are targets for cost displacement.

There are many instances of increased workloads for employees at all levels as a result of such efficiency drives. Whether it be teachers (from kindergarten through to university), administrators, welfare officers or managers, the story is the same: increased hours, increased case load, increased stress, and reduced support from relief or support staff or from colleagues who have spare capacity that might be brought in to help out when needed. The evidence for this comes from many sources: surveys of employees (e.g. Hammer 1994); wide support for industrial action to protect working conditions (for example, by Victorian teachers in 1995); from official reports that see increased workloads as a positive or at least a necessary thing (e.g. the 1995 Karpin Report on management education); and from the personal knowledge of almost anyone who has several years work experience.

Often the displacement of costs onto clients and employees occurs together, and this is signalled by the rhetoric of 'client focus'. This approach to planning, management and work simultaneously does two things. It defines clients in a functional and one-dimensional way, so that only their most immediate needs and the most directly measurable services provided for them are taken into account. It also encourages employees in the service organisation to work harder 'for the clients' sake' — which is actually for top management's sake, once that organisation's mission has been defined in client focus terms.

Efficiency or effectiveness?

This chapter has assumed that technical efficiency is actually carefully assessed and used as the basis of restructuring decisions in public sector organisations. Yet the ANAO has found that often there are no satisfactory costings of contracting out versus carrying out processes within the organisation, and that managers may develop a commitment to contracting out that supplants decisions that should be based on adequate cost–benefit analysis (Coleman 1993, p. 17).

Even if such costings have been thoroughly done, any increase in narrowly defined efficiency can actually increase the displaced and hidden costs by more than the 'on budget' savings, as has been argued earlier. That is, increased technical efficiency (as measured by the organisation's budget) may go hand in hand with decreased social effectiveness. As well, costs are displaced onto less organised and less powerful groups (which is why they are singled out to carry the extra costs), so the displacement also increases inequality. In the private sector technical efficiency ('the bottom line') may be an end in itself — for better or for worse. But in the public sector the end should be social effectiveness, and managerialism does not deliver this.

From this perspective the slogan 'value for money' that drives the managerialist push for efficiency has an ironic edge to it. In terms of the outcomes that public sector organisations are able to provide, value means much more than the costs of outputs, and value for money means much more than cost saving or an improved cost–benefit ratio. The public sector is able to provide much social value in and for the society. It can contribute to building public goods such as equity, justice and enhanced citizenship, and to reducing public bads such as pollution and social instability. Its contribution to these social and public values is a measure of its real effectiveness. However, an effective public sector that makes this contribution to social value is going to cost money.

So 'value for money' should become the slogan of all those who recognise that social values can only be defended and extended provided people, as a society, are prepared to pay for it. The real value of the social benefits that make up the public interest need to be emphasised and brought into focus. Only then will political discourse allow people to appreciate that through expenditure on a public sector that is effective as well as efficient can they as a society build the things they value. It is not just taxpayers who want to minimise costs: it is citizens who want to be able to take responsibility for social and political decisions about what they are willing to pay in order to achieve the things they value.

References

Alford, John & Considine, Mark 1994, 'Public sector employment contracts', in John Alford & Deidre O'Neill (eds), *The Contract State: Public Management in Kennett's Victoria*, Deakin University Press, Geelong.

Alford, John et al. 1994, 'The contract state', in John Alford & Deidre O'Neill (eds), *The Contract State: Public Management in Kennett's Victoria*, Deakin University Press, Geelong.

Beauris, Vic 1993, 'Probity and pitfalls: tendering and purchasing case studies', in Jane Coulter (ed.), *Doing More With Less? Contracting Out and Efficiency in the Public Sector*, Public Sector Research Centre, University of New South Wales, Sydney.

Birnbauer, Bill 1995, 'Looking for the right direction', *Age*, 17 February, p. 13.

Codd, Mike 1991, *Federal Public Sector Management Reforms—Recent History and Current Priorities*, Public Service Commission, Occasional Paper No. 11, AGPS, Canberra.

Coleman, Russell 1993, 'Some ANAO perspectives on contracting out in the public sector', in Jane Coulter (ed.), *Doing More With Less? Contracting Out and Efficiency in the Public Sector*, Public Sector Research Centre, University of New South Wales, Sydney.

Considine, Mark 1988, 'The corporate management framework as administrative science: a critique', *Australian Journal of Public Administration*, vol. 47, no. 1, pp. 4–18.

Evatt Research Centre 1989, *State of Siege*, Pluto Press, Sydney.

——1990, *Breach of Contract*, Pluto Press, Sydney.

Ferrari, Justine 1995, 'Prosecutor to examine doctor's fee transfers', *Australian*, 25 April, p. 4.

Gerrand, Valerie 1993, *The Patient Majority: Health Policy and Services for Women*, Deakin Series in Public Policy and Administration, no. 4, Deakin University, Geelong.

Hammer, Marie D. 1994, 'Effects of per capita funding on Victorian kindergartens', Kindergarten Teachers' Association of Victoria, Melbourne.

Jones, Grant 1993, 'An overview of Commonwealth Government policy', in Jane Coulter (ed.), *Doing More With Less? Contracting Out and Efficiency in the Public Sector*, Public Sector Research Centre, University of New South Wales, Sydney.

Keating, Michael 1990, 'Managing for results in the public interest', *Australian Journal of Public Administration*, vol. 49, no. 4, pp. 387–98.

Messiter, Gordon 1993, 'Contracting out in the New South Wales public sector: CSG as a case study', in Jane Coulter (ed.), *Doing More With Less? Contracting Out and Efficiency in the Public Sector*, Public Sector Research Centre, University of New South Wales, Sydney.

Montague, M. 1993, *The Report of the Inquiry Into the Increasing Costs of Disability*, Office of the Public Advocate, Melbourne.

Osborne, D. & Gaebler, T. 1993, *Reinventing Government: How the Entrepreneurial Spirit is Transforming the Public Sector*, Plume, New York.

Parker, Lee & James, Guthrie 1990, 'Public sector accounting and the challenge of managerialism', in John Forster & John Wanna (eds), *Budgetary Management and Control: The Public Sector in Australasia*, Macmillan, South Melbourne.

Victorian Commission of Audit (VCA) 1993, *Report*, vol. 2, The Graphics Centre, Melbourne.

Weller, P. & Lewis, C. 1989, 'Corporate management: background and dilemmas', in G. Davis, P. Weller & C. Lewis, *Corporate Management in Australia*, Macmillan, Melbourne.

Part III

Undermining the Public Sector

Crown

She knew he needed
this softness
came to the gates
at lunch
with gardenias
curlicues of flesh.
He turned to the
open furnace
tossed them in
had ideas of blooms
setting solid in an
emblem for an empire.

Instead steam

This was the way
it had always been
in his fibro house
the economy of
the exchange
flushing their
weary faces.

Susan Bower

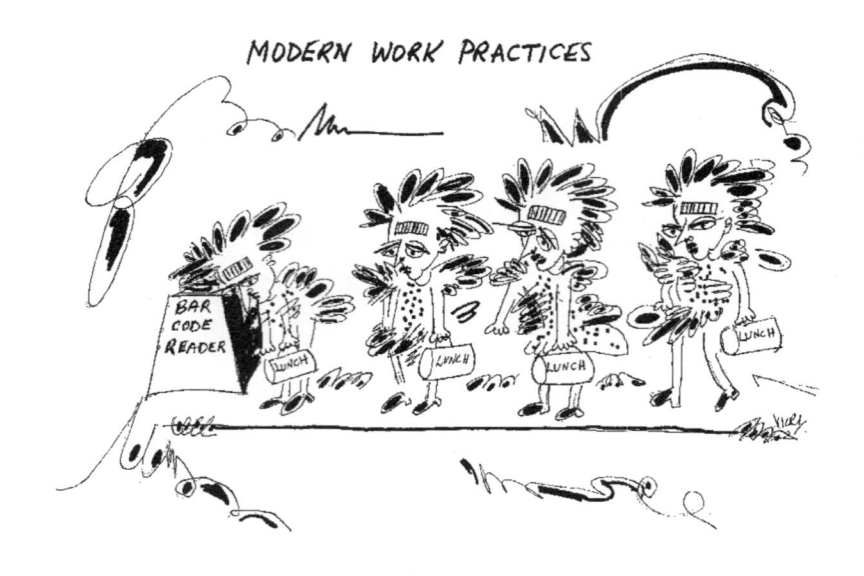

Downward/Onward/Upward?

The old Paley house collapsed
in a clang-bang of dust —
a pachyderm dropped to its knees
& belly-rolled sideward,
face contorted, head limp, chin grounded,
as tiny black drop-lidded deep-hurt eyes
each pearled a string of tears.

As the tar roof accordioned down
into the white board siding,
a steamy effluence arose
from the cellar's roots.
Phantom children of another time
skipped through the wreckage,
then hid breathless & agape
as the scrapers cleansed the land
of scrap, &, pronto-presto!
huge buckets poured a many layered
mammoth honeycomb on site —
another prison-grey domicile
for a thousand robots.

Henry S. Maas (from *Tide Pools & Swoosh Holes* 1988)

8.
Management of Higher Education Policy

Jane Marceau

This chapter suggests that understanding trends in the management of universities requires understanding the impact of the language of management as the tool for debate. The 1980s and early 1990s saw a change from a focus on policy to a focus on process. In this, education was not the only area affected. When decision-makers advocate particular directions for policy change they now feel obliged to translate their proposals into a more apparently 'neutral' language, a technocratic tongue that appears to take the politics out of policy. Derived from the province of rational economics and beginning as a legitimating device for policy directions selected, the language rapidly came to use the policy 'implementation' doctrines summarised in the word 'managerialism' to set an agenda for change which became increasingly hard to combat because of the apparently obvious or motherhood rationality of the concepts.

The goals of education

Education has always been a legitimate and important area of government action, albeit in Australia more at state than federal level until the last two or three decades. Education policy, and especially policy change, was usually expressed in terms of content rather than process, terms such as 'social justice' and 'equality' or 'equal opportunity', the language of politics.

Now, however, especially at Federal Government level in Australia, the language used to discuss education reduces policy questions to degrees of conformity with two common criteria: efficiency and effectiveness. This reduction is achieved by the use of the 'language of management' in both the development and the justification of the policy directions selected rather than simply the implementation of choices made.

Instead of recognising the problems openly, however, policy-makers have increasingly come to interfere in the internal workings of the system as though managerial changes would be enough to reconcile major goal differences. The focus is on the running of the system rather than on the objectives. Over time the goals of policy swing between emphasising the instrumental and expressive, between education for what the economy and society are thought to 'need' and what individuals want and need beyond the demands of the labour market. As educational goals have again swung towards the instrumental so, too, the language of management has come to dominate discussion. The way in which policies are implemented, financed, developed and evaluated influence what is recognised as appropriate 'organisational knowledge' and become essential parts of the policy adopted.

Theories and models

As Carol Weiss (1977) has recognised, inside every policy decision is an implicit causal model. Every time policy-makers develop and ultimately choose between alternative courses of policy action they are using a theory. That theory is necessary to interpret the world, to explain why it is operating as it is and to deduce what is necessary to get the world to change in the way desired. Policy-makers always operate with such theories, theories mostly based on 'ordinary knowledge', pragmatic knowledge derived from experience, social practice, observed correlations or half-remembered ideas. But sometimes a discourse structured from particular elements comes to dominate, becoming the widely agreed vehicle for expressing policy ideas. This has become the case with the language of management.

The concepts and the theory used to create policy form an internally coherent paradigm, a collection of value orientations, theories, techniques, and criteria for selecting problems and defining acceptable solutions on which analysts more or less tacitly agree (Kuhn 1962). Policy decisions are made within a policy paradigm in the same way that scientific discourse occurs within a scientific paradigm. One paradigm is usually dominant and is used by the controlling areas of government to mould decisions made in the 'follower' segments, such as education. The paradigm now dominant in policies for higher education is that associated with rational economics and managerialism. That paradigm provides the lens for analysing connections between issues of public concern and for determining the advice given to policy-makers. The problem is that the lens disguises fundamental choices and encourages focus on process rather than content. Three decades ago university education was a *consumption* good whose value was linked to belief in a broad liberal education as the basis of the proper citizen. Since then, higher education has come to be seen again as predominantly a *production* good: a service activity, essentially *reactive* to the forces or 'needs' of other social areas. The question then is not the goals of education but how educational institutions serve the goals set by others.

The importance of the broad political agenda

Broad political concerns shape not only the education policy which *is* adopted but also keep certain education issues *off* the policy agenda. The centrality of politics is particularly clear when major reforms of the system are undertaken or even contemplated. This is true both of reforms which aim to widen equality of opportunity and of reforms aimed at reinforcing the link between education and perceived economic interests. While Gough Whitlam proclaimed that 'the most rapidly growing sector of public spending under a Labor government will be education ... [as] ... *the great instrument for the promotion of equality* ...' (quoted Mathews 1983, p. 149, emphasis added) the Hawke government of 1983 emphasised the role of central government in managing the economy. Economic restructuring became the thrust of most government policy, and economic goals largely replaced social progress as legitimation for policy choices. Higher education has been bent to the task while at the same time suffering real losses in resources. Economy as well as economics has become the test of legitimate policy in all fields. The great dependence of education policy both on the economy and on the controllers of government economic policy has become clear. When pensions, health and, above all, unemployment costs are politically more salient, education policy is, perhaps understandably, the poor relation.

Since education is greatly dependent on a state's willingness to incur massive expenditure to achieve change in the social sphere as a whole, it is not surprising that where measured outcomes apparently do not give 'value-for-money' education, policy is redirected. If higher education apparently fails on the production count it cannot maintain a strong position on any other platform, and attention is focused on production and employment rather than broader social outcomes.

Education policy is being scrutinised in terms of outputs rather than inputs, a change of focus made easier by the loss of the vision of education as a social leader rather than follower. Once education defines its role as reactive to events and trends in other social spheres it is judged by the criteria applying to policies in those other areas. To survive as a large-scale spender in an era of public sector thrift, the education system must use the languages of dominant policy fields and shift its policy and evaluation justifications accordingly.

But education has been given three enormous tasks: social integration, equalisation of opportunity and economic training. Education is bound to fail on many counts, becoming highly vulnerable to interference in its operations by state and other players interested in clearly definable results. Political decisions in areas outside education shape both processes and outcomes within education and education's own values as the system is forced to justify the public expenditure received in terms not of its own choosing but in terms emerging from a different policy paradigm. Playing by the rules of the game implied by the use of the language will not be enough, however, to escape from the trap of multiple goals to be achieved on reduced resources.

The language of management and policy in education

In his book on the economist mandarins who dominate public policy-making in Australia's federal capital, Canberra, Michael Pusey has pointed to the extent to which the functioning of the market has become the criterion against which all policy proposals are examined (Pusey 1991).

There are several reasons for this dominance. First, like money in the market, the language of the management of money plays a levelling and 'neutralising' role in the policy process. Governments play both politics and policy, and ministers representing widely divergent policy areas must win major battles in cabinet. Political leaders must not only present the case for policy changes, especially for desired initiatives, but they must provide a language in which their proposals can be compared with the propositions of others. In a crowded policy arena and in a context of fiscal restraint, proposals for expenditure on defence, social security, the arts and education must vie for space in both discussions and in budgets. To do this they must be seen as occupying a common arena. For the debate to be undertaken at all a common language of evaluation must be provided.

Second, the development of certain social sciences has led to a focus on quantitative data as the basis of social analysis. The discipline of economics provides powerful tools for dealing with the enormous complexity of the societies and economies with which ministers and their advisers grapple. Models simplifying social phenomena and supported by apparently irrefutable quantitative data indicate the flow-on effects of particular decisions, both immediately and in the longer term. In a crowded policy space where no new policy can be brought in without affecting an existing one or creating new issues, and in a situation of fiscal constraint when governments want full value for every dollar spent, such models are obviously attractive to overworked decision-makers.

To some degree, however, the means of arriving at policy decisions have begun to subvert the ends, because the means can be measured while the ends require other judgments. The emphasis on quantitative tools crowds out more qualitative data, discourages broader thinking and subverts the agenda by pushing towards certainty and measurability of outcome.

Policy-makers, too, use models. A common one describes the process as a series of stages:
- creation of an agenda (salience of an issue);
- preparation of alternative options for action;
- choice of options and legitimation of the choices made;
- implementation of options;
- monitoring and evaluation;
- feedback, termination or recommencement;
- legitimation of decisions taken.

This model began as an analytical tool but has acquired normative overtones, seen in its name, the 'rational' model of public decision-making. While its limitations are well documented and recognised, the model allows people trying to change policy directions to make plausible claims about using the approach 'best' suited to analysing policy options within an area or between and across areas in the current political and economic environment.

The third reason for its pre-eminence as the language of government, then, is that economics provides a unifying knowledge which fits well with the acceptable forms of legitimation associated with belief in rational decision-making; it seems to be taking the 'politics' out of policy. While policy-makers know that most policy decisions are political, personal and ultimately chancy, they also know that they are supposed to make their recommendations seem the 'logical' outcome of rationally developed and considered alternatives. As long as dominant sources of policy advice, such as the Treasury and the Department of Finance, use the 'rationalist' approach, the others, such as education, must use it too.

The 'stages' model outlined indicates the division of the policy process into areas of politics and areas of rationality. It can be seen where the quantifying and standardising approaches of rational economics are indeed appropriate and powerful tools for analysing complex policy areas.

This approach has increasingly taken over the additional stages where the politics of the issue involving recognition of important social and cultural values have normally been the criteria used for the choices. The criteria associated with rationality are now applied both to selecting and legitimating the choice of the items to put in central place on the political agenda (among the many that call for attention and scarce political time) and to justifying the options selected.

A further and especially important inroad into the political side of decision-making is also being made. After policy options have been selected the same criteria are applied again during the stages of implementation and evaluation. It is here that the other language of the 1980s, that of 'managerialism', takes over and may distort the evaluation process. Managerialism is the organisational equivalent of economic rationalism and seeks to apply the same rather limited notions of allocative efficiency and policy effectiveness.

It is at this level that the impact on educational institutions is clear. Managerialism stresses the need for transparent budgeting and getting value for money. While the first is unexceptional, the second raises major issues of value, timing and the interests of the beneficiaries of the policies concerned. It tends to lead to over-rapid evaluation and policy termination because the real rate of social change that is possible through most policy decisions is much slower than is imagined by observers tending to rational expectations. The language of economics and management ignores factors in policy success or failure associated with organisational limitations (such as time, scale and specificity) and assumes that organisations designed for one set of goals can be rapidly redeployed to answer another set of imperatives. It is this issue in particular with which universities are having to come to grips.

All public policies that are systematically thought out include implicit theories about action (Weiss 1977), theories about how the world is organised, how the relations between social groups are structured, which forces create economic and social patterns, and about individual motivation. These implicit theories have been as diverse as the areas in which they are found. In contrast, the language of management has made it possible to bring together into one corpus criteria used for evaluating policies in arenas where the state has played different roles and where policies have been devised and operated with different theories of action. The users of the new language have succeeded in making indisputable what are, in fact, highly diverse and debatable assumptions about how a society, in this case Australian society, works.

Trying to use a set of common concepts and a common language to describe, assess and make recommendations for change in very different arenas of public action forces policy thought to run along often inappropriately narrow channels. Equally important, managerialist language reduces the likelihood of recognition of the legitimacy of particular values and political beliefs in the construction of public policies and inhibits appeal to such values as major guides for selecting action. Thus, for instance, where once words and concepts such as 'social justice' were used as the unifying language and criteria for action, 'efficiency' and 'effectiveness' are now used, concepts not about goals but means. These concepts have their place but should be subject to guidance and direction. They should not be the sole parameters for evaluation.

Public policies are made through compromise and conflict rather than fact and consensus. The language with which the complex issue of policy-making is discussed must be broader than the language of management, but the political language has become impoverished, making alternative proposals hard to formulate.

The language of management and higher education policy in Australia

In the process of change since the 1980s, policies for education in particular — and for higher education more especially — have increasingly taken on an imperative rather than an exhortatory, stimulatory or permissive tone. The major reforms of 1987 transformed Australian higher education with little consultation with the constituencies. This was a political decision with an economic, not a social justice or particularly educational motivation. Since that time, the Federal Government has become increasingly interventionist, while using the rhetoric of 'letting the institutions manage'. Quality exercises are an excellent case in point.

Minister Peter Baldwin's approach, as outlined in a 1991 speech, has given rise to the creation of a whole new language unknown to university administrators who thought their role was to facilitate knowledge production and transmission in line with the wishes of their peers. One document produced for the government was forced to include a glossary to explain to readers such terms as management province, mission drift, niche migration and a host of different aspects of 'quality': assessment, assurance, audit, control, culture, improvement, management and planning (Piper 1993, p. 7).

These terms are not without organisational impact. Quality management, the report goes on to explain, requires mission statements, value statements and vision statements, aims, goals, objectives, targets and strategies. It requires rules and regulations, codes of practice, goal-setting, briefing and exhortation, staff performance review, training, incentives and rewards. It requires management maps and procedures for evaluating practice which, in turn, require subdivisions designed to test efficiency, effectiveness, economy and policy evaluation and reference to the seven C's: comprehensiveness, communication, cogency, coherence, consonance, constancy and consequence (Piper 1993, p. 33). The author admits that the 'final proof of quality management is the quality of the organisation, the merit of its mission and the efficiency with which it pursues that mission' but fears that 'relying solely on that final proof may be impractical'. The government has judged that 'the quality of universities in general would be enhanced ... by the widespread adoption of institutional quality assurance procedures. To this end, the Minister's policy is to reward good quality management systems' (Piper 1993, p. 33).

In this list of management exhortations, transformed into imperatives by the promise of a share of an extra $70 million, remarkably little attention is given to aspects of teaching, learning and research that involve allocating *more* rather than less time and money. Thus, students are asked to evaluate their existing courses but not to evaluate them against potential courses endowed with smaller classes, more individual tuition, greater interaction with staff actively engaged in well-funded research, who are not stretched by an ever-increasing administrative burden, and who are supported by excellent library facilities. In other words, students are being asked to evaluate courses supplied only within the current financial state, not to imagine an even better course or a better funded system. Students are, in effect, being asked to evaluate their courses without critical information on resources available or about alternative uses of available funds. The quality of intellectual life is nowhere mentioned. Nor is there any evaluation at all of what several studies have shown — that students of an earlier generation valued as a central part of their university experience the time and space for thought, debate, personal development through relaxed interaction with peers, and a strong sense of community among the student body (Marceau 1994).

The language of management has, so far, taken centre stage in the ways in which universities now have to rethink their work and role. It has taken so much of the time and space of staff that it has controlled the entire process of higher education. Once intended for the *implementation* of agreed educational policies, it instead *determines the agenda*. The imperatives disguised within it are transforming the organisational structures to which they apply and forcing reconstruction of a common kind. While the rhetoric of politicians focuses on encouraging the diversity of the system and promotes a notion of university autonomy, the implementation of the policies creates a powerful tendency towards uniformity and a uni-dimensional criterion of success. Even more important, the language in which the organisational edicts of managerialism is couched has become the vehicle used for the justification and legitimation of activities by the universities themselves as they have been deceived into compliance with the dominant policy paradigm. They no longer seem to have an alternative mode of expressing their aims.

Conclusion

This chapter has made two essential points. The first is that education policy can only be understood when broader political concerns are taken into account. Western societies long used the education system for social and political ends wider than the economic, which meant that policy progress was measured, to the degree that it was measured at all, through evaluations of a broader kind. Now, however, economic management dominates the agenda and, hence, evaluation also.

This has meant that the language of management has taken over additional stages of the policy process. Beginning as a language of option evaluation, the tenets of rational economics and managerialism now play major roles in the creation of the agenda and thus in the choice of areas in which the government intervenes. These tenets have further shaped both the timing and the parameters of evaluation of the operation of complex social institutions, notably those of the education system. Since the goals of the system are increasingly defined as instrumental and narrow, so the criteria of evaluation have narrowed. Since quantification is the essence of this approach, the establishments concerned are being forced to define their activities in ways which permit such quantification. While it is clear that publicly funded institutions should be accountable to the government as proxy for the taxpayer, it is less clear that it is beneficial to confine a multi-faceted process within the bounds now imposed. This is especially the case because education is an arena assigned multiple and perhaps irreconcilable goals by modern western societies. As policy-makers veer between favouring instrumental and expressive goals, and new social needs appear, educational institutions need to retain the flexibility to respond effectively and to determine both their own roles and the best means of fulfilling them. It is thus imperative that higher education institutions maintain a debate couched in other terms and justify their activities using broader criteria.

The chapter points out that the apparently neutral language of policy discussion serves to narrow policy analysis by so forcing attention on implementation issues that eyes are distracted from a more diverse education policy agenda. As Simon Marginson says, budgetary and political cycles are short and, therefore, encourage the obsession with efficiency at the expense of productivity (1993, pp. 116–17). Quoting the OECD, Marginson notes that the main danger in education policy in the 1990s is the excessive emphasis on the short term at the expense of education's longer term contribution which is often indirect and less easy to measure than its costs (Marginson 1993, p. 117, quoting OECD 1990, p. 87). The short-term management view which has proved so damaging to Australian industry may be undermining higher education as well.

References

Bourdieu, P. & Passeron, J. C. 1970, *La Reproduction*, Editions de Minuit, Paris.

Istance, D. 1985, *Education in the Modern World*, OECD, Paris.

Kuhn, T. 1962, *The Structure of Scientific Revolutions*, Chicago University Press, Chicago.

Marceau, J. 1989, 'The Australian business sector: skills, tasks and technologies', in D. Pope & L. Alston (eds), *Australia's Greatest Asset: Human Resources in the Nineteenth and Twentieth Centuries*, Federation Press, Sydney, pp. 220–38.

―― 1994, Interview with past students of Cambridge University, *Cam*, June.

Marginson, S. 1993, *Education and Public Policy in Australia*, Cambridge University Press, Melbourne.

Piper, J. 1993, *Quality Management in Universities*, Report prepared for the Department of Employment, Education and Training, AGPS, Canberra.

Pusey, M. 1991, *Economic Rationalism in Canberra: A Nation-building State Changes its Mind*, Cambridge University Press, Melbourne.

Quality Education Research Council (QERC) 1985, *Quality in Education*, Report, AGPS, Canberra.

Schools Commission 1980, *Equality of Educational Opportunity: Diversity and Choice*, Schools Commission & State Education Departments, Canberra.

Stewart, J. 1982, 'Guidelines to policy derivation', in S. Leach & J. Stewart, *Approaches in Public Policy*, Allen & Unwin, London, pp. 24–35.

Weiss, C. 1977, *Using Social Science in Public Policy Making*, Lexington Books, Lexington, Mass.

9.
Managerialised Health Care

Alan Davis

There have been some intriguing changes going on since the mid-1980s that promise to enliven the debate on health care in Australia. As usual this is presaged by grumbling from the medical profession about the changes that are being pressed on them, and other professions in Australia, by governments of different political persuasions, that increasingly challenge traditional modes of professional organisation and practice. In this chapter some of the major changes will be discussed, with particular concentration on the ways in which 'economic rationalism' and 'the new managerialism' are together remaking all public sector services.

The threat to medical dominance

A number of complaints can be heard from the medical profession that give texture to what they see as the origins of their sense of dis-ease. Not only are there too many doctors being produced to work in an increasingly crowded marketplace, but other health care occupations are getting restless and demanding to be treated as equals in the health care division of labour. Such insubordination takes the form either of suggestions that they too should be permitted to treat patients in their own right without the help and guidance of a doctor, or that some of the things they do are incapable of being understood or directed by those outside their own profession. Just as the medical profession insists on autonomy and self-regulation, so too are other health care professions asserting their independent status and explicitly rejecting the authority of the medical profession to set and enforce the boundaries within which they do their work. Patients are perceived both as misusing health care (claimed to be a result of a lack of financial responsibility for treatment brought about by bulk billing), and as being less docile and more likely to take legal action for redress in the courts if they are not satisfied with the treatment and outcome that results from it. This leads to suggestions that 'defensive medicine' will become the dominant form of cautious medical practice as insurance premiums rise to cover the payouts. State-funded health care complaints units now deal with complaints against harassed health care institutions and professionals without sympathy, allegedly fuelling some patients' discontents, by mediating and resolving some and taking legal action with others. The greatest threats are seen as coming from public underfunding of health care that creates a permanent pressure to work within limited budgets, and that leaves hospitals with closed emergency departments, and closed beds and operating theatres. The waiting lists that result, along with the medical emergency that could not be treated due to closures or lack of appropriate beds, excite media comment and politicians' ire.

These kinds of complaints suggest an embattled medical profession besieged by troubles caused by others that seek to erode their rightful authority both socially (in the sense of controlling and commanding the actions of others) and culturally (in the sense of their right to say what is truly illness and what is the appropriate treatment) (Coburn 1993a, b). With this the professional autonomy that gives the profession control over the organisation and terms of the work that they do is also diminished. The picture is overdrawn of course, and there are many reasons why dis-ease is not yet professional decline. For a start it assumes a rather static model of professions that sees them as at a peak from which they can only decline, rather than more accurately as occupations that have continually remade themselves in the context of the changing state of the marketplace for services over the centuries, and the different dominant institutional regimes in which they practised their arts.

Within the hospital alone, over the past 200 years there have been major shifts in the dominance of various groups and segments within the professions, as hospitals moved from ecclesiastical control with a religious mission and the care of souls, to secular institutions based on the application of scientific knowledge and technology to the human body. In the process, control of hospitals by religious orders gave way to their direction by boards of wealthy bourgeois patrons. Lay control then shifted to medically dominated control over what went on inside the hospital, and increasingly, state control of hospitals with support from public revenues (Perrow 1962; Davis & George 1993). In each of these situations the medical profession has been forced to renew its claims to authority and autonomy against aristocratic clients or patients who knew as much about medicine as they did, philanthropists who regarded them as their social inferiors, religious competitors who challenged the efficacy of science in human affairs, and the state that now demands cost control, efficiency and strategic vision in the medical workplace (Starr 1982).

Unlike many other occupations, in the process of expansion of markets for medical care in the nineteenth century, and through the growth of state intervention in social life, the medical profession was able to achieve an enviable position which left it effectively in control of its own training and licensing, and gave it a high degree of autonomy in its work. The profession alone set the standards of what was appropriate health care, set its own fees (having fought off contract practice imposed by the Friendly societies — see Green & Cromwell 1984), and is still held in high regard by the general public who view it as having a legitimate right to influence the setting and executing of health care policies (Willis 1993; Lupton et al. 1991). These developments have not been without critics arguing that this social position, which is depicted in the profession's self-descriptions as one of social benevolence, altruism and service, has in practice covered those who have used it to seek high material rewards. Professional closure and self-regulation produce both good and poor standards of work, but lack of peer control leaves poor work unchecked and uncorrected, and sometimes even covered up by a professional closing of ranks in the face of critics (Brante 1988). Others have commented on the dubiousness of the claims of esoteric knowledge made by the medical profession to justify its exclusivity (Alvesson 1993; Fores, Glover & Lawrence 1991). Rather than social responsibility, and an ethic of service, some members of the profession have used its powerful position to exert inappropriate social control over areas of vulnerable people's lives. Their social insulation and dedication to technological fixes leads to health care without any knowledge or sympathy for most patients' social situation or life (Turner 1987). To paraphrase Shaw, the medical profession is a good example of an unholy conspiracy against the patient.

Other forms of criticism have centred on the inability of those who pay for health care to control what is done with the money once it gets into the health care system, where the final pattern of expenditure emerges from the multiplicity of decisions that are made in respect of patients, referrals, technology, drugs, services and treatment. Each decision generates a cost borne by the Medicare levy and general taxation revenues. Clinical autonomy ensures that these decisions are made by medical practitioners according to criteria set by them. Only other medically qualified people can legitimately comment on the appropriateness of the treatment given, the test performed, and the referral made. Eighty per cent of health care spending goes into hospitals, nursing homes, pharmaceuticals and medical practitioners, and about 8 per cent of GDP goes on health in Australia (Duckett 1992, pp. 140, 155). The amount that is committed to health care is not insignificant, even if by international standards Australia falls in the middle of the health care spending patterns of OECD countries.

While there is good reason to doubt a professional apocalypse, there are some signs that these discontents are a prelude to greater ones. Changes in the organisation of work in health care are similar to those already accomplished in other public sector organisations. In health care this may well finally disrupt the postwar settlement that had governments giving amounts of money to health care while letting the health care profession spend it as it saw fit by continuing to grant clinical autonomy. But the introduction of universal health care in the form of Medibank and then Medicare, and the sheer size of the health care budget, has attracted the attention of governments to the possibilities that high levels of funding for health care from the public sector might also offer the possibility of greater control over the patterns of health care expenditure.

The new public sector management

In the 1970s and 1980s this wish for greater government control coincided with a more general trend towards a new form of management of the public sector, in which the role of the manager was seen as crucial in helping a new organisational dynamism to emerge. Management-consultant-led, the private sector was seen as offering models for a reinvigorated public sector management that would abolish the passive, sclerotic bureaucracies that were seen to hinder change and throttle innovation (Hoggett 1991; Hood 1991). The right-wing economic rhetoric that surrounded the new liberalism promised that markets would set everyone free from the dead weight of state planning and mediocre services provided by arrogant officials guaranteed a lifetime of service for doing nothing. This was to be done by taking the virtues that the market supposedly created (dynamism, entrepreneurial spirit, risk taking, concern for the customer who pays for the service, hard work) and transporting both the form and the content of market rationality inside the reformed public sector. This rationality would remake everyday practices and attitudes to work, respect for economy and budgets, and align hearts and minds to a new organisational culture.

The major components of the new public management are identified by Hood (1991) as a privileging of the managerial role in organisations over the service provision role, and the elaboration of explicit standards and measures of performance in quantitative terms that set specific targets for personnel. All units and people should be able to specify how their individual goals and those of their units fit into the corporate plan of the organisation. There is a greater emphasis placed on output controls, with rewards and resources being allocated to successful performance and away from decline and failure. Here the emphasis is on getting results in the short term, rather than worrying too much about how they are achieved. Devolution of budgets to units allows the unbundling of monolithic and impenetrable bureaucracies that hide waste and inefficiency at the same time as it creates a new cadre of managers in the devolved units. Operating with one–line budgets, and decentralised in their dealings with other units, the contribution of each unit member to the achievement of the unit's goals are visible and able to be monitored. Some functions disappear altogether as they are 'out–sourced' by competitive tender at lower cost, such as cleaning, payroll management, waste removal, domiciliary services, maintenance. The creation of a top management stratum concerned with strategic visions is matched by a shedding of middle-level managers that were required in the old public sector to transfer information up and down the hierarchy. This is increasingly done by electronic data control and systems monitoring. The slim, flatter organisational shape is continually looking for ways to save money by eliminating unnecessary activity, raising labour discipline and commitment, and reducing the number of people employed, while maintaining the same level of goal expectations of each unit.

Management stresses the value of private sector practices which demand greater labour flexibility as well as relying on more public relations output to change the ways people think about the organisation. In the organisational rhetoric a new emphasis is placed on a vocabulary that reflects enterprise and action rather than tradition or service. A new vocabulary emerges of 'downsizing' instead of sackings, 'lean and mean' profiles, people 'working smart', 'multi–tasking', 'multiskilling', and 'delayering', as well as the jargon of management science and consultants that circulate JIT (just in time), OD (organisational development), MBO (management by objectives), QC's (quality circles), TQM (total quality management), and HRM (human resources management) among others. Needless to say, these have not all been popular at the same time; rather there seems to be a consistent pattern of consultant-promoted panaceas being pushed, with little long-term evaluation as to their effectiveness, and each one abandoned as the next takes hold. It might be suggested that this fecundity is more a result of the desperateness of the market for new management ideas, the transience of managers' interests, and the procedural (packages) orientation of sellers of management ideas than of the compelling intellectual content of any of the ideas on offer (Gill & Whittle 1992; Hood 1991).

According to the apologists and hagiographers, the new managers are visionaries, bringing about a veritable cultural revolution in the way public sector services are thought about and designed (Hood 1991;

Guest 1990; Peters & Waterman 1982). The new manager reanimates the organisation with his (invariably his) vision and imposes on it its new mission (Bourgeois & Brodwin 1991).The New South Wales Department of Health Discussion Paper 'A Healthy Future' (1994, p. 5) contains, for example, a statement that the health care system needs a 'vision', and calls for a focus on customers, staff, high quality outcomes, providing value for money and improved decision-making. Littered through the rest of the document are references to strategic plans, outcome measures and customers (but never patients). Typically for this genre, it ends with the pious hope that it will generate discussion and constructive comment, and a customer questionnaire to be returned to the corporate planning unit.

The new manager clearly desires efficiency, economy, excellence, enterprise and effectiveness, and will use consultants to make sure he gets it from his staff (Harrow & Willcocks 1990). In the process staff will have their talents unleashed, and creativity will be rewarded. The new manager inspires, cajoles, campaigns to get what he wants; rules are no longer useful, instead commitment is sought. For the new manager cares about people, not about chains of command; the organisation values all its staff, although it still pays some more than others. Structures inhibit; instead it is networks or teams that do the work, while leadership is installed instead of control, and the new organisational values and culture replaces position and status as staff go through the new training programs that induct them into the mysterious transformative world of TQM, 'international benchmarking' or 'best practice' (Wilmott 1993). As the New South Wales document says, 'a new style of leadership, a more strategic management, a reinvigorated staff and a successful organisation ...' will result.

The front line is praised for its commitment to the customer providing it supplies services at the cheapest possible cost and with the least human resources (du Gay & Salaman 1992). The new manager works hard to remove the inward-looking provider or professional focus and installs a customer-oriented, outward-looking concern to ensure the organisation does well in the eyes of stakeholders and purchasers of services. A flexible, internally elaborated and differentiated organisation adjusted to the twin priorities of economy–efficiency and customer need (and hopefully quality too) is designed to emerge from this. Decentralisation of decision-making and the devolution of budgets make the front line service providers take on new roles, expanded responsibilities, and new identities which give primacy to the 'mission' of the organisation over the old style service ideals or professional values that were oriented to individualised care, the present realities of the patient, a desire to do the best possible for the patient, advocacy for that patient, and the primacy of the patient's needs over the organisation's routines or economies (Stoeckle & Reiser 1992).

The workers are to provide the most appropriate form of service at the lowest cost possible as they are forced by the logic of their situation (i.e. to manage with what they are given and no more) to internalise the conflict that exists between what the patient might need and what the organisation can afford to deliver. The true measure of the success of the new public sector management is the extent to which economically rational behaviour is installed throughout the organisation, in manager, clerk and professional worker alike. Competing evaluative standards that might impose alternative logics on the practice of professional work, such as notions of duty, rights, collegiality, service, obligation, care, compassion, or even need that once provided the rhetoric for public service are eliminated, as all share the same cultural ideals as the economically rational manager.

Public services — have they changed?

A number of critiques exist of these kinds of developments suggesting that much of the change is rhetorical rather than substantial, that employees learn to clothe their actions in new sets of words while continuing to do the same old things. This may be partly correct, but rhetoric also has its force by the way it encourages people to see the world and define its content differently. Clearly there are also major problems in imputing consumer sovereignty to patients because of their inability to know what is best for them in the way of treatment. Trust is an important part of the relationship between health care provider and user. Services can only be delivered in a relationship; they are not like goods where consumption can be separated from the relationship. Health care services invoke and are sustained in complex ongoing reciprocities in a way that buying a microwave is not. Payment is typically indirect, and services are provided according to what the provider thinks is needed. Public services are also justified by reference to the intangible public good that they perform for the moral and spiritual welfare of society as a whole. These differences between the private and public sector raise questions about the appropriateness as well as effectiveness of private sector management models in the public services (Saunders & Harris 1990; Ackroyd et al. 1989). Nevertheless, corporatisation has proceeded widely in the public sector in Australia, UK and New Zealand alike, and health care has not been immune to these changed imperatives of management and the market (Dent 1993).

It may be argued that this is an overdrawn picture, that there are a number of obvious difficulties with the transformations suggested, not the least being the ability of the powerful corporate organisation of the medical profession to resist such challenges to its professional and collegial values. It can do this either by crude power plays, by strikes and removal of services (such as the NSW doctors' dispute), by colonisation of management positions (Hunter 1994 suggests that the Achilles heel of health services managerialism is the gravitation of medical practitioners to positions in management hierarchies that render them penetrable by professional values), or by threat of an en masse exit to the private health care sector. These possibilities are given by medicine's position as a dominant occupation which cannot be replaced, one that is simultaneously in the public health care sector but not necessarily of it. This ensures that a conflict of value positions and the possibility of debate and reconciliation is still possible in a health care system that has not been reduced to the primacy of economic values for the assessment of human lives. But given that the size of the private market for health care is decreasing as more and more people refuse to carry private health insurance, so the opportunities to exit the public sector go down quite dramatically as the patients are just not there to generate for the medical practitioner a viable income from private health provision alone. Not only do patients like bulk billing, but so now does the Liberal Party and the majority of medical practitioners whose annual income it guarantees.

Within the public sector the state is now continually asserting its right to influence the terms and conditions under which payments are set, for example changing the rebate system in Medicare to reduce the payment for pathology tests to the top three in a requested battery. This will either force doctors to be more alert to the gap that patients will have to pay, or order fewer tests. There are restrictions on what can be prescribed and claimed under the Pharmaceutical Benefits Scheme, with pressure to substitute cheaper generic drugs for name brands unless the prescriber orders otherwise. Requests for expensive new drugs to be imported for patients have been rejected by the Canberra bureaucrats on the grounds of expense. Payments for general practitioners are linked to training undertaken with the Royal College of General Practitioners under another government initiative, and a report on training for medical specialties from Professor Peter Baume was savaged by the profession for suggesting that the colleges should tackle what he saw as the undersupply of, for example, general surgeons or orthopaedic surgeons. The suggestion to open up specialist education came from the government in an attempt to undermine the specialists' power conferred by their small numbers.

Organisation of health care

Alongside these changes are others in the way that health care is organised — with closures of hospitals, redesignation of functions, transfer of some to the private sector, tiering of hospitals, and the explicit rationalisation of services and closure of small units, and transfer of beds to under-resourced areas. There are also attempts to shift costs away from state budgets to the Commonwealth, for example by running fewer outpatients clinics and referring patients to the private sector, where bills will be paid by Medicare and not the hospital, or restricting the dispensing of drugs in hospitals so that the cost is transferred to the Prescribed Benefits Schedule (PBS). Also there are attempts to use private capital to accelerate the building of new facilities, with the private sector building and running new hospitals or prison medical services under contracts with state governments. Refusal to increase funding results in periodic closures of beds, wards and operating theatres in hospitals, and staff vacancies unfilled as area authorities attempt to balance their books. Area boards responsible for planning, funding and accounting for that expenditure in New South Wales have imposed on their areas new management structures, many of which employ doctors in managerial roles. The number of non-medically qualified managers, planners, accountants, computer experts, and epidemiologists employed to provide the information and strategic planning for an integrated health service has also been increased.

All these trends can probably be weathered by a determined and united medical profession. But the changes that will not prove so easy to circumvent are those that threaten control over core elements of medical practice. There are already irksome restrictions on which drugs can be prescribed through the PBS, and monitoring of prescribing levels and patterns; significant deviations from professional norms are followed up by requests from Canberra for further information. If this proves unsatisfactory further action can be taken to limit that doctor's medical practice. The introduction of case mix and DRGs (diagnostic related groups) also significantly alter the patterns of medical practice. Introduced to permit identification of 'outliers' in hospital stays and treatment patterns, their use as a device for the allocation of prospective funding for the mixture of cases anticipated by the hospital can only lead to attempts to shift admissions towards the highest tariff and influence diagnoses in order to maximise income. Pressure is to be exerted on the medical staff to provide treatment at the lowest cost and shortest duration to minimise costs.

Other staff in the hospital have their work similarly restructured in relation to DRGs, so that, for example, in the case of social work it is the clinical diagnosis that gains the income for that patient while social work is expected to aid the earliest removal of the patient from hospital in order to minimise costs. A number of studies from the USA suggest that early discharge from hospital is one result, along with refusal to let into hospital some people who only generate costs and where profits are hard to make (Ruggie 1992). Patient 'dumping' is not unheard of in the private sector in the USA, that is, turfing the patient out of the facility once the payment for that patient from Medicare or Medicaid is exceeded, along with other strategies to minimise costs such as hiring underqualified staff and letting staff–patient ratios drift upwards beyond the legal maximum (Bogdanich 1991). Under such cost constraints, health care staff are under continued cost pressure and under surveillance to make sure that unnecessary or unpaid medical work is removed from hospital practice. It is perverse that a measure designed to bring in cost control to public sector health care budgets and reduce political controls has also had the effect of increasing the level and intensity of government intervention through the increased monitoring and compliance required to make DRGs work (Ruggie 1992).

Some of the changes have been of benefit to the patient: greater use of outpatient treatments, more use of day surgery, and shorter hospital stays. But the danger remains that the pressure for earlier discharges may well lead to sicker people being put back into the community, stretching already inadequately funded community based services to cover a larger and sicker population. This becomes cost shifting, rather than cost saving, with the patient the loser. Where admissions are hard to achieve there will be pressure to admit more people as emergencies, and to displace people from emergency departments into primary care either in the public or private sector. Again this is cost shifting rather than cost saving. There are also costs brought about by the sheer intensity of the work in terms of stress and distress of staff who are asked always to do more with the same amount and to carry a managerial load.

Outcome measures

The shift towards outcome measures also potentially goes to the heart of medical practice, with research used to identify the outcomes of various forms of medical treatment. Diagnoses and costs are made visible in prospective payments systems. It needs but a further step to move from generating comparative health care costs per patient per facility in order to identify high and low cost services, to identifying what treatments should be refused to which groups of patients. By using such research correlating diagnoses and treatments and outcomes of success or failure as measured by mortality or morbidity, a catalogue of effective, relatively ineffective and even unsafe treatments is revealed. What would emerge as inappropriate use of some treatments on some types of patients would then not generate any payments for the treatment facility. Those engaged in making such determinations in New South Wales in October 1994 were a mixture of health economists, public health doctors, Department of Health staff, hospital administrators and medical academics. In an article entitled 'Cents to decide if a life is worth saving' in the *Sydney Morning*

Herald of 14 October 1994, Alicia Larriera identifies the key issue as the loss of the patient's primary advocate, the one person that could normally be expected to lobby hard to give them the best chance of treatment to ease their illness irrespective of their social or clinical status, in favour of an abstract calculation based on monetary considerations that make life into something decided by a ready reckoner. Not surprisingly, the Australian Medical Association (AMA) and the Labor Party showed some appreciation of the implications of this for a doctor–patient relationship in which the doctor did not act on the patient's behalf, but instead used cost calculations to decide whether or not treatment was given. This raises the further issue of the bioethics of such crude forms of rationing, where the doctor could no longer be assumed to be working in the patient's interest, but in the interest of cost reduction for the general taxpayer. Those patients able to pay would of course exit promptly to the private sector to get the treatment their doctor thought best in the circumstances.

Managed markets

There have also been suggestions that Australia might benefit from the introduction of managed markets that split the provision of health care from the funding of it. By moving towards a system like that currently under way in the UK, a market is introduced that induces changed behaviour from health care professionals as they share an interest in maintaining the economic viability of their employing organisation (Ham 1994; Harrison & Wistow 1992; Hudson 1992). Their continued employment and service expansion depends on how well they do in attracting customers and satisfying them. Hospitals that give poor service at high cost will have no takers for their contracts, and lack of revenue will result in their closure. Purchasers of services are not the patients. The market is rigged so that the general practitioner or district health authority acts as fundholder and enters into contracts with providers to get the most service for their patients at lowest cost; unspent funds can be retained and invested by the fundholder for its own benefit, for example to buy new equipment or pay higher salaries. The objective is to circumvent the providers' professional control of the National Health Service and to impose on the professions involved a consciousness of enterprise and entrepreneurship that will cut waiting lists, shake up traditional patterns of practice, force innovation in delivering treatment and care, introduce competition with private providers such as private hospitals, clinics and nursing homes, and overall improve the quality of services that 'customers' receive. The competition is between segments of the professions to maximise their units' income while providing an adequate service at the lowest possible cost. Already it has led to hospital closures, service closures, sackings and rehiring of nursing staff at lower salaries, and contracts let out over large distances at great inconvenience to patients. There is now a marked disparity between those patients whose doctors opted to become fundholders for whom the health services compete, and those who are not fundholders' patients who make up a second tier of people who have to wait for their operations or consultations. It leads to a two-tier health service in which valuable patients receive good care and less valuable ones do not. Here again economic rationality and managerialism undermine clinical autonomy in favour of health care directed by economic considerations alone.

Finally, the introduction of electronic means of surveillance now permit the collection and collation of large amounts of data on the internal practices of staff in organisations. Medical Management Information Systems provide speedy reports on the state of play inside medical systems. Much information now routinely collected can also be routinely reshuffled and processed into new forms that will reveal, for example, how much of a unit's budget has been spent on what kinds of activity. This depends on the size of the files (the number of subjects and items of useful information), the degree of centralisation and cross-referencing potential that the system has, the time taken to process it and to use it to steer behaviour in the direction that managers want, and the relative visibility of subject (i.e. the number of times they impinge on collection points in the information flow) and their potential for subversion and resistance (Dandeker 1990; Feinglass & Salmon 1990). Such information allows the managers to have at their fingertips information not available to others in the system and gives a means of monitoring front-line compliance with strategic decisions made by the dominant coalition in the organisation (Golding 1991). Add other information, such as customer surveys of satisfaction with services, and systematic medical audits to standardise practice and examine deviations from expected outcomes, and the effect is to make medical work less invisible and more open to direction through budgetary manipulation and cost cutting.

Conclusion

Threats to medical dominance in health care would increase if alternative sources of cheaper health care were available. As yet there is little sign that alternative medicine or other health care professions could fill such a gap. The longer that a united medical profession is able to fight off economic rationalism and managerialism in health services the more likely we are to see competing values articulated and informed ethical debates held on what is desirable and what is not, rather than an obsolete MBA-based commander system (Bourgeois & Brodwin 1991). This is a machismo management style that cuts, burns and slashes while demanding commitment to the new corporate culture and a health care marketplace that is governed by a logic of cost rather than care and compassion.

The medical profession alone can deliver the community from these outcomes. Indeed there are many ways in which the medical profession should be reformed both in its training and practice to make it more responsive to patients' needs and to the diverse social circumstances of those it serves, rather than relying on the cruel stereotype and dismissive and brusque handling of patients at their most vulnerable to get through their chosen punishing schedule of work. There is no reason why doctors cannot learn from complaints (complaints about the physician's manner were 250 per cent more frequent than those about medical misdiagnosis in Nettleton and Harding's 1994 study of complaints in the UK). Nor is there any reason why patients should not be much more involved in the treatment they receive and the planning of health care services. The definitions of health and illness in Australia will remain those promoted by the medical profession as most people still respect the cultural and cognitive authority of the orthodox medical practitioner, even as they consult their alternative ones in parallel. What remain largely ignored are the social changes that need to be made to bring about a better chance for people to lead a healthy life in which they regain some control over the social institutions that make them sick.

Wealth and health are still closely correlated, as are poverty and ill-health. The organisations that shed staff to flatten their profile contributed to increased unemployment, and to the creation of an ever more intensely exploited contract work force delivering services at lower rates of pay than when they were on staff. The labour market increasingly reflects a division between good jobs which are secure and pay well, and part-time or contract positions that include little in the way of occupational welfare (Pulkingham 1992). This too shows itself in health and illness patterns that consistently display a gradient of ill-health, with those with most security, autonomy and pay doing best in achieving a decent standard of living and good health. Aboriginal health is a scandal that still awaits redress, with managerialism and free markets being unlikely solutions to the health problems that beset Aboriginal people. Solutions are more likely to come from designing services that incorporate Aboriginal perspectives and values, and which empower through participation of the groups served in the provision of the service.

People still do little to relate their health to their environment either globally or locally, where an ecological view of health would alert them to the contingent nature of human life and the ways in which economic growth rates threaten their existence and future health (McMichael 1993). There is little sign of Australia moving towards greater use of public transport. Woodchipping continues, soil erosion and depletion is still occurring on a large scale, waterways bloom with algae, and wildlife disappears from everywhere but zoos. The longterm effects of climatic and environmental change remain uncertain in their effects on the human body (e.g. through increased exposure to ultraviolet rays, with skin damage, depressed immune systems and corneal problems), and exposure to new diseases and vectors for disease may thrive in changed Australian climatic conditions. HIV, the Ebola virus, and new resistant strains of tuberculosis and more virulent bacteria all show that the natural world has not stood still in its effects on health. The danger, as ever, is to remain infatuated with the politics and economics of health care, and assume that economists have the answer to all the problems of human existence in their economic calculus of the value of life.

References

Ackroyd, S. et al. 1989, 'Public services and their management', *Journal of Management Studies*, vol. 26, pp. 603–19.
Alvesson, M. 1991, 'Organizational symbolism and ideology', *Journal of Management Studies*, vol. 28, pp. 207–25.
—— 1993, 'Organizations as rhetoric', *Journal of Management Studies*, vol. 30, pp. 999–1015.
Bogdanich, W. 1991, *The Great White Lie*, Simon & Schuster, New York.
Bourgeois, L. & Brodwin, D. 1984, 'Strategic implementation', *Strategic Management Journal*, vol. 5, pp. 241–64.
Brante, T. 1988, 'Sociological approaches to the professions', *Acta Sociologica*, vol. 31, pp. 119–42.
Coburn, D. 1993a, 'State authority, medical dominance and trends in the regulation of the health professions: the Ontario case', *Social Science and Medicine*, vol. 37, pp. 129–38.
—— 1993b, 'Professional powers in decline', in F. Hafferty & J. McKinlay (eds), *The Changing Medical Profession*, Oxford University Press, New York.
Dandeker, C. 1990, *Surveillance, Power and Modernity*, Polity in asociation with Basil Blackwell, London.
Davis, A. & George, J. 1993, *States of Health*, Harper & Row, Sydney.
Dent, M. 1993, 'Professionalism, educated labour and the state: hospital medicine and the new managerialism', *Sociological Review*, May, pp. 244–73.
Duckett, S. 1992, 'Financing of health care', in H. Gardner (ed.), *Health Policy*, Churchill Livingstone, Melbourne.
du Gay, P. & Salaman, G. 1992, 'The culture of the customer', *Journal of Management Studies*, vol. 29, pp. 615–33.
Feinglass, J. & Salmon, W. 1990, 'Corporatization of medicine' *International, Journal of Health Services*, vol. 20, pp. 233–52.
Fores, M. et al. 1991, 'Professionalism and rationality', *Sociology*, vol. 25, pp. 79–100.

Gill, J. & Whittle, S. 1992, 'Management by panacea', *Journal of Management Studies*, vol. 30, pp. 281–95.
Golding, D. 1991, 'Some everyday management rituals in management control', *Journal of Management Studies*, vol. 28, pp. 569–83.
Green, D. & Cromwell, L. 1984, *Mutual Aid Welfare State*, Allen & Unwin, Sydney.
Guest, D. 1990, 'Human resource management and the American Dream', *Journal of Management Studies*, vol. 27, pp. 377–97.
Ham, C. 1994, 'Reforming health services', *Social Policy and Administration*, vol. 28, pp. 293–8.
Harrison, S. & Wistow, G. 1992, 'The purchaser provider split in English health care', *Policy and Politics*, vol. 20, pp. 123–30.
Harrow, J. & Willcocks, L. 1990, 'Public services management', *Journal of Management Studies*, vol. 27, pp. 281–304.
Hoggett, P. 1991, 'A new management in the public sector?', *Policy and Politics*, vol. 19, pp. 243–56.
Hudson, B. 1992, 'Quasi markets in health and social care in Britain', *Policy and Politics*, vol. 20, pp. 131–42.
Hunter, D. 1994, 'From tribalism to corporatism', in J. Gabe et al. (eds), *Challenging Medicine*, Routledge, New York.
Lupton, D. et al. 1991, 'Caveat emptor or blissful ignorance?', *Social Science and Medicine*, vol. 33, pp. 559–68.
McMichael, M. 1993, *Planetary Overload*, Cambridge University Press, New York.
Nettleton, S. & Harding, G. 1994, 'Protesting patients', *Sociology of Health and Illness*, vol. 16, no. 1, pp. 38–61.
Perrow, C. 1962, 'The analysis of goals in complex organisations', *American Sociological Review*, vol. 26, pp. 854–66.
Peters, T. & Waterman, R. 1982, *In Search of Excellence*, Harper & Row, New York.
Ruggie, M. 1992, 'The paradox of Liberal intervention', *American Journal of Sociology*, vol. 97, pp. 919–44.
Saunders, P. & Harris, C. 1990, 'Privatization and the consumer', *Sociology*, vol. 24, pp. 57–75.
Sewell, G. & Wilkinson, B. 1992, 'Someone to watch over me', *Sociology*, vol. 26, pp. 271–89.
Starr, P. 1982, *The Social Transformation of American Medicine*, Basic Books, New York.
Stoeckle, J. & Reiser, J. 1992, 'The corporate organization of hospital work', *Annals of Internal Medicine*, vol. 116, pp. 407–13.
Turner, B. 1987, *Medical Power and Social Knowledge*, Sage, New York.
Willis, E. 1993, 'The medical profession in Australia', in F. Hafferty & J. McKinlay (eds), *The Changing Medical Profession*, Oxford University Press, New York.
Willmott, H. 1993, 'Strength is ignorance, slavery is freedom', *Journal of Management Studies*, vol. 30, pp. 515–52.

10.
Mangerialising Local Government

Stephen Albin

Managerialism has become an orthodox social, economic and organisational cure-all. It will lead to efficiencies in government administration which will free up resources to meet ever-increasing demands — doing more with less. The logic appears straightforward. However, like most prescribed medicine it treats the symptoms and not the cause.

The managerialism cure-all is continuing to converge on local government. Changes in legislation by state governments and policies by organisational élites, are making local government more exposed to the managerialist threat.

Local government has the opportunity to re-chart the course of government in Australia. In social democracies such as Sweden and liberal democracies such as the USA there is evidence of local government being a hive of innovation (see Osborne & Gabler 1992). Local government in Australia has a capacity to redefine the desirable aspects of 'government' and managerialism can stifle this capacity by fragmenting local government organisations into agencies of control. In doing this, managerialism is likely to create deep-seated and long-term organisational problems which will raise serious questions about the legitimacy of government.

What is managerialism?

Managerialism has been promoted in Australia since the early 1980s. Nonetheless, just a cursory scan of economic, social and organisational climates of Australian government shows that the managerialist rhetoric cannot be legitimised by resultant experience. For instance, during this period, Australia had double-digit inflation closely paralleled by double-digit unemployment. At the local level, governments have been virtually bankrupt trying to deal with increasing demands placed on them. At the organisational level, perceptions are that more and more workers are suffering from stress and other work-related illness as they succumb to the increasing pressures of work.

These human costs are not acknowledged by the managerialists, who continue to promote their views to larger audiences. For this reason it is particularly difficult to arrive at a testable definition of managerialism. Possibly, the best way to arrive at a definition is to take the concept back to public choice theory and New Right ideology.

Public choice and managerialism

Managerialism has been pursued in government ever since public choice theory provided a framework to examine government failure to provide goods and services in an apparently efficient manner. The key to the public choice account is that under bureaucratic transfers the government will tend to oversupply outputs. Whereas a profit-seeking, market-based monopolist offers units of output for a price, the government supplies output in exchange for a total budget. However, the relationship between budget and output does not necessarily ensure that outputs will be oversupplied. When combined with the incentive structures associated with traditional government production, budgets will be fully maximised and so, too, will outputs.

This is all predicated on a rather contentious assumption that individual bureaucrats will seek to maximise their budgets because, almost universally in western polities, the salaries of officials working in government are closely related to the budgets they administer and control. Moreover, controlling higher budgets means expanded promotion opportunities and higher remuneration (Niskanen 1973). This is only limited by the constraint that on average they must supply the quality of service expected by the politicians.

Public choice provides the much-needed intellectual support for managerialist ideology. The simple fact is that managerialism is directed at changing traditional bureaucratic organisational incentives to reduce outputs and thereby lower taxes. The explicit assumption is that private sector incentive structures are far superior to those which are manifest in government. According to managerialist orthodoxy, government should be more like the private sector and thus exposed to competitive markets.

Contracting out

There has been a history of managerialism in local government which may predate other managerial initiatives in other levels of government.

Managerialism began in earnest in the early 1980s with contracting out. By the late 1980s over 55 per cent of local councils contracted out at least one of their functions (Evatt Research Centre 1990, p. 49). With compulsory competitive tendering introduced by the Kennett government in Victoria and to follow in all other states, contracting out is likely to be the normal way for councils to deliver services.

Other managerialist trademarks have been, and are continuing to be, foisted on staff in local government. Total quality management, customer service, performance measurement and benchmarking are the current jargon.

As the debate is ideologically charged — with claims about the good of the private sector versus the good of the public sector — so is the research. Much of it is polarised by the private versus public dichotomy, with results providing few useful conclusions.

While many claims have been made that contracting out yields significant savings, quoted figures, ranging from 6 per cent up to as much as 20 per cent, can only be supported by anecdotal evidence at the margin. About half or more councils in Australia have moved back to providing services in-house.

But the significant point behind all these wild claims about savings is what constitutes a saving to the organisation. If savings are based on fundamental success factors for the public organisation (i.e., taxes paid by residents and the range of services delivered by the organisation) there is no evidence to support the claim that contracting out is beneficial. For instance, it would be impossible that contracting the garbage service would lead to taxpayers having a 20 per cent reduction in rates or a 20 per cent greater range of services.

If savings are defined as the reduction in the costs of delivering a specific service, there is potential for a one-off saving which normally reflects the costs of workers' compensation, holiday-leave loading and other benefits enjoyed by the outdoor work force. But interestingly, these savings do not find their way to the organisation's financial statements. The reason is that the savings are subsumed in employing contract supervisors on far higher salaries (Albin 1992). Therefore, savings and contracting out claims are based on limiting the definitions of costs to the organisation and disregarding the extensive impact on conditions for the outdoor work force.

These comments are based on a study conducted in 1992 which aimed to remove ideological bias (Albin 1992). One hundred local governments across Australia were surveyed in detail to identify whether contracting out led to the benefits touted by managerialists. It was found that contracting out did not confer any identifiable gains to ratepayers or communities in terms of reduced local taxes, nor did it lead to a wider range of services being provided. Councils which contracted out charged higher local taxes. Additionally, the difference between the cost of councils providing services internally or through contracting was not significant enough to determine which was cheaper. On all counts managerialism did not measure up.

There were, however, significant distributional consequences at the organisational level. In councils that contracted services, there were fewer outdoor workers (as a proportion of total staff) and a far greater number of engineers (as a proportion of total staff) than those that produced the service internally. It could, therefore, be concluded that when a council moves to contracting out, outdoor workers are shed and replaced by professional engineers to supervise contract work.

This casts a new light on managerialism. The fact that managerialism is shrouded in the language of efficiency and public interest is a mere smokescreen. In the case of local government, managerialism is more about reshaping the organisation into a control agency for the benefit of professional staff and to the detriment of lower skilled outdoor workers.

Managerialism as a form of control

The influence of New Right ideology on managerial practice may be seen in the writing of Dunleavy. Instead of pursuing mechanisms to further the public interest, Dunleavy has developed a bureau-shaping model in which he proposes that senior managers change organisational arrangements to further their own private interest. In *Explaining the Privatisation Boom* (1986) he claims that senior managers use contracting out to shape their organisation into pure control agencies.

> The bureau shaping model predicts that policy level staff will try to shift their agency, as far as possible to an ideal type of pure control agency, hiving off implementation functions ... automating routine jobs in order to liberate resources ... and to insulate key decision areas from public scrutiny or participation. (Dunleavy 1986, p. 21)

Dunleavy contends that the welfare of managers is very closely aligned to the status and character of their agency, which is due more to the activities of the agency than the size of the budget. He asks, 'why should a Director of Technical Services in a Local Authority care if refuse collection is privatised, thereby removing the need for her to manage some of the best organised and most militant public service workers?' (Dunleavy 1986, p. 21).

Moving into the managerialism fold offers the senior manager the opportunity to reduce the number of blue-collar workers and expand the number of supervisory and professional positions, which increases his or her control and thereby improves the agency's status and character. Additionally, contracting out affords senior managers more control over contract workers who can easily be sacked or replaced if they question decisions or challenge authority. Herein lies the appeal of managerialism.

The evidence suggests that the effects of managerialism are organisational control, professional rent-seeking and prestige. This behaviour can also explain why managerialism has such widespread support among politicians, businessmen and bureaucrats alike. The politicians and business interests are enticed by the prospects of savings. For politicians it means no tax increases while being able to satisfy community interests; for businessmen it means lower taxes. In local government both expectations have been proved to be fallacious.

To the government professional, managerialism means control over militant workers, greater prospects for career and salary advancement and hiving off all the mundane routine work and creating prestigious supervisory units. However, it needs to be established whether this is an intentional outcome or whether it is the result of unrelated circumstances. Although the bureau-shaping framework is logically consistent, like the managerialist discussions, it is ideologically charged. It is difficult to accept the notion of a sinister controlling manager when there are many other people who are party to such decisions (politicians, general managers and sometimes unions and workers). Bureau-shaping, while providing a consistent framework for explaining local government privatisation, leaves out the important reference to decision-making within the overall dynamic of an organisation.

Nonetheless, the organisational impacts of managerialism have taken their toll. Across the country there are countless stories about organisational gridlock and low staff morale within local government.

Explanations for incorrect diagnosis

So far, the managerialist agenda has been unveiled and some of the myths that surround it exposed. To identify where it went wrong is a little more complex. The managerialist agenda is obliging government organisations to acknowledge their location in a competitive market.

The complexity, and perhaps the answer to their incorrect prescriptions, lies in the organisational dynamic. Questions on what happens to the organisation when incentive structures are changed are rarely considered by the managerialist. Managerialism examines internal incentive structures and their relationship to outputs. However, the organisation is made up of more than just incentive structures. People in local government socialise and learn in the organisations where they work. The way they are treated at work impacts on their family life and everyday life. Not everyone is in an organisation to mould their career paths and implement policies which are not in the broader public interest. Essentially, most people have a desire to do a good job without ulterior motives. Humanitarian sentiment still survives in local government and offsets the excesses of managerialism.

Increasing pressures were placed on local government during the early 1990s. Higher community demands and expectations have been placed on councils throughout Australia. The rise in community services provided by local governments is evidence of this. For example, between 1980 and 1991 real term per capita expenditure on community services increased from $14.90 to $25.39 in New South Wales. Over the same period, real term per capita expenditure on roads went from $157 to $169 (ABS 1994).

While the community is demanding more services, local government revenue has been severely constrained. Local government employees have been trying to deliver more services to the community with fewer resources.

Because employees are genuinely trying to meet these demands, they are under a great deal of pressure: not to go over budget, to stay at work longer, and to ensure that politicians and managers and the local community are satisfied. When offered the managerialism cure-all, most rational (albeit myopic) managers would jump at the chance. This is exactly what has happened since 1990.

Unfortunately, the managerialist doctrine tells managers that they must control, and control they do. They follow all the documented steps (of contracting out, of privatising, of strategic planning, of restructuring activities) but then find the organisation is in a worse position than when they began the exercise.

People who have embarked on this course generally have no underhand motive; they are just looking for a solution to all the pressures in the workplace. Managerialism offers problem-solving methods used in everyday life: identify a specific problem and set up appropriate organisational responses. The dilemma is that once this process is undertaken the result is a fragmented organisation which has lost sight of its purpose.

Corporate planners are now putting back the fragments by developing cross-program linkages and further organisational restructuring. To do this is futile. It is like putting the pieces of a broken mirror together with glue and expecting to see a true reflection.

What is needed is to look at the problem from a totally different perspective. Instead of scrutinising outputs and restructuring organisations to change incentives, the organisation's most important asset — people — should be looked at.

The issues that need to be addressed are how to get people once again to feel part of the organisation, not just as some commodity that can be cast aside when pressure has taken its toll. Only then will organisational productivity and quality of outputs improve. Instead of using the managerialist logic, 'if it moves privatise it; if it doesn't, restructure it', the organisation has to be viewed as people working in teams to achieve shared goals.

Government organisations (and the people within them) are confronted with many pressures. People working in government have always had to deal with pressures, but the primary difference between then and now is that the pressures are different. Typically, government organisations were designed to deal with big problems; the Federal Government was extremely effective at mobilising resources for a war, and similarly local government for a bridge collapse. But now a community not only wants the local council to fix the collapsed bridge but also asks for sustainable development, more child care and more recreational facilities. In the mid-1980s local government would not have become involved in these issues but today there is real and pressing community expectation of government involvement. These expectations are not matched by a necessary commitment to increased taxation.

An opportunity for learning

Local government has not changed the focus of its organisations to meet these new pressures. It is trying to set up new child care centres and meet community expectations with the same organisational technology used to repair broken bridges. Control is important in dealing with broken bridges but not when meeting community needs. Managerialism is taking the outdated organisational technology to the limit by fragmenting organisations and setting up more control clearance points.

To deal with the changing pressures placed on government there is a need to develop new organisational technology which brings people back into the organisation. It should focus on making the organisation flexible, adaptive and innovative to best meet changing community expectations. Only when people in organisations are encouraged to learn in the workplace will local government cope with changing community expectations and increasing pressures.

Employees need to be part of building a shared vision for the organisation, to be encouraged to be innovative, not chastised for making mistakes, and given opportunities rigorously to challenge all assumptions that they bring to their day-to-day work; and then learn as a team (Senge 1992).

Developing an environment which facilitates learning in an organisation has the potential benefit of high morale, quality output and greater clarity about the purpose of the organisation. That environment can encompass the broader dimensions of humanitarian concerns which involve not only a commitment to serve the public but also the enrichment of the experience of being at work.

References

Albin, S. 1992, *Bureau Shaping and Contracting Out : The Case of Australian Local Government*, Discussion Paper No. 29, ANU, Canberra.

Australian Bureau of Statistics (ABS) 1994, *Standardised Local Government Statistics,* ABS, Canberra.

Downs, A. 1957, *An Economic Theory of Democracy*, Random House, New York.

Dunleavy, P. 1986, 'Explaining the privatisation boom: public choice versus radical approaches', *Public Administration*, no. 64, pp. 13–34.

Evatt Research Centre 1990, *Breach of Contract: Privatisation and the Management of Australian Local Government*, Pluto Press, Sydney.

Gerritsen, R. & Albin, S. 1992, 'Privatisation: economic cure-all or ideological dogma?', in *Markets, Morals and Manifestos: Fightback! and the Politics of Economic Rationalism in the 1990s*, Institute for Science and Technology Policy, Murdoch University, Perth.

Niskanen, W. 1973, *Bureaucracy and Representative Government*, Aldine Atherton, New York.

Osborne, D. & Gabler, E. 1992, *Reinventing Government*, Addison-Wesley, Reading, Mass.

Senge, P. 1992, *The Fifth Discipline*, Random House, Sydney.

11.
Jeff Kennett's Anti-Government

Mike Salvaris

If government is about people and their well-being, then what Jeff Kennett heads could best be described as an 'anti-government'. In action, it is primarily concerned to reduce the size and traditional functions of government as an agency of human well-being and community services. In style and philosophy it treats government 'like a limited stock-company or a weak auxiliary to the market system' (Self 1990).

The human cost of Kennett's radical, small-government program has been extraordinarily severe and can be measured in different ways: in the breadth and depth of cuts in community services, government spending and public employment; in a general loss of morale, independence and competence in the public sector; in the decreased value and efficiency of public assets owned by the Victorian people; and in various conventional socioeconomic indicators of well-being.

But one broader and less obvious cost may prove more serious in the long term: the cost to democracy and citizenship. So-called 'management reforms', which the government claims are essential to restore financial efficiency and economic growth, have been increasingly accompanied by measures which undermine democratic processes, civil rights, open government and the independence of public officials. The Victorian experience is not new; a similar pattern has been observed in Britain, for example, by Hillyard and Percy-Smith (1988). They conclude that 'developments towards more intensive forms of social control [were] crucially linked to the deepening economic crisis'.

The impact on citizenship in Victoria is hard to measure, but nonetheless real. The signs of damage to the broader social fabric of the state are beginning to show in multiply disadvantaged communities (such as small country towns); in particular socioeconomic groups (young unemployed people in industrial suburbs); and, more generally, in diminished social solidarity and a weaker civic ethic. This effect has also been seen elsewhere, notably in Britain, North America and New Zealand. As Turner (1993) explains:

> The monetaristic and managerial revolutions of the 1980s have regarded inflation as the principal enemy of a sound economy and as a consequence every attack on inflation has directly or indirectly been an attack on the principles of citizenship within the welfare State.

The human impact[1]

In its first two years in office after election in October 1992 the Kennett government made the most severe cuts to government spending and employment in Victoria's postwar history. Annual spending has been slashed by about $1.1 billion or 10 per cent in real terms.[2] Most of this has been in community services such as education, health, welfare and public transport (but notably not police). In the main government sector 41 000 jobs have been lost, or about 20 per cent of the entire work force; in public corporations another 15 000.

A massive program of privatisation is under way. At the top of the scale this includes selling off the three pivotal state corporations which supply water, electricity and gas. The largest of these, the State Electricity Commission, has a gross value of about $13 billion and is already one of the world's cheapest and most efficient electricity providers. All three are likely to be sold to overseas owners,[3] despite opinion polls showing that 66 per cent of all Victorians oppose any sale of these corporations, and 90 per cent oppose overseas sale.[4] Further down the list, low security prisons and public bus services are being privatised, local governments required to submit up to 50 per cent of all municipal services for private tender, and hundreds of smaller government services sold or transferred to private contractors.

The impact on human services has been wide-ranging. Large and small programs have been affected in almost all policy fields, with no apparent regard for need or social priority. Funding has been cut to schools and kindergartens; Family Planning clinics have been closed. Community-based services have been especially penalised, from peak agencies such as the Victorian Council of Social Service (funding reduced by about 33 per cent), through to Citizens Advice bureaus (cut 25 per cent), community health centres and tenants advice services, and down to small programs like cottage homes for the intellectually disabled and the 'lollypop ladies' who supervise school crossings.

Public education has been hit particularly hard: nearly 8000 teachers and 3700 school cleaners have been made redundant, and 260 state schools forcibly closed. Victorian school retention rates, previously the highest in Australia, are now close to the lowest. Average class sizes have increased from twenty-three to twenty-six. In 1994, 10 700 pupils dropped out of state school enrolment lists despite a government forecast that they would increase.

Melbourne's public transport system is visibly running down; in 1993–94 it lost 10 million customers. A national survey on youth homelessness in 1994[5] showed that Victoria now has the nation's highest rate of homeless youth in secondary schools. Increases in tuberculosis (by 25 per cent) and water contamination reported in 1994 have been partly traced to greater homelessness and reduced spending on infrastructure maintenance; if water is further privatised, the British experience suggests these health problems will dramatically worsen.[6]

Where government services have remained in public hands, the systematic introduction of commercial principles has replaced universalism and equity as core service values. A prime example is the 'casemix' system, which makes hospitals across the state bid against each other for particular medical procedures, and forces patients to go where they are most cheaply provided. Case mix has been criticised for 'treating conditions, not people', but this is not surprising in a system where hospital managements now commonly refer to patients as REUs or 'revenue earning units', and where, alone among all states, Victorians are now charged by the minute for emergency phone advice on poisoning.[7] In many cases fees have been introduced surreptitiously for services that were once free — such as parks and gardens, now charged for through municipal and water board levies.

At the same time, and despite its attacks on the former government for doing the same, the Kennett government has sharply increased state taxes and charges.[8] Many increases are highly regressive in their impact. A new flat tax of $100 (the 'State deficit levy') was imposed on all householders regardless of means or property value — very like Mrs Thatcher's poll tax and not much more popular. This was justified to the electorate on patently political grounds, as an essential corrective to the financial mismanagement of the previous Labor government. There have been big increases in many other household taxes and charges, from public transport (up 8 per cent), gas (13 per cent), electricity tariffs (up $64), petrol (3 cents a litre) and car registration (up by $70).

Like its British and New Zealand counterparts, the Kennett government claimed that public sector cuts would speed up the state's economic recovery, but the opposite has proved to be the case. The quite predictable consequence of huge cuts in government employment and spending during a recession has been to worsen unemployment, reduce economic output and thus slow down the recovery in both public and private sectors of the economy. For nearly eight years Victoria had Australia's lowest unemployment rate: in just three years it went from lowest to highest, peaking at over 12.3 per cent in mid-1993. The rate of growth of the state economy from September 1993 to June 1994 was fully 20 per cent lower than the average for other states (3.5 per cent of Gross State Product, compared with 4.5 per cent). In 1993–94 the net growth in full-time jobs for the rest of Australia was 200 000, while in Victoria it was virtually zero (but part-time jobs grew disproportionately). It is true that by 1995 the state's economy was recovering; but the pain of unemployment and recession has certainly been much longer and deeper because of government cuts. Faced with clear evidence for this, both the premier and the treasurer shifted their position, eventually conceding the link after initial denials, but then following the Thatcher gambit: 'there is no alternative'. Not all Victorians accepted this; in the two years to September 1994 a record number migrated from the state.

The impact on democracy and citizenship

The list of coercive and undemocratic measures sanctioned by the Victorian government is long. It ranges from the obvious (increased police powers, public attacks on independent officials, the dismantling of democratic structures) to the covert (secrecy, cronyism, and many forms of low-level bullying). When the government has been required to justify these measures it has generally done so on some quasi-managerial ground, such as efficient administration, sound financial management, commercial confidentiality, state economic development or simply 'strong government' (although the underlying rationale may be quite different).

Police powers have increased in Victoria. In 1994 eight Victorians were shot by police, by far the highest state rate; five of the victims were former psychiatric patients. Since 1993 police violence in peaceful demonstrations has increased notably, with a growing use of baton charges and lethal neckholds. The police commissioner now concedes that there is 'a culture of aggression' in the force. In a 1994 police raid on a gay nightclub over 400 people were strip-searched and many lined up naked against the walls. Compulsory fingerprinting of minors has been introduced. Journalists are now forbidden to interview prisoners. Prisons are being privatised.

The government has removed important democratic structures. Elected local governments have been abolished and replaced by state-appointed commissioners. This was claimed to be a temporary 'efficiency' measure, but the government's purpose was transparently to bypass possible dissent by democratic councils from a number of controversial state measures: council amalgamations, deregulated planning and development, forced spending cuts and the contracting out of local services. A new planning code has reduced the right of residents and communities to participate in local decisions. The state Industrial Relations Commission and the Accident Compensation Tribunal have been abolished, and the tribunal judges sacked. The premier himself has proposed that parliamentary by-elections be replaced by a process of government appointment.

Established rights of many individuals and groups have been weakened. Early in its term the government brought down extensive industrial legislation directed at workers within the state jurisdiction: this had the effect of removing existing industrial rights, worsening work conditions, reducing pay and leave entitlements and requiring workers to sign individual work contracts. This legislation has been partly blocked by federal courts; but workers' compensation and superannuation rights have been substantially reduced. Not unrelatedly, at an International Labour Organisation conference in Scandinavia in 1993, the two most serious international breaches of teachers' industrial conditions noted by the conference occurred in Chile and Victoria.[9] In thirty separate amendments to the state constitution, the government has limited existing rights of administrative appeal against specific and controversial government programs, such as school closures and the Grand Prix motorcycle racetrack development. When in 1994 a court dismissed obstruction charges against the Alexandra Parade freeway extension because no Environment Effect Statement (EES) had been issued and the extension was therefore unlawful, Planning Minister Robert Maclellan simply legislated to remove the EES requirement. In other cases, confidential criminal records have been released to commercial contractors operating Transport Accident Commission computer systems. Funds for legal aid have been reduced. In 1994 Premier Kennett supported the Tasmanian government's attempts to block the application of United Nations human rights to gays.

There is a long record of official bullying, mainly in the form of government attacks on independent public officials and agencies, aimed to suppress dissent and ensure compliance. The director of Public Prosecutions, Bernard Bongiorno, was a strongly independent officer who had taken a firm stand on police shootings and white-collar crime. Following a quite improper suggestion by Kennett on national television that a man charged with murder was guilty, Bongiorno stated that the remark prejudiced the man's right to a fair trial, and proposed possible contempt of court proceedings against the premier. Soon after, he was pressured to resign after a personal attack by the premier and a secret 'restructure' of his office by the attorney-general, who evidently lied publicly to conceal it.[10] A similar fate befell the outspoken commissioner for Equal Opportunity, Moira

Rayner. She was publicly criticised by the premier for making an antidiscrimination order protecting women prisoners from being removed to Pentridge, a prison for males. Soon after, the government announced the abolition of her position, falsely claiming that Rayner supported the 'restructure' of her office. State Coroner Hallenstein resigned after a long public brawl and strong criticism by the premier: he also had been critical of police. The government tried but failed to require the auditor-general and the state ombudsman (who are both responsible to the Parliament) to sign short-term contracts.

Two distinguished Family Court judges were attacked by the premier after expressing concern about the effects of government cuts on child welfare. The funding of the Office of the Public Advocate was partly cut after it criticised the impact of cuts on its severely disadvantaged clients. The Victorian Law Reform Commission was closed down by the attorney-general, reportedly on the basis of a long-standing personal enmity. The chief magistrate of the Children's Court was asked to resign (and did so) following his criticism of government cuts to children's services. After orders by the Equal Opportunity Board preventing government closure of the Northland Aboriginal school were twice upheld on appeal, the premier announced that the Equal Opportunity Board's powers would be reviewed to prevent it from 'hindering the lawfully elected government'. In mid-1993 the premier was prosecuted for selling wine from the premier's office without a licence (to raise funds for the Liberal Party), and Kennett strongly criticised the liquor commissioner; the commission announced there would be no legal consequences of the premier's actions; several months later the government did not renew the commissioner's appointment when it became due for renewal. In 1994, during the elections to reinstate the sacked Geelong Council, the premier threatened to sack the new council if it did not approve a foreshore redevelopment plan he supported. The office of prison chaplain at Pentridge was put out to tender after the incumbent criticised prison administration and refused to sign a confidentiality contract. Community groups in health and housing which received government funding have had their funds cut for criticising government. For several years the premier himself has kept up a quite virulent attack on two of the government's key media critics: the *Age* newspaper[11] and ABC-TV's *7.30 Report* (whose popular presenter Mary Delahunty resigned after a government ban on ministerial interviews).

There have been many other less spectacular but more systematic examples of coercion within the public sector. State public sector workers have been under steadily increasing pressure to sign individual work contracts which, on the whole, are detrimental to their interests or traditional notions of 'public service' (Alford 1994). Senior executive contracts include performance indicators linked to various rewards and penalties. Department heads receive bonuses for the number of staff reductions they achieve. State school principals are rewarded for amalgamating schools and punished for teacher illnesses; the rewards include subsidies to educate their children at private schools. Conversely, principals who criticise the effects of education cuts or the government's controversial Schools of the Future program have been strongly disciplined.

At the same time government itself has steadily become more secretive and less accountable. Freedom of Information laws have been weakened. Claims of 'commercial confidentiality' are increasingly used to prevent citizens finding out the real costs of the major developments funded by their taxes. The premier has refused to disclose details of the huge bonuses provided for top public servants, claiming that these are 'private matters' between the government and the individuals concerned. Serious doubts have been raised about the probity of tender processes for major projects such as the Crown Casino and the Grand Prix, partly controlled by a close personal friend of the premier and former treasurer of the Liberal Party. The term 'cronyism' has been increasingly used to describe the close links between the government and its key friends and advisers in business.

Marketing the Kennett program

By 1995 there were few Victorians whose lives were not touched in some way by two years of radical small-government surgery, whether as parents or teachers, patients, train travellers, trade unionists, municipal voters or ordinary householders. As early as November 1992 over 100 000 people marched on State Parliament in the biggest civil protest since the Vietnam War. With so many people hurt and aggrieved, how has it all been allowed to happen?

The public justification for such apparently 'anti-people' programs has typically been couched in the value-free language of management, most commonly expressed as the need for tough decisions. This is an image the premier himself, a marketing consultant by trade, obviously finds congenial. Speaking at an international seminar, Kennett claimed that the Victorian government was a world leader because it had rejected populism; it 'had revolutionised public administration in Australia by not compromising its goals for the sake of interest groups'[12] (or 'people', as others might describe them).

But tough managers need to find tough problems, especially if they have already decided on tough solutions. In a seminal study, Noam Chomsky (1989) showed how the citizens of modern democracies are often persuaded to acquiesce in measures harmful to their own interests, not by monolithic state propaganda systems, but by the skilful creation of legitimating myths or 'necessary illusions' by powerful

THE ECONOMY SAYS

The economy says, "close the hospital."

The economy says, "build a freeway through the schoolyard."

The economy says, "cut down the forest."

The economy says, "you are all afraid of me... you are broken people... you do what I require... nothing is above me... no person can stand up to me... you are my slaves... you all run for me..."

The economy says, "build a racetrack in the park."

And then the economy says "So get stuffed; you and your values and your feelings— GET STUFFED!"

Leunig

institutions. Hayward (1994) applies a similar analysis to the Kennett government.

The art of successful government electorally is all about manufacturing problems which can then be solved. The trick is to pick the right issue, sell it as a problem, and then be seen to solve it. It matters not whether the problem is real. Nor does it matter whether the solution actually solves the problem. All that matters is the perception of reality, not reality itself. The Kennett government has so far demonstrated considerable flair in its ability to manufacture and then solve mythical problems.

The particular 'management problem' that the Kennett government has created with the help of powerful institutions such as the media and Right-wing think-tanks is the crisis of government finances. This can be summed up as: 'Labor has bankrupted the State. Desperate measures are needed'.

For over six years the Coalition pursued this theme relentlessly and single-mindedly, first in opposition and then in government. In that time, almost every adverse event in the life of Victoria had somehow been linked to this problem. In the media the theme has been constantly reiterated and reinforced by the élite opinion-makers in the financial and editorial pages and echoed by secondary pundits to the point where it is now an unchallenged orthodoxy. There have been remarkably few systematic attempts to question the prevailing wisdom or present a serious contrary case (Ken Davidson of the *Age* has been an exception). It has been a dramatic example of a failure of media responsibility on a matter of unquestionable importance (Crooks & Webber 1993).

In this one-sided climate of opinion, and with an increasingly supine and dispirited Labor Opposition, it is therefore not surprising that the financial necessity of the Kennett cuts appears to have been widely accepted by ordinary Victorians although, as opinion polls have shown, there are some considerable qualifications. Few people have any detailed understanding of the nature of the supposed 'crisis' of public debt, and many express strong reluctance about the cuts and a preference for maintaining specified services (health, education, and others), by increased taxes if necessary.

In Chomsky's and Hayward's terms, Victoria's 'financial crisis' has been a clear-cut case of a necessary illusion or a manufactured problem. To assert this, of course, is not to claim that there never was any problem, or that there is not even a kernel of truth in the government's claims. As Chomsky argues, the most effective illusions are those which build on some existing fact or prejudice. The New Right campaign for small government was widely accepted because it tapped into powerful populism on such themes as 'bloated bureaucracies', 'government waste' and 'dole bludgers'.

However, two points can be made with less qualification. The Kennett government's claims about the so-called financial crisis and the need for such extensive cuts have been grossly exaggerated, and are in some vital respects inaccurate and dishonest. More importantly, it seems clear that the Kennett government set about the task of inflating this 'crisis' systematically and deliberately in order to create a climate that would legitimate a predetermined and less public ideological agenda. It is this agenda — a commitment to small government and privatisation as political goals — rather than an honest 'managerial' response to an undeniable crisis which has motivated its unprecedented attack on the Victorian public sector.

Of course, the use of some variant of the financial crisis argument to drive politically predetermined small government programs is not a purely Victorian invention, although as a political form it may have peaked under the Kennett government. A similar pattern can be found in several other Anglo-Saxon countries such as New Zealand, Canada and Britain, where New Right governments have orchestrated economic and public finance crises to legitimate harsh cost-cutting and privatisation (see Chorney et al. 1993; Kelsey 1993).

Stripped of rhetoric and hysteria, the factual claims on which the government based its case for massive cuts and privatisation can essentially be reduced to four:

1. the State government was close to bankruptcy because of critical and unprecedented levels of public debt incurred by the previous Labor government;
2. public sector spending and the size of the public work force had become 'bloated' and excessive under Labor;
3. privatising the state's major utilities (gas, water, electricity) was not only essential to restore state finances but would lead to better service for the public;
4. cuts in public spending would speed up the overall recovery of the state's economy.

Not one of these statements is substantially true. The issues are complex, and a fair treatment of them requires much more space than a single short chapter, but it may still be useful here to summarise some of the key facts and arguments and point to more detailed supporting studies.

By 1991 Victorian public finances were indeed under some pressure. Public debt levels were fairly high relative to those of other states, although low historically. For several years state revenue had been consistently lower than predicted, essentially because of three factors: the economic recession; cuts in Commonwealth grants to the states; and a self-imposed ceiling (the Cain Labor government had promised to keep taxes and charges to the level of inflation). Public debt had increased partly because of increased borrowing to cover the shortfall in revenue (unusual but, in a recession, economically defensible); and partly as a result of private sector debts which the State Bank (like many others) inherited from the excesses of the 1980s. As a result, interest payments by the state were at fairly high levels, although not excessive historically or internationally.

But these stresses need to be carefully set in context. A fair analysis of government finances requires an examination of comparative and historical levels of public debt, spending and interest; that is, how big are they compared with those of other states, or with previous Victorian levels? How do they compare with levels deemed safe by other governments, or by credit agencies? Or by the private sector? A fair assessment of debt necessarily requires comparing the size of the debt with the assets which guarantee that debt. Whether interest paid is excessive depends on the future revenue available to pay it, as well as the value of, and likely return on, the investment for which the debt is contracted. On the whole most of these essential details were ignored in the shrill sloganising.

The following points are a summary only, but they make it very difficult to sustain the argument that the state was facing a crisis of public finances warranting the most severe cuts and wholesale privatisation.

First, throughout the most relevant period (1988–92) the state government's actual credit rating as assessed by the largest private credit agency (Standard and Poor) was never less than AA, meaning the state had a 'very strong' capacity to pay its interest and repay its debt. Second, Victoria's public debt levels in this period, while marginally higher than a decade earlier, were half the level they had been in the 1960s, less than half the level of those of the average European government, and about a quarter the level of the average large private sector corporation's. Interest payment levels were relatively high, compared with the previous decade (reflecting high levels in general interest rates) but not in comparison with the levels some decades before. Despite media focus on 'speculative debt', a very high proportion of the debt always consisted of traditional borrowings to finance community infrastructure. Most importantly, the value of Victoria's assets at all times was about three times that of its debts. The claim that Victoria was anywhere near insolvent at any time is absurd.

The claim that Victoria's public sector spending and public employment was excessive and had been bloated under Labor governments was particularly dishonest. From 1985 to 1992 Victorian public sector spending was actually the lowest of all states and its public sector work force the second smallest. Much the largest increase in the state public work force had occurred in the decade of Liberal government from 1972 to 1982, when it increased by 108 000 or 66 per cent, compared with an increase of 9000 or about 3 per cent in the Labor decade to 1992.

The main official evidence the government relied on to support its claims was the 1993 report of the Audit Commission. This body was set up by the government; it was chaired by a director of a leading right-wing think-tank notorious for its support of small government, and its report was mainly written by a former Kennett adviser. Not surprisingly, it was attacked as biased and political by several economic commentators as well as the distinguished New South Wales accountancy professor, Bob Walker.

(Readers seeking more detailed supporting articles and studies should refer to: Barker 1993; Crooks & Webber 1993; Hayward 1993, 1994; Langmore 1993; Salvaris 1993a, 1993b, 1993c. These include an analysis of the claimed public benefits of privatising Victoria's utilities.)

Ideology of an anti-government

What motivates the Kennett government? What are its underlying values? On the surface, and in countless glossy pamphlets delivered to Victorian homes at public expense, there is a steady stream of breathless, managerial hype ('We're getting the state *moving* again'). Deeper down, it is a fundamentally negative government, a government about cutting and closing down, about hardship and sacrifice, a government that must abolish public holidays because 'there is no option'. If ordinary Victorians were asked to name one positive thing the government has done for people they would be hard pressed. Businesspeople might dutifully echo the 'moving State' line, but the truth is that Victoria's economic recovery would have happened anyway; the Kennett program merely delayed it.

On its own admission, the politics of the Kennett government are indeed managerialist, but this is not itself a sufficient explanation. More deeply, the government is driven by a kind of bleak fundamentalism about government and society, a politics that is essentially loveless, authoritarian and punitive. Every so often these somewhat brutish philosophical antecedents manage to break through the marketing veneer.

Some commentators have described the government as essentially a two-man operation, with the premier as chief executive and the treasurer, Alan Stockdale, as resident ideologue (Stockdale has close links with right-wing think-tanks and spent a short period in residence at a British think-tank). In the five years preceding their election success, both men publicly espoused the full New Right position on small government (cuts, privatisation, de-unionisation), and both expressed fundamentalist beliefs which at times seemed to equate 'big government' with original sin. (However, as the election drew closer, and victory seemed assured, both became notably vaguer and less strident.)

As early as 1985, well before any suggestion of a state financial crisis, Jeff Kennett made an extraordinary speech likening Victoria to Argentina, and predicting that if the rush to big government were not halted, we might expect to see death squads in the streets of Melbourne (Kennett 1985). He committed himself then to providing 'a radical alternative ... of systematic and continuing restraint in government' and spoke of 'the need to cut the cost of government and free up the economy and the society', promising to 'totally revise the role and power of government'. At that time, he declared that he would cut the Victorian public sector by 15 per cent (about 48 000 people); and he made a similar promise in 1988.

Kennett's 'philosophy of government' is now expressed in more statesmanlike tones, but then it was more direct. In 1991 he proclaimed that: 'Governments are a sponge on society. They take from the wealth creators.' Public servants, he said, 'don't produce a dollar of wealth'.

In a tortuous but revealing explanation of his views on social equity, and presumably of the values which drive his government's human service programs, Kennett said in 1991: 'There is no such thing as equality. We live in a competitive world. If you try and make the fat man thin, then the thin man ultimately dies. We have to encourage the fat man to become fatter so that the thin man becomes fatter.' A strange meeting of Milton Friedman and Jenny Craig.

Writing about Margaret Thatcher's government, Peter Self (1990) argues that its 'essentially egoistic and negative view' of political behaviour became a self-fulfilling prophecy increasingly removed from any clear standard of good government. Good government, he says:

> requires a kind of generosity ... [an] active and public-spirited citizenry and ... a shared public philosophy ... which can combat the short-run pressures of the electoral cycle ... These conditions may be hard to attain ... but a philosophy which treats government as functioning like a limited stock company or a weak auxiliary to the market system, cannot offer any viable alternative to the continuing search for good government. Market ideology can offer nothing but political and moral degeneration. (Self 1990, p. 10)

Notes

1. Material in this and the following section draws on a wide range of sources; no single authoritative source is available listing all the cuts and budget changes. Principal sources used include newspaper reports 1992–95 (especially the *Age*); Victorian Budget papers for the period; and Hayward 1993. Material not found in these sources, in most cases is sourced in individual notes.
2. By comparison, real spending cuts of 3 per cent in Labor's 1988–89 bud-

get were described at the time as 'the lowest rate of growth in Government spending since the early 1960s'.
3. A smaller-scale program to privatise the utilities had already begun under the previous ALP state government.
4. McNair poll reported in the *Age*, 4 February 1995.
5. *Age*, 22 November 1994.
6. *Age*, 26 July 1994; *Sunday Age*, 18 September 1994; *Frontline*, February 1995.
7. *Age*, 16 January 1995.
8. Over the three years to 1995 state revenue will have increased by about 13 per cent in real terms, a rate higher than that in Labor's last three years.
9. Source: Professor John Smythe, Flinders University, Adelaide, as reported to the author.
10. This issue was extensively reported in the ABC-TV *Four Corners* program on 10 April 1995. In subsequent media coverage it was claimed that both the attorney-general (Jan Wade) and the premier intervened directly to prevent the contempt prosecution.
11. In one incident Kennett urged all Victorians to 'tear up their copies of the paper', while the *Age* editor accused the premier of 'behaving like a bully who can't get his own way' (*Age*, 10 June 1994).
12. *Age*, 17 February 1995.

References

Alford, J. et al. 1994, *The Contract State: Public Management and the Kennett Government*, Deakin University, Geelong.
Barker, G. 1993, 'Crisis? What crisis?', *Age*, 10 April.
'The big drip' 1995, *Frontline*, February.
Chomsky, N. 1989, *Necessary Illusions*, Pluto Press, London.
Chorney, H, Hotson, J. & Seccareccia, M. 1993, *The Deficit Made Me Do It*, Canadian Centre for Policy Alternatives, Ottawa.
Crooks, M. & Webber M. 1993, *State Finances and Public Policy in Victoria*, The Victoria Foundation, Northcote.
Hayward, D. 1993, 'The Kennett cuts: how necessary are they?', *Journal of Australian Political Economy*, December.
——1994, 'The Kennett cuts: who will pick up the Tab?', *Frontline*, November.
Kelsey, J. 1993, *Rolling Back the State*, Bridget Williams, Wellington.
Kennett, J. 1985, 'Victoria at the cross roads', speech to CEDA, 1 February.
Langmore, J. 1993, 'Kennett's false crisis on debt', *Age*, 27 January.
Salvaris, M. 1993a, 'Victoria's necessary illusions', *Frontline*, February.
——1993b, 'Cooking the books', *Frontline*, June.
——1993c, 'In a political war, truth is the first casualty', paper delivered at the annual conference of the Victorian Council of Social Service, Melbourne, 21 June.
Self, P. 1990, 'Market ideology and good government', *Current Affairs Bulletin*, September, pp. 4–10.
Turner, B. 1993, *Citizenship and Social Theory*, Sage, London.

12.
New Mandarins New Zealand Style

Grant Duncan

Managerialism may be defined as the reform process by which public policy adopts marketing and business management concepts and techniques. Typically, it is associated with neo-liberal, individualist economic reforms, though this is not always the case.

In New Zealand the key pieces of public sector law passed by the fourth Labour government to effect these managerialist reforms are the State Sector Act 1988 and the Public Finance Act 1989.

The State Sector Act 1988 puts into effect the principle 'let the managers manage', while the Public Finance Act 1989 says 'let them manage with accountability to Parliament'. In theory, there should now be a public service which is able to operate free from ministerial intervention in day-to-day business such as recruitment. Managers should be free to choose what resources are most appropriate and cost-effective for their own operational needs and, every six months, they should report to Parliament on how efficiently and effectively they have achieved the 'outputs' purchased by government.

This chapter examines the process by which a state sector social worker's performance is held accountable to organisational objectives. It addresses two main questions concerning the implementation of managerialism: what do these systems do to guarantee the quality of social services, and how do they impact on the work of professionals?

Managerialism in practice

The organisational model which seems to be applied universally by the managerialist restructuring may be called a 'top-down performance control model'. How this model works in practice can be illustrated in some detail within a social work agency, the New Zealand Children and Young Persons' Service (NZCYPS), linking outcomes, outputs and the Key Performance Indicators (KPIs) which are used to control and evaluate the activities of the individual worker. Given the frequent criticism that fiscally determined managerialist reforms directly threaten the quality of social services, it is how this performance control system attempts to manage and evaluate the quality of outputs that is examined here.

NZCYPS is responsible for promoting five socially desirable outcomes based on government policy. For example, outcomes 2 and 3 are as follows:

> Children and young persons are safe within their family group, and are protected where their safety or well-being cannot be guaranteed.

> The community is protected from children and young persons whose behaviour is harmful. (NZCYPS 1994, p. 19)

As representative of policy objectives for which the New Zealand government may be held accountable, these statements have several interesting properties. There is no standard by which achievement of the outcome may be measured. No research is being undertaken to ascertain the degree to which New Zealand's performance in relation to these social outcomes may be improving or deteriorating. There is no means by which anyone can with any degree of confidence assert that the organisational outputs of the NZCYPS (the next level of analysis) contribute to the achievement of these highly desirable outcomes. In short, it is impossible to give a reasoned account of whether or not public administration is achieving public policy.

What can be more easily assessed are outputs, measures of actual organisational activity. It may not be certain that this administrative and service 'busy-ness' contributes to anything socially worthwhile, but at least Parliament can know whether the organisation is doing what it is paid to do. Thus, within the framework of managerial jargon that is now commonplace, the 'output classes' which government 'purchases' from NZCYPS (as well as other third sector 'providers') are: 1. public awareness services; 2. risk identification and management; 3. family resolution services; 4. residential and caregiver services; 5. adoption and information services. The daily activities of an individual social worker are accounted for within one or more of these output classes. Each output class is further broken down into individual outputs. For example, family resolution services includes the outputs of informal resolution and family group conferences.

Each output is then further broken down into a series of 'key actions' to be performed by the social worker. For instance, informal resolution includes: a. family–Whanau agreements negotiated; b. family–Whanau agreements reviewed before a three-month period has elapsed; c. assessment of intervention success (no further action required), or failure (extend for three months, refer for family group conference). Should a family group conference be required, then a further series of key actions will be implemented and documented under that output.

The quantity and quality of these actions are controlled and accounted for. The documentation and measurement of performance are used to compare individual and organisational performance against set standards of quantity and quality. It is the issue of service quality which is the focus of this chapter, although it deserves to be mentioned that anecdotal reports clearly suggest that NZCYPS is unable to cope with the sheer quantity of cases, especially in Auckland.

Quality assurance or quality control?

Before examining how service quality is controlled at NZCYPS, it is important to make a few remarks about service quality in general. There is no absolute or objective measure of the quality of a service. Quality is what it is perceived to be. For management purposes, however, quality is usually defined in relation to the needs which a service is intended to satisfy, and its ability to do so. 'Needs', of course, are those of the customer or consumer.

When there are a number of individuals and agencies with conflicting interests involved in a social service (such as the protection of an abused child) there will potentially be an equal number of evaluations of the quality of that service. This is further complicated by the fact that statutory social services have many clients who are under coercion. Those measures of service quality favoured by the private service sector, for instance customer satisfaction and loyalty, are not as meaningful in this context. In general, however, the manner in which any service organisation chooses to measure its performance will depend on the standards and objectives it sets itself, as well as on the costs involved in measuring certain kinds of variables. There are no universally applicable measures of service quality.

In its 1994–95 business plan, a key management strategy for NZCYPS was to 'research what clients' expectations are ... and, in tandem, to carry out a national "client satisfaction survey" ' (NZCYPS 1994, p. 9). Although problematic, this approach will give some indicators of service performance. The non-financial performance measurement to be looked at more closely, however, is that which controls and evaluates individual and organisational productivity at the level of outputs.

The 1994–95 business plan gives both quantitative and qualitative performance standards for each class of outputs. Internal documents go into even more detail, measuring the performance of individuals in their achievement of these standards. Two things become apparent from studying these documents. The planned quantity of outputs is related solely to cost (i.e. how much 'busy-ness' is affordable) rather than to any analysis of actual needs in the community. For instance, under the output class residential care services, the quantitative performance standard for the number of beds in residential care services is ninety-nine. It is widely known, however, that there are insufficient residential care beds, with the result that many young people who have been arrested or remanded by the courts are not able to be kept in custody. The number ninety-nine happens to be the number available, and no plans are in evidence to increase this number in order to meet needs.

It may well be argued that there could be no end to demand based on perceived community needs, and hence no limit to potential expenditure. Rationing of resources will always be required. When an organisational performance standard is simply based on what happens to be available now, however, the observer may justifiably conclude that organisational policy has no genuine commitment to service improvement.

As for qualitative performance standards, there is an evident emphasis on timeliness and case closure. For instance, for informal family resolution services, the social worker is expected to review the agreement within the accepted three-month period in all cases. He or she should have finalised an agreement with no further action necessary within three months in 75 per cent of cases.

Certainly there are important professional reasons for seeking a timely and effective service in facilitating family agreements. But the incentive for the individual worker who wishes to be a high achiever is to focus on short-term goals and to keep casework relatively simple and circumscribed so that the file can be closed within a few months. The reaching of an agreement seems to be paramount, with no long-term qualitative assessment. A family agreement may easily be reached by imposing the least possible commitment on its members, but the long-term benefits for the family may be less satisfactory.

Once an agreement has been reached, the possibilities for effectively carrying it out will be constrained by restricted finances. Social workers will often have to argue for funding for services such as counselling, and the lack of funds frequently results in service provision which is, from a professional viewpoint, less than satisfying.

The emphasis on outputs creates a further barrier to a high-quality, client-centred service. For instance, an individual child and her family may, as clients of NZCYPS, move through risk identification to family resolution to caregiver services. That is, they may 'consume' services within different classes of outputs. Each class of outputs is funded and managed separately by the organisation. So, for instance, if risk identification is particularly efficient, resulting in a larger than expected number of child clients at risk, there is no guarantee that funding of family resolution services will be sufficient to cope with the quantity of cases. Funding is not integrated according to identified needs. The splitting of funding into measurable outputs does, on the other hand, allow for more exacting control of organisational 'busy-ness' and expenditure.

Some social work offices have gone so far as to split teams of social workers into output classes. Hence, a single client may pass through the hands of several different workers. This form of office organisation is clearly created for bureaucratic convenience rather than the interests of a client-centred service.

Despite attempts at implementing qualitative performance standards, there is no evidence that the performance control system implemented in NZCYPS is leading to improvements in the quality of social work services. It is impossible to judge whether NZCYPS is achieving the social service goals of ensuring the well-being of children, for example. There appears to be an obsession with satisfying internal and political financial agendas. Such organisational introversion is the opposite of the outward-looking, client-centred attitude which would be needed for genuine improvement in service quality.

Efficiency before quality

Despite the emphasis on qualitative performance standards, service delivery at NZCYPS is clearly driven by a diminishing fiscal commitment from central government. These fiscal objectives are achieved administratively by the organisational model which has come to be known as 'managerialism'. The 'customer' or 'purchaser of services' who is really being served, therefore, is central government, not the consumer of the end product (families and children). The real objectives and needs of families seem tangential to an overall objective of efficient social control with the emphasis on achieving a budget surplus and debt reduction.

The quality goals of these social services become lost when the organisation is forced to achieve financial goals first. Even in the private sector it is now recognised that high performance in non-financial, customer-service variables is paramount. Achievement of service quality goals, in a context where more customers mean more revenue, rather than the opposite, will usually lead to satisfactory financial, bottom-line performance. In a non-profit social service, however, the performance incentives are clearly quite differently structured. High achievement from the organisation as a whole and from individual workers will be more dependent on altruistic professional values. It is evident from discussions with NZCYPS workers that the emphasis on financial goals and restrictions along with managerial control has led to a demoralisation of professional staff due to the denigration of these internalised professional values.

Managerialism has effected what Pollitt (1990) refers to as 'neo-Taylorism'. The example of NZCYPS supports this claim. Frederick Taylor (1856–1915) is thought of in the standard management literature as one of the fathers of modern management (Bartol & Martin 1991). The effect of Taylor's 'scientific management' was to place greater control over the planning and measurement of work in the hands of managers. The conceptualisation of work would belong exclusively to management, while the physical achievement of the job would belong to the worker. This division of labour meant less autonomy for the worker in deciding what to do, how to do it and when. Although human service work cannot be as tightly controlled managerially as car assembly, the technology of managerialism is certainly taking us down the path of scientific management. Taylor advocated methods to analyse a worker's tasks into the smallest possible individual components, thus allowing the ability to measure and control each individual action.

A clash of cultures

What has resulted from this managerial reform at NZCYPS may be characterised as a clash of cultures. The concept of organisational culture is a rather vague and slippery one, but nonetheless useful in conceptualising situations such as this. Organisational culture may be defined as the behavioural norms and psychological attitudes which are consciously or unconsciously enacted by organisational members as they seek to understand their collective structure and identity through formal and informal events such as meetings, organisational charts, and written and unwritten rules. An important part of this will be the process by which practices are defined as normative or deviant (which may be expressed as acceptable or unacceptable, effective or ineffective, appropriate or inappropriate). It is also important to remember that a culture is very rarely unitary and cohesive. Within one organisation there will be competing and conflicting sub-cultures which attempt to assert their own values and norms as dominant.

The clash of cultures at NZCYPS is between a managerial culture and a professional social work culture. The system described illustrates the dominance of a Taylorist managerial culture, determined by a policy environment which has largely accepted neo-liberal economic rationalism as its ruling ideology. Structurally, this culture emphasises hierarchical control, financial costs and subordination to managerial and political objectives.

Within this organisation there is also an alternative culture at work. It is based more on the professional values of altruism, social equity and justice, which are the very values which draw people into the field of social work. Structurally, this culture is likely to prefer a flatter organisation with consensual decision-making as well as individual professional autonomy. This would include the ability of professional staff to have direct control over an allocated budget.

The managerialist prescription of a top-down performance control system may be appropriate for the New Zealand Income Support Service, whose task is the administration and delivery of welfare benefits. It is production-oriented and its performance can be more meaningfully quantified. As Alford (1993) argues, however, the managerialist movement in public administration has taken little account of contingency theory, which holds that the most appropriate structure for an organisation depends on its tasks, technology and environment. Elsewhere (Duncan 1994) it has been argued that core state social services such as NZCYPS illustrate the limits to the appropriate application of the managerialist paradigm. Certainly the dissension between managerial and social work cultures displayed in that organisation and the inappropriateness of its qualitative performance control system suggest that other changes are needed. Further reform should be based on a quite different paradigm than that which has completely altered the public service in New Zealand since the mid-1980s.

'The new mandarins'

One of the promises held out by the reformists in the 1980s was that the old systems of bureaucratic control and political privilege would be broken down. New Zealanders would be given a country of greater equality of opportunity and greater flexibility for the needs and aspirations of diverse communities. However, the comments of Peter Self on the British experience apply equally well to New Zealand:

> the market system has led not to more diffusion but to increasing concentrations of economic power. The international reach of capitalism has outdistanced the capacity of national governments to control its [sic] activities or to pursue independent policies. Some governments, especially in the English-speaking countries, have chosen deliberately to move with the tide and to favour and encourage market forces while cutting back the responsibilities of government. If the liberal thesis about state and markets is right, the effect should have been a strengthening of political liberty. The example of Britain suggests otherwise ... (Self 1993, p. 244)

New Zealand, to the surprise of many commentators such as Self, has been a particularly rigorous example of this process of concentration of power. The liberal promise of greater freedom has been deflected into enforced responsibilities for state workers and their clients, while the opportunities for self-determination were reserved for a new generation of the rich and powerful. Easton (1993) narrates this process as it has occurred in the New Zealand economy as a whole. In the public services illustrated in this chapter, it should be clear that what has resulted is a top-down control and uniformity produced by a 'reformed' system of administration. This system seeks to enforce all social objectives and values into the overarching needs of debt management. Cultural diversity and equality of opportunity are well down the list of priorities for the new class of mandarins who now administer.

These new managers experience greater autonomy in decision-making than ever before. This has been achieved at the expense of the professional autonomy of social workers. The state's social workers now find that the professional discretion available to them on the job has been severely curtailed. Earlier attempts to introduce bicultural power-sharing (O'Reilly & Wood 1991) have been reined in and the promise of equal employment opportunities under the State Sector Act has not been met (Walsh & Dickson 1994). Each individual staff member's survival within the organisation depends more than ever on his or her attitudes 'fitting in' with those of the managerial élite.

The role of bureaucracy in society

Public choice theory has been employed by liberal 'reformers' to reconstruct the notion of bureaucratic organisational rationality, and hence to redefine the very role and value of the public bureaucracy within the society which supports it.

Public sector reform in the 1980s attempted to depart from the stereotype and fixed notions of Weber's model (Weber 1970) in that: a. the individual office manager is given greater flexibility to determine salaries in accordance with individual achievement, and remuneration policies are less inflexible (or more easily manipulated); b. the policy of promotion on the basis of seniority is no longer considered appropriate and achievement alone is (in theory) taken into account, although the factor of 'experience' must correlate with seniority; c. security of tenure is no longer guaranteed; and d. individual officials are accorded greater freedom to determine how they will achieve the set objectives. Weber's principles of a clearly defined sphere of competence for the bureau and a free contractual relationship of employment are, on the other hand, given even greater importance by managerialist reforms.

Although the actual implementation of these reforms in the industrialised nations varies, managerialism does not altogether reject Weber's basic model of the bureaucracy. Indeed the underlying principles of economic rationalism and efficiency would have been quite familiar to Weber. Where the managerialist state administration begins to differ from Weber's observations is in its subordination of impartial administrative rationality to the dictates of supposedly 'value-free' economic rationality. In the name of 'more effective management', however, managerialist techniques increase rather than decrease bureaucratic controls over workers while empowering senior managers. While tightening performance controls, managerialism also advocates 'the *de*-bureaucratization of employment relationships' (Pollitt 1993, p. 16) by removing security and allowing managerial flexibility in determining salary levels. Employees thus lose a degree of both professional autonomy and security in their conditions of employment.

'Administration' may have been replaced by 'management' and many practices may have changed, but there is still a bureaucracy in the Weberian understanding of the concept. Centralised regulatory control of state policy does require bureaucratic organisation. This necessity will remain — with or without critics such as Niskanen (1973) who anathematises the bureau manager and idealises the 'self-interested businessman'.

Neo-liberal rhetoric is apparently anti-state control and anti-bureaucracy. In practice, neo-liberal managerialist methods rely heavily on bureaucratic control and 'compulsory accountability'. The bureaucracy may be slimmer, but it would be self-deceiving to call it anything but a bureaucracy, in a form which Weber would have found comprehensible.

The fundamental value of bureaucracy, as portrayed by Weber (1970), remains that of rationality. The question is: whose rationality will decide what the bureau is to produce and how will such production be achieved? Will it be the economic rationality of the dominant individualist, neo-liberal ideology or the justice-oriented rationality of collective responsibility and civil rights?

Conclusion

The human costs of managerialism have been not only on the state's clients and beneficiaries, but also on many of its front-line workers. The managerialist prescription for organisational restructuring has been inappropriate for the specific tasks and personnel of a social work department. A more suitable model would be a kind of 'professional bureaucracy' (Mintzberg 1989) with a flat hierarchy, wide span of control, and consensual decision-making based on peer support and supervision. In this model, budgets would be allocated down to the front-line level. Hence, the kind of managerial autonomy which is enjoyed only by the élite would be transferred into front-line professional autonomy.

The predominance of neo-liberal ideology and economic rationalism may have given greater clarity to the objectives of those state services with social outcomes. Overriding economic objectives have, however, left service quality in a doubtful position, and the standards set by NZCYPS do not give any basis for adequate evaluation. While professional accountability is to be welcomed as a principle, the increasingly bureaucratised control over the work of professionals at NZCYPS is manifestly inappropriate for the objectives of social work and for the responsibilities of service to a vulnerable public.

References

Alford, J. 1993, 'Towards a new public management model: beyond "managerialism" and its critics', *Australian Journal of Public Administration*, vol. 52, no. 2, pp. 135–48.

Bartol, K. M. & Martin, D. C. 1991, *Management*, McGraw-Hill, New York.

Duncan, G. 1994, Managerialism and the distinction between business management and public administration, unpublished paper, Massey University, Albany.

Easton, B. 1993, 'From Rogernomics to Ruthanasia', in S. Rees, G. Rodley, & F. Stilwell, *Beyond the Market: Alternatives to Economic Rationalism*, Pluto Press, Sydney, pp. 149–62.

Mintzberg, H. 1993, *Mintzberg on Management*, Free Press, New York.

Niskanen, W. A. 1973, *Bureaucracy: Servant or Master?*, Institute of Economic Affairs, London.

NZCYPS (New Zealand Children and Young Persons' Service) 1994, *Business Plan 1994–95*, NZCYPS, Wellington.

O'Reilly, T. & Wood, D. 1991, 'Biculturalism and the public sector', in J. Boston, et al. (eds), *Reshaping the State: New Zealand's Bureaucratic Revolution*, Oxford University Press, Auckland, pp. 320–42.

Pollitt, C. 1990, *Managerialism and the Public Services: the Anglo-American Experience*, Basil Blackwell, Oxford.

——1993, *Managerialism and the Public Services: Cuts or Cultural Change in the 1990s?*, Blackwell, Oxford.

Self, P. 1993, *Government by the Market? The Politics of Public Choice*, Macmillan, London.

Walsh, P. & Dickson, J. 1994, 'The emperor's new clothes: the uncertain fate of equal employment opportunities in the New Zealand public sector, 1988–1992', *New Zealand Journal of Industrial Relations*, vol. 19, no. 1, pp. 35–52.

Weber, M. 1970, 'Bureaucracy' in H. H. Gerth & C. Wright Mills (eds), *From Max Weber: Essays in Sociology*, Routledge & Kegan Paul, London.

Part IV

Counting Human Costs

Barking at the Thunder

There's a common human level you can strike with any people
if you don't impose on them, or scare them, or sound strange.
On their own ground works best, with your legs bent if they're men.
It's near impossible not to play up to the other sex
but if you can not, they sometimes forget yours, for minutes:
you can be just human, sharing. Even mad folk and toffs
and others who have trouble getting off stage can be soothed
into it. Outside this, things all slope towards war.

I was always good at it. It was the best I could do,
and it saved me, a few times. I always liked to watch
it gather on a group, or be there between two
and stay —
till a frown hunted it, or a joke against, really anything.
I've known honest men who thought you could box this
what? solidarity, and have it to share with all people
and dishonest buggers out to corner it for their lot.

Les Murray
(extract from Book II of a verse novel in progress)

Humanity

What a fair world were ours for verse to paint,
If Power could live at ease with self-restraint!

...

For the poor Many, measured out by rules
Fetched with cupidity from heartless schools,
That to an Idol, falsely called 'the Wealth
Of Nations', sacrifice a People's health,
Body and mind and soul; a thirst so keen
Is ever urging on the vast machine
Of sleepless Labour, 'mid whose dizzy wheels
The Power least prized is that which thinks and feels

William Wordsworth (from 'Humanity' 1829)

STAKEHOLDER AND TEAM

13.
Dismantling Child Welfare

Gary Hough

In Victoria, as in other states in Australia in the first half of the 1980s, the adoption of managerialist approaches, technologies and values was promoted by a Labor government. This original quest for better management of state welfare services was founded not so much on reductions of expenditures, but on delivering more from a static revenue base. While the original emphasis on short-term objectives and policies may have been intended to preserve the legitimacy of child and family services, these short-term objectives have led to an erosion of the value of providing a service.

This chapter discusses the organisational construction of child protection, a field which has received greater managerial attention than some other areas of practice and which, in many ways, reflects the managerial conception of state welfare. During a second wave of managerialism, from the late 1980s, it has become clearer that managerialism is not about doing the same things more cheaply or better. On the contrary, it is about doing fundamentally different things as it transforms services to make them fit within the understandings and technologies that the generalist managers plan to bring to them.

Supply-led welfare

Since the mid-1980s welfare workers' practices have been continually subjected to rationalisation and managerial reorganisation. This reorganisation has been based on an implicit assumption that before coming under the new managerial gaze, their practices were irrational or pre-rational. This has happened within a framework of 'supply-led welfare' (Jones & Novak 1993) where policies and practice principles are shaped by resources available rather than by identifiable need.

Since the late 1980s, but particularly since 1992, the welfare sector has absorbed massive cuts, and gate-keeping and rationing have increasingly become central tasks for social workers. In Victoria these cuts have been targeted at broad family support programs and at advocacy and community development activities. This has invited friction between workers and service users as the emphasis on decision-making rather than notions of partnership, on restrictiveness rather than support, and on client control rather than sharing, has led to greater use of compulsory measures against clients, and to more social distance between workers and service users. In turn, the service users identify social and welfare workers with agencies which do not meet their needs.

It should not be assumed that a golden era in state welfare service delivery existed previously. To an extent, state public welfare provision has always been heavily bureaucratised and directed in ways that obstructed and compromised the service ideals that practitioners initially brought to their work. But this trend has been massively amplified as the values and technologies of managerialism dominate not only management or administration but the policy and practice domains as well.

Supply-led welfare is about much more than cuts to services. In some areas, where widespread social anxiety or even moral panics about violence can be discerned, there have been substantial increases in allocations, or redirection of resources. In particular areas like corrections, some areas of mental health, and of course child protection, a new role for state welfare can be seen in the proliferation of interventions aimed at violent or potentially dangerous individuals who infringe, or are likely to infringe, the rights of other individuals. During the second wave of managerialism, state welfare practice shifted to more targeted, judgmental and authoritarian interventions to social problems in a context of greater social anxiety about law and order, sexuality and the erosion of the traditional family.

Although the contemporary expression of state welfare as an army of investigators and case managers enacting narrow, outcome-based interventions may make sense to the corporate managers, such a configuration offers no social vision. The attempt to relieve social anxieties by targeting resources to the risky cases can only promise a short-term blanketing of problems; the next media scandal is just around the corner. When it arrives, criticism and responsibility will be directed at the workers, with the senior managers using the opportunity to put an even heavier layer of administrative law over welfare practice.

Enquiries into contemporary child protection practice lead to the view that the present system is unsustainable, not only on moral and ethical grounds but also in administrative and resource terms. Those most involved with this system, the workers and the clients, know that a practice which presents child abuse as a self-contained problem separate from issues of gender, poverty, substance abuse, mental illness, and intellectual disability makes no sense at all. Nor does a practice which revolves around a disconnected set of abuse assessment episodes, which is all too often what the service looks like. For the clients and the front-line workers, monitoring and surveillance, rather than support and help, are central features of a system developed within the frameworks of managerialism.

Managerialism and welfare policy

Child protection probably provides the best example of the managerial appropriation of policy. The policy construction of child protection practice in Australia, as in the USA and UK, relies on a mandatory reporting system, involuntary clients, an extended network of individual case management services involving public and private agencies, and a concentration on the deficiencies of individual care-givers. This formulation of child protection presents it as an individual, classless, gender-blind, culturally inclusive, individually caused phenomenon which can be responded to within an after-the-fact, investigative paradigm.

While child protection staff would wish to balance vigilance and investigation with prevention and family support services, broad social, political and managerial attitudes have conspired to locate abuse in the realm of parent failures. To a significant extent, child abuse policy has developed around media scandals about atypical cases. This has led to massive disjunctions in the system so that, for instance, only sexual and physical abuse are subject to mandatory reporting in Victoria, yet neglect has always been, and continues to be, the biggest category of reported cases.

Mandatory reporting has not been generally supported by practitioners in the field. But it offers a good example of the kind of organisational solution which seems to appeal, precisely because it conforms to culturally sanctioned myths about the value of control and coordination. In a similar way, a child abuse register has been implemented in Victoria, notwithstanding overseas research which indicates that the children who end up on such registers are not markedly different from the general population (Campbell 1991).

The central place of enquiries into child abuse scandals in developing policy is clear. Official child death enquiries have been conducted by lawyers, politicians and administrators who have framed problems and solutions within the organising imperatives of their own discourses and technologies. With the breakdown of social consensus, the intensification of social anxieties, the need to attribute blame, and a search for culprits and scapegoats, governments will direct anxieties along certain paths. Individualisation of the issue leads to blaming the individuals most involved: parents and social workers (Cooper 1993). The government's distancing of itself from its social work agents enabled the public to displace its anger for the whole state to just a part of it; instead of enhancing social work it preferred to regulate it (Blom-Cooper 1991).

Parenthetically, it is worth noting Parton's (1991) contention that the twin discourses of law and managerialism now dominate the field of child and family welfare; people in social sciences and social work are told what their contribution will be and when it will take place. An example of this was evident in the murder of James Bulger in the UK where the sole role for those professionals who used social-science-based knowledge was in establishing the child perpetrators' fitness to plead.

Howe (1992) has referred to the 'translation' of social problems whereby different actors can reframe problems within a context of certainty and thereby gain occupational power as politically and organisationally valued actors. In the field of child protection, solutions were developed within a single conceptual outlook. This reframed the central problem from returning families to competent functioning, to protecting children from violence (or, more luridly, to stop parents from killing or sexually abusing their children).

In Victoria, the development of this policy paradigm during the 1980s coincided with the rise of managerialism. The process has been similar in the rest of Australia and, indeed, in the UK, the USA, Canada and New Zealand. The child-saving crusade has not developed to the same extent in non-English-speaking countries, which have not so wholeheartedly embraced the New Right economic and social agendas. Parton (1991) attributes this to the fact that in those societies the social consensus between the state and its citizens has not been so severely ruptured. The role of state agents has remained more supportive of citizens and, therefore, less resisted and contested.

In Victoria, as in the rest of Australia and in the UK particularly, the new administrative arrangements have formed structures to promote some solutions to social problems over others and some kinds of social interests over others (McCullough 1988). The increasing, and apparently unthinking, focus on the protective function as the core business of the state welfare system reflects the way in which generalist managers have understood social work. Howe (1992) suggests that in bringing their technologies to this 'core business', the generalist managers have placed welfare workers not as family caseworkers, but as investigators; their managers as designers of surveillance systems rather than casework consultants.

Parents have become objects of enquiry. Their behaviour must be predicted, and in the shift from therapy and welfare to surveillance and control, firm protective steps require authoritative and intrusive interventions. The anxiety for a technical language and the need for a regular and reliable management system encouraged bureaucratic forms of practice to investigate cases in a uniform and systematic manner. In child welfare in particular, procedural guidelines have proliferated with the managerial need to control the 'quality' of practice (Howe 1992).

In some crucial sites, at least, social work in welfare bureaucracies has changed and assumed a new role. It has gained a focus on danger and lost rehabilitation, support and empowerment as central working constructs. The increasingly overt forms of control of practice are most evident in the areas — such as child protection — which generate the greatest social anxiety (Howe 1986).

In order to reduce anxiety, minimise uncertainty, and manage the work, corporate managers who face the dilemmas of statutory social work are likely to understand the environment and the clients in a particular way. Social workers, on the other hand, have always known that indeterminacy and uncertainty are inherent in occupations which confront moral issues and social problems (Howe 1986), and that public welfare agencies provide a fertile breeding ground for organisational uncertainty (Brannon 1985). Child abuse reveals suffering that is incontrovertible and often preventable, and inaction cannot be defended. But as those with an understanding of the field and a practice history in it have continually pointed out, children suffer for complex reasons and there are no simple solutions.

Even when the conceptual dead-end of the present approach is recognised as a 'cuckoo in the nest', remorselessly consuming ever more resources (Stevenson 1992), the inability of managerialists to understand the importance of policy and practice perspectives makes it unlikely that fundamental changes will take place. Workers in the sector and managers within the state Department of Health and Community Services with a knowledge of the terrain of the work have despaired at the generalist managers' inability to recognise the importance of primary care services and networks. They watch with some bemusement as the generalist managers belatedly recognise the importance of diverting people from the abuse assessment system. The high number of inappropriate referrals to the child protection service is related to the escalating scarcity of any other appropriate services. But rather than signifying a return to a more policy orientated approach, the new emphasis is described and understood as a rationalisation of primary care services. Moreover, it is being driven by yet another generalist manager with no background or experience in welfare policy or practice.

What seems like the familiar managerial hubris is a reminder that managerialism is part of a political project to bring about far-reaching changes in human service organisations and that 'a record of involvement in, knowledge of, and commitment to a field of service is viewed as of secondary importance, or even as a liability' (Jones & May 1992, p. 389). This issue lies at the heart of the managerial degradation of social service work. It is witnessing a crude program of social engineering.

Managerialism and welfare practice

Conflicts about the nature of welfare work, and the ways in which knowledge about it is utilised, have been at the centre of debates about the aims, skills and purposes of such services. The managerial reconstruction of welfare work may be characterised as an attempt to lay them to rest and to impose a managerialist solution which is highly interventionist. Notwithstanding the frequent rhetoric about innovation and flexibility, the forms of organisation introduced across the public sector proclaim the rules of a practice built on models of management in the private sector. This assumption is often implicit and sometimes explicit, as in the following statement:

> CSV 'production lines' share a common logic with a manufacturing 'custom shop' building one-off products to order, but employing mass production methods to a significant extent. Whether the product is physical objects or human services, the logic of organization and control is identical. When that logic is violated things go wrong. (Community Services Victoria, *Annual Report 1990–91*, p. 5)

This statement sounds silly, but it reveals the pervasive presence of what Ingersoll and Adams (1986) call the 'managerial meta-myth'. Its core components are: an assumption that all work processes can and should be rationalised (i.e. broken into comprehensible constitutive parts that can be completely controlled); that the means for attaining organisational objectives deserve maximum attention, with the result that the objectives quickly become subordinated to the means; and that efficiency and predictability are more important than any other consideration.

A fundamental clash exists between the *managerial precept of operation* and the *occupational principle* which emphasises intrinsic standards of work or service.

'One stop shop' practice

By 1989 the official vision for Community Services Victoria required all workers to concentrate on products rather than processes. Corporate strategy revolved around the creation of a 'one stop shop' approach, the elimination of professional or workplace boundaries, and the use of information technology to develop a generic case management system. The vision for the department was specifically modelled on an analogy with the travel industry, and the strategic initiatives were united around a view that 'belief systems in the department were too locally focussed. People in child-care were about child-care; people in IDS were about intellectual disability services ... The corporate resource that the whole provided was not something which was widely recognized' (Baird 1991, p. 11).

The simplistic one stop shop model is a natural outcome of misguided managerial dogma. First, rather than attempting to understand the nature of the work, design rules are imported from other fields with which the generalist managers are more comfortable. Second, while welfare practice has struggled to hold to principles of flexibility, difference and individualisation, managerialists value predictability, regularisation and sameness above all else. They will then seek, through a command model, to impose their views. As they reconfigure the work, they impose their definitions about its nature and meaning, and they sever the connection to real-world problems which the workers have been striving to address. Third, in an organisation in which the idea of management has such totemic power, context-bound knowledge will be devalued. The resulting rationalist monocultures will be even more dysfunctional in a field like community services, which has a predominantly female work force.

Deskilling

In Victoria contemporary welfare work at the front line has been consistently deskilled as the 'product' is changed, by higher design, from a complex one to one that is readily assessed and controlled. Traditional emphases of service work like empowerment, problem resolution, utilisation of all available options, confidentiality, advocacy, and social change are unlikely to appear in record-keeping or even in the practice of social workers. Quality practice is redefined as quality control, with flexibility being discouraged by a standardised framework. Concomitantly, there will be a reduced need for skilled workers, as in crucial areas of practice the worker loses control of her own work and a deskilling cycle ensues (Karger 1986; Cousins 1987).

A management control system is developing that will monitor more closely the performance of both workers and service users. This might be regarded as benign, as was implicit in the managerialists' underpinning assumptions. But both sets of actors are constructed by the organisation as objects to be manipulated, stereotyped, and silenced. Howe (1986) has characterised this new public welfare practice as 'procrustean': seeking to enforce conformity with a theory by violent methods.

In child protection, the assumption that cases of maltreatment can be counted, predicted and measured as products or outputs, leads to the system distorting and denying a problem which can only be recognized through the inclusion of subjective social processes. 'Social' work must attempt to draw clients into the sphere of government through investments in individual lives, and the forging of alignments between the personal projects of citizens and images of social order (Miller & Rose 1990, p. 8).

Conclusion

The imperatives of corporate managerialism should never be seen as completely beside the point. Regularised and predictable modes of coordination are what makes social organisation possible. Efficiency and effectiveness are important issues for state welfare organisations. However, to elevate efficiency to a first-order good is to lose sight of what the efficiency is meant to achieve.

The wilful single-mindedness of managerialism has led to profoundly negative consequences in state welfare services:

1. Its logic leads to a less skilled labour force. Discretion, flexibility and skills necessary to innovate and meet the wider needs of clients are being lost.
2. Through the use of the central metaphor of the machine, managerialism inevitably leads to a critical devaluing of process.
3. It has produced a more disaffected and alienated work force, where workers' diminished control over the content, structure, pace and outcome of work has combined to make it difficult to retain a commitment to service ethics and ideals, and to critically reflect on practice. Workers are likely to be alienated from their labour and from their personal history (Fabricant & Burghardt 1992, p. 203) and, as deskilling escalates, will increasingly be given the impression that their work is stupid and dishonourable.
4. The command model does not provide mechanisms to learn from day-to-day front-line experience nor a learning environment which can deliver a complex program of care.

There can be no easy solutions, but the starting point is to recognise that, while they do not totally prevent good work from continuing, managerialists offer a banal social vision, they hinder effectiveness, and they create real distress in the lives of those they touch.

References

Baird, J. 1991, 'John Paterson and Community Services Victoria', Case Study Services, prepared within the Graduate School of Management, University of Melbourne.
Blom-Cooper, L. 1991, 'Hidden agendas and moral messages: social workers

and the press', in B. Franklin & N. Parton (eds), *Social Work, the Media and Public Relations,* Routledge, London, pp. 129–37.
Brannon, Dianne 1985, 'Decision making in public welfare: scientific management meets organized anarchy', *Administration in Social Work,* no. 9, pp. 23–33.
Campbell, M. 1991, 'Children at risk: how different are children on child abuse registers?', *British Journal of Social Work,* no. 21, pp. 259–75.
Cooper, D. 1993, *Child Abuse Revisited,* Open University Press, Buckingham.
Cousins, Christine 1987, *Controlling Social Welfare: A Sociology of State Welfare Work and Organization,* Wheatsheaf, Sussex.
Fabricant, M. & Burghardt, S. 1992, *The Welfare State Crisis and the Transformation of Social Service Work,* M. E. Sharpe, Armonck, New York.
Howe, D. 1986, *Social Workers and Their Practice in Welfare Bureaucracies,* Gower, Aldershot.
—— 1992, 'Child abuse and the bureaucratization of social work', *Sociological Review,* vol. 40, no. 3, pp. 491–580.
Ingersoll, V. & Adams, G. 1986, 'Beyond organizational boundaries: exploring the managerial metamyth', *Administration and Society,* no. 18, pp. 360–81.
Jones, A. & May, J. 1992, *Working in Human Service Organizations,* Longman Cheshire, Melbourne.
Jones, C. & Novak, T. 1993, 'Social work today', *British Journal of Social Work,* vol. 23, no. 3, pp. 195–212.
Karger, H. J. 1986, 'The deskilling of social workers: an examination of the impact of the industrial model of production on the delivery of social services', *Journal of Sociology and Social Welfare,* no. 13, pp. 115–29.
McCullough, A. 1988, 'Organization theory and administrative change', *Australian Journal of Public Administration,* vol. 47, no. 2, pp. 137–46.
Miller, P. & Rose, N. 1990, 'Governing economic life', *Economy and Society,* vol. 19, no. 1, pp. 1–31.
Morgan, G. 1990, *Organizations in Society,* Macmillan, London.
Parton, N. 1991, *Governing the Family: Child Care, Child Protection and the State,* Macmillan, London.
Stevenson, O. 1992, 'Social work intervention to protect children: aspects of research and practice', *Child Abuse Review,* no. 1, pp. 19–32.

14.
Human Costs: A View From Within

Col Face

The years since 1987 have witnessed a systematic demoralisation and, to a certain extent, a dismantling of the state welfare department in New South Wales — the Department of Community Services (DOCS).

This occurred to the accompaniment of a new rhetoric and a new 'style' of management, one which promised greater efficiency and a reduction in red tape and waste, with a resultant benefit to clients. The claim of providing a new customer focus has proved to be nothing but a smokescreen.

The catchcry of productivity and efficiency accompanied a number of 'restructures' resulting in cuts to the work force and a reduction in real dollar terms of funding to non-government services. The staff cuts were accompanied by the introduction of new technology and the Senior Executive Service (SES). The cumulative effect of these actions was to reduce services to the individuals, families and children DOCS claims to serve, while government propaganda created an expectation of better access to high quality services. The net result is a work force, in both government and non-government welfare services, that feels used, ignored, devalued and under increasing stress.

The stress is due to increased workloads in child abuse, a 60 per cent increase in notifications of abuse, and substitute care. The increased workload included an increase in the complexity and seriousness of the cases. In disability services there have also been more clients needing services, but only minimal growth in funding. The pressure felt by families and people with disabilities is keenly experienced by workers trying to assist them.

The thrust to scale down the work force was carried out in a way that was dehumanising for the work force. DOCS showed a complete lack of concern for its staff, despite government rhetoric of 'managing better by putting people first'. Offices were closed without discussion, consultation or even advance notice. On 15 August 1991 staff were simply given a brown envelope that included details of a new departmental structure and their non-existent jobs. That was an advance on the 1988 restructures when staff read of changes and closures in the *Sydney Morning Herald*.

Since the late 1980s the annual allocations to funded community organisations have not included allowances for inflation, nor for additional liabilities (such as superannuation or training levy). Some services had to implement a new award, including new employment conditions and increased salary rates for their staff (Social and Community Services Award (SACS)), without additional funds from DOCS. The demand for services increased but the expectation of better services was not met by additional funding.

The costs borne, personally and at a service level, by staff of DOCS and the management committee members and staff of the funded services have been enormous. The flow on to their clients is almost incalculable, particularly as many of the clients are the most marginalised in the state. The department employs in excess of 8000 staff and has an annual budget of about $1 billion.

Three tenets drove the decision-makers at the senior levels of DOCS. Based on the political philosophy of a conservative government, these included a new style of management, the introduction of information technology systems, and a steady progression towards privatisation of DOCS services.

The managerial dogma derived its base from former Premier Greiner's experience in his business administration studies in the USA. The emphasis was on efficiency and improved productivity and the transfer out of the public sector, or the abandonment of certain tasks deemed to be non-core activities.

New managerial dogma

The election of Nick Greiner in 1988, the first conservative premier of New South Wales for more than a decade, brought with it a much publicised drive towards greater efficiency and effectiveness in the New South Wales public sector. The welfare and community services sector was not exempt from this drive.

The new government introduced 'productivity savings'. These were reductions to the budget of government departments, progressively over a three-year cycle, totalling 4.5 per cent. There were also 'portfolio' savings. These varied from one minister to another and were incentives for ministers to outdo each other in cutting back budgets. The exceptions were increased funding for computerisation, particularly where greater efficiencies could be achieved with new technology. For DOCS, 9 per cent portfolio savings were imposed from 1987 to 1990, totalling an annual recurrent figure of more than $40 million.

The introduction of the SES brought senior public servants into line with political expectations. The new Chief Executive Officers (CEOs) either willingly embraced the new approach or were astute enough to realise where their futures lay. As a result, the government had little difficulty implementing the targeted cuts. There was also a popular belief that the contracts of the SES included a bonus for achieving the cuts.

There was a range of budget cuts across the community services sector. DOCS underwent a number of restructures, some quite widespread, others within particular units or branches of the central office. The Property and Finance Branch of DOCS has had eight or nine changes and restructures since 1985. This has done little to achieve efficiency within the departments, with some staff and branches having had a question mark over their futures for more than a year.

Further restructures in 1988 and 1991 witnessed major closures of units and cuts to jobs, while the integration of disability services was accompanied with very little administrative support being transferred from the Department of Health. These restructures were driven by the government-imposed productivity savings of $40 million. The resultant implementation brought about large-scale loss of experienced and dedicated staff. More significantly, it reduced the number of experienced managerial staff.

It is ironic that the union covering the majority of public servants, the Public Service Association of New South Wales, won pay rises on the basis of productivity gains proudly listed by CEOs in their annual reports in 1989, 1990 and 1991. The productivity was achieved, but at a high cost.

The drive for efficiency introduced an additional layer of bureaucracy into the department. Before 1991, managers of districts had access to their supervisor, who had direct access to the central office. In a traditional department for child protection and substitute care, staff were accountable to their manager, to regional office, and then to the central office. The disability services staff were responsible via their manager to the area manager, who reported to central directors in DOCS. There were two layers between the worker and the centre.

The 1991 structure had four unit layers: district, area, divisional, and central office. The drive to efficiency and effectiveness distanced the central policy-makers and decision-makers one step further from the front-line staff.

New chief executive officer

A new CEO for DOCS arrived in 1993 and progressively brought new directors into the central office of DOCS. He also created additional positions at the SES level while workloads increased at the coalface. Field staff face more cases of greater complexity. Growth has been in the number of 'chiefs', not the 'Indians'. There is a clear perception by staff throughout DOCS that the new directors have progressively centralised authority and decision-making, while passing more responsibility and work to other layers within the department. This exacerbated a feeling of powerlessness among staff of DOCS. All the work and responsibility are at one level; power and authority remain at a higher level of the organisation.

A 'review of roles and functions', a further restructuring of DOCS, was attempted in 1994. Commonly called a 'Clayton's restructure', it was promoted by the CEO as an opportunity to 'put right' the previous attempts at fixing DOCS. Yet the four tiers remain.

The first steps taken after that review were to prepare and promote a human resources (HR) strategy and to review and upgrade area managers. The area managers hold key positions of responsibility for operations and service provision in twenty areas across New South Wales.

The HR strategy promoted, among other things, the training and development of staff. The theory was that competencies should be prepared for specific jobs, for example, district officers, residential care staff or area managers. Selection, training and development of staff should then follow accordingly.

The practice did not follow the theory. The area managers' positions were reviewed and regraded (some to SES level). They were recruited by an international commercial recruitment firm (Morgan and Banks) and only six of the twenty positions were filled by current area managers. This was seen by staff and the community sector as yet another restructure and it is believed that the CEO used the opportunity to introduce new people ostensibly having the corporate leadership and style he requires. With only 30 per cent retaining their jobs, 70 per cent were thus removed, many despite 'very satisfactory' performance appraisals and long careers.

The area managers were the crucial managerial positions that bore the brunt of the implementation of the ill-conceived 1991 restructure. Most area managers had worked long and hard, well above the 40 hours per week for which they were paid, to make the ill-fitting structure work. They received much criticism that was directed at the department following the restructures and worked hard to rebuild morale and commitment among staff and the powerful lobby groups. For most there was no mention of unsatisfactory service or unsuitability for the new, appropriately valued positions. A clear message was sent throughout the organisation: comply with the new managerial model espoused by the CEO and his new directors, or do not plan for a career with DOCS.

This latest restructure in DOCS followed earlier 'scorched earth' approaches at managerial level. Only five or six senior managers out of sixty or seventy have survived since 1985. This includes regional directors, area managers, operation managers and central office directors and branch managers. The loss of expertise and historical wisdom has been profound. Some view this as another clear sign to encourage any competent managers to pursue their careers elsewhere.

The new four-tier structure cocoons the CEO and his central directors from the problems experienced on a day-to-day basis by the direct service staff. The perception in local units is that the executive of DOCS does not want to be faced with day-to-day problems of child abuse or people with disabilities and will systematically get rid of those who raise questions.

The CEO has a vision and a clear belief in the future direction of DOCS, which he articulates at different times. However, his continued promotion of his vision for community services in Australia reinforces the perception of staff that he is far removed from the daily operational decisions of his staff. His preoccupation with Commonwealth–state negotiations, and Council of Australian Governments (COAG) deliberations distance him from the real concerns and pressures of his frontline staff.

Such perceptions are reinforced by the new style of the generic manager. The new manager brings skills in financial and personnel management and good public relations. There is no longer a requirement for any substantial program knowledge or experience in serving the public as in child protection, substitute care or disability services. Nor do staff see that a commitment to clients is a prerequisite for managerial jobs.

This new managerialism has its own terminology and underlying constructs. Clients and their needs are viewed as inputs and outcomes. It is necessary to quantify everything, with the Client Information System (CIS) and Disability Client Database (DCD) used in tandem with a Workload Management System (WMS) to quantify and cost all aspects of DOCS work. This feeds the state Treasury's demand for departments to quantify and cost on a program budgeting model.

Performance is also quantified, with set benchmarks for the number of cases that staff should deal with on average, irrespective of the needs of the client. The number of abused children, the number of foster parents, the number of children needing therapy, the average amount of time in initial assessments, the amount of time in supporting families with a child with a disability all had to be documented for the attainment of mythical goals or 'benchmarks'.

Although outcomes are measurable, the work in disability services, child protection, family and adolescent work does not really fit the mould developed for the private sector manufacturing experience. Total quality management, despite its application with a degree of missionary zeal by some, is hard to apply. Human services work needs to retain some part of the human to make it a service.

This terminology creates a further gulf between the staff who deal with children and families in crisis and the DOCS executive, who deals with the 'big picture'. There is a subtle pressure to use the terms and conform, or feel right out of it.

New technology

The strong, and somewhat unfettered, embrace of new technology was driven by the new managerialism promoted by the New South Wales conservative government. This move to computerisation of a number of systems since 1986 embraced client databases and tracking systems, a payroll–personnel system, financial and accounting systems, motor vehicle management, word-processing packages and spreadsheets.

Client Information System

There was a basic logic in trying to hold, on a state-wide basis, information about child abuse victims and their families to assist with the early identification of children at risk. There are many families who are mobile, and the usefulness of having a database that is readily accessible across the state seemed sensible.

The early specifications included a database with a capacity to capture basic data about children and their alleged abuser. It included a capacity for recording detailed information or reports if the officer wanted to use it. The system promised data that could be extracted to allow local staff and their supervisors to monitor and juggle workloads.

Ironically, the promised advantage of using the CIS to replace paper files was not achieved. There is still no simple word-processing capacity on the CIS, so even a simple court report has to be done separately, on a different terminal, and stored in a paper file.

There are a number of problems with the CIS from a service provider's perspective. The district officer (DO) is the field worker responsible for investigating child abuse and taking matters before the court, where necessary, to protect the child(ren). However, before he or she can take any action, the relevant data must be entered onto the CIS and approved by the manager. Staff feel they cannot get on with their job and that their professionalism is compromised. As a result the frustration levels are very high, putting another nail in the coffin of morale.

Notwithstanding the theoretical debate on the changes in the thrust and focus of field worker's jobs, skills are also a major problem. An ability to type and familiarity with computer systems is still not an essential requirement of field workers' positions. Although many of the department's field staff when recruited had no computer literacy or typing skills, there has been no systematic attempt to upgrade the skills of workers to meet this new type of work. There was a token offer of Typequick, a computer-based tutor disk, for those with enough time to study it.

Staff feel inept. They must serve the computer, whether the CIS or the Payroll system, and yet they have not been given the basic skills to fulfil this new requirement. The fact that data on the CIS are used to analyse workloads and impacts on resource allocation adds pressure to the field worker to spend more time keeping the CIS fed.

Payments to foster carers also depend on regular updating of the CIS, to feed the Substitute Care Payment System (SPS). If a DO does not enter a 'change of placement', the carer may not be paid. This places the DO in a double bind; no computer work, no payment for the carer and placement breakdown, yet with no attention to the casework there is an equal chance of placement breakdown. The DO feels additional pressure and frustration generated by the CIS.

The reason for the SPS system was the cutting of clerical jobs during the 1991 restructure. There were no longer clerical and administrative staff to do the processing of claims, so along came multiskilling for the DOs. Multiskilling really means multi-tasking or simply additional tasks. This offered little consolation for staff who cared about the deteriorating standards of care.

The inclusion of the disability services within the portfolio of DOCS ensured that this program was not denied the benefits of the new technology. Data demands that had not been evident within the Health Department were discovered. A whole new database was established to satisfy the central office's appetite for information.

The benefit to the service providers and consumers was not initially evident, but they were assured by the ever-growing central office branches that, like motherhood, new technology was a good thing. An enormous amount of work was put into establishing the database, and getting it up and running. However, the first efforts in 1992 were not very successful, and much more was required to bring it up to date in 1993. By 1995 it was still not very reliable.

One problem for DOCS with its implementation was the stand taken by direct service providers in many areas not to give up time spent in direct service provision for entering data onto a computer. Additional resources had to be provided to ensure that the DCD was completed. The major problems with keeping the DCD up to date have persisted.

The move from a manual accounting system to a statewide network took several years. The first step saw a system moved from the central to regional offices, of which there were ten. This was to be replaced by an on-line system that linked the major service centres (district centres and residential care units) through the regional office to the central office. The specifications were drawn up, the staff consulted and involved and tenders let. The system was developed and refined and was about to be implemented when DOCS went through yet another restructure in 1991.

One of the most significant problems with the Financial Management System (FMS) was the chasm between its development before 1991, and its implementation post-1991, with massive reductions in clerical and administrative staff levels in all DOCS offices, Community Service Centres (CSCs), regional, and area offices. In some CSCs the staff was cut from an administrative officer, senior clerks and three or four clerical support staff to two clerical officers. The clerical officers had no authority to make any payments or do accounts; these were now processed by the managers and sent to area offices.

An implication was the increased administrative responsibility for the managers while they simultaneously lost immediate control over their finances. The managers were not even given access to the FMS to check their unit's expenditure and financial records.

The combined Payroll and Personnel system was also developed before the 1991 restructure and introduced after it. As a result of the deletion of clerical and administrative staff, additional tasks were given to managers, or 'hands on' staff such as house managers, which are not substantive positions. This has taken them away from supervision of client work or from direct services.

The 1991 restructure left field staff with minimal access to clerical support. More time had to be spent by the DOs doing clerical and keyboard work without appropriate training. More time was spent on the computers, leaving less for client services. A staff climate survey in 1992 found that the staff felt that technology was one of the worst aspects of their work.

Privatisation

A hallmark of conservative governments in western democratic countries since the 1980s has been the sale of assets and privatisation of services. This trend is continuing in the welfare sector in New South Wales, causing further anxiety among staff, who fear that those who are still left with a job after numerous restructures will see their jobs move over to the private, non-government sector.

A number of services were privatised. The audit function was put out

CONTINUOUS IMPROVEMENT

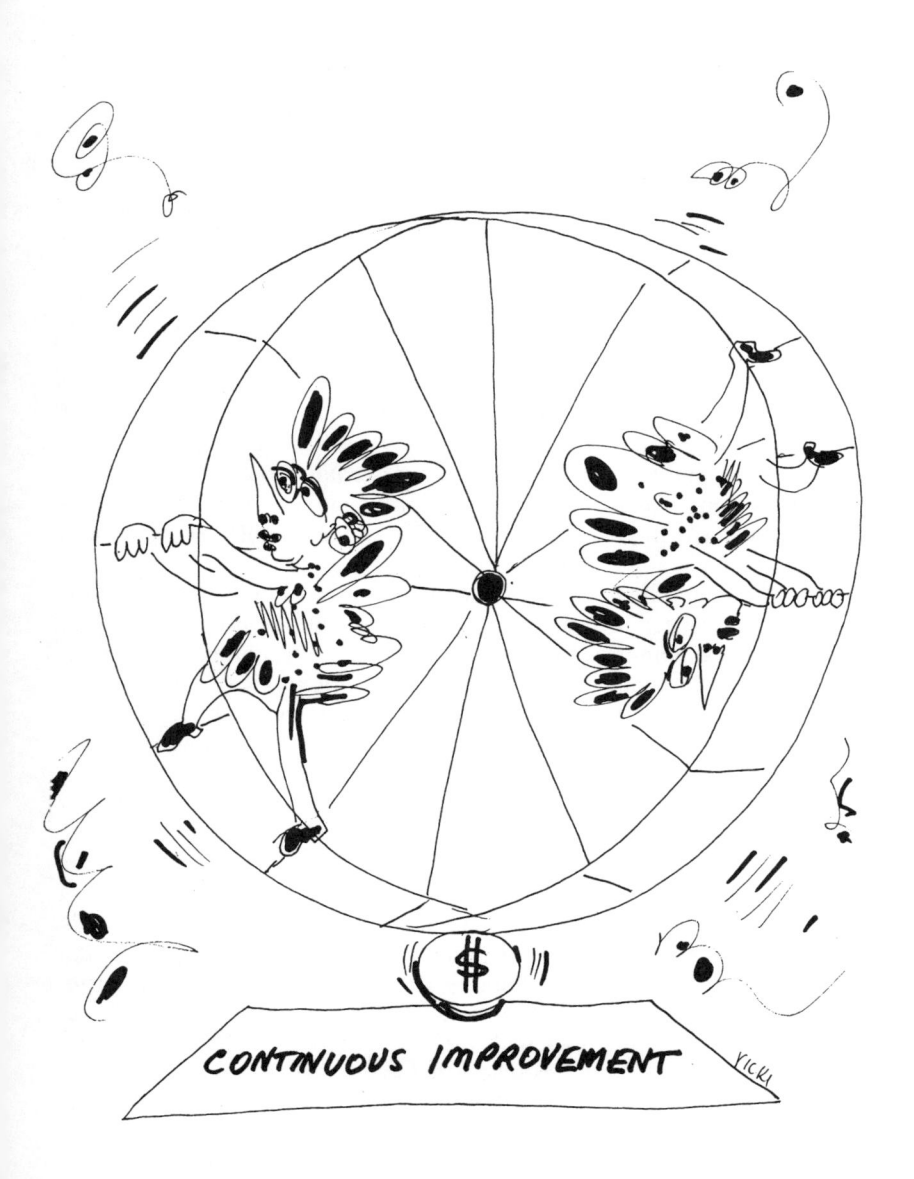

to tender, and a number of private international firms have taken up the contract, employing ex-DOCS staff to manage the auditing of DOCS.

The management of the motor vehicle fleet was put out to tender, and is now privatised, at a monthly cost of about $15 to $20 per vehicle. This occurred after clerical jobs were cut in 1991, yet with little change in workload for DOCS staff. The previous director of finance and property in DOCS is working for the successful company after the new CEO decided to terminate his contract.

The next wave to go private was substitute care services. About fifteen DOCS units of varying sizes (from houses for five to eighty residents) were closed during 1994, and the funds provided to non-government agencies. These agencies, which include many of the large churches, such as the Baptist and Catholic churches, and traditional agencies such as Barnardos, now run residential services for wards of the state.

The plan, which follows a review of services and production of a report to the minister (the Usher Report), foreshadows the transfer of more than $65 million from DOCS-provided services to private agencies. The report was compiled by a ministerially appointed committee largely comprising private agency representatives which recommended, not surprisingly, that government services should be closed and replaced by non-government services.

The replacement of large institutions by small homes was clouded by the privatisation strategy. The starting point, the needs of children and the young in need of care, was lost in a political imperative: funding private agencies. The government's ideological position was implemented by SES, who had the outcomes built into their contracts. The issue of quality of care was used to justify the political decision. The jury is still out on this issue.

DOs and their managers can spend many days seeking a place for a child requiring substitute care. All energy at the policy and planning level in DOCS at central and divisional offices has gone into the Usher implementation, with the redistribution of resources to the private sector. There has been no government commitment to meeting children's needs in the wider community, and certainly no growth to meet the increased demand. This demand was also fuelled by an effective freeze in admissions to DOCS residential units since 1992. The ban on admissions was imposed with the Usher Report, and this has taken placements out of the substitute care system, which was progressively wound down. The anecdotal evidence suggests that the 'too hard' cases are left with DOCS to patch up.

Staff also see ex-DOCS managers working for some of the non-government agencies on higher salaries with more attractive packages and fringe benefits. They get more funds to provide services than DOCS once provided. Staff see many dollars thrown at politically sensitive cases so that private agencies can do for more money what DOCS once did with far less.

The same privatisation trend happens with disability services, as new programs go to the private sector. In 1994 the Post-school Options Program for school leavers with severe and multiple disabilities was put out to tender. The new services were offered to, and taken up by, non-government agencies. However, no one was interested in providing services for some specific young people, particularly those with severe and multiple disabilities, and DOCS set up a new service to meet their needs.

There is a fear that large DOCS residential units will be privatised during a process of 'transition planning' under new disability legislation. The move from large public residential units to small non-government houses occurred with the substitute care services of DOCS, and is a precedent for disability services.

Staff are concerned for those clients who are 'too hard', and fear that there will be a residue of the most disadvantaged left to the public sector for care. There appears to be no way out of the legal, and moral, responsibility. DOCS will continue as the last port of call, or a dumping ground for the private agencies, further demoralising staff. The adoption and legal services within DOCS are still under review and may be privatised.

Impacts and costs

It is difficult to measure the impact and cost on the DOCS staff and clients of the three managerial tenets that underlie the provision of welfare service in New South Wales. Several objective measures have surfaced, including a staff climate survey commissioned in 1992 and contracted to a private company, Towers Perrin. The results were devastating: DOCS were below the Australian and Sector benchmarks on all fourteen measures:

- The overall mood could only be described as negative, particularly in comparison with the Australian workforce or Health and Community Services industry benchmarks.

- The large shortfall of favourable responses in most critical Key Measures is considered by Towers Perrin to be of major concern and an indicator of poor organisational health. (Towers Perrin 1992, 'Staff Climate Survey 1992, Summary Report')

The senior executive undertook to re-survey staff after twelve months. Three years later, in 1995, the staff were still waiting for the second survey. They believed that morale had deteriorated even further than in 1992, and that the CEO was afraid to find out how 'sick' his organisation had become.

Major program changes when stability required

The need for stability and calm was highlighted by the staff climate survey. However, neither appears on the agenda of the CEO or his new directors. The overriding concern seems to be justification of their large SES salaries.

Implementation of the Usher Report continues to bring more changes. This has implications for staff, foster carers and children in care.

The *New South Wales Disability Act 1993* requires all services, both government and private, to comply with the standards of the Act. The initial timeframe had to be altered because it was not possible for staff and management of services to meet the deadlines.

DOCS management have still to make funds available to finance the changes. There is about $40 million available from the Commonwealth, which is carried over from previous years. There are questions as to when this will be made available, and why it is still held at central office level.

Workloads

From 1987 workloads continued to grow, particularly in child abuse, with one child death a month over the past eighteen. This has led to sporadic outbursts of industrial action in various parts of the state, and the political imperative to 'fix it', particularly before the New South Wales election. The negotiations for an after-hours service had stretched on and on for years, since the mid- to late-1980s, but were suddenly resolved in December 1994, three months before the 1995 New South Wales election.

There appears to be no systematic approach to addressing the increased workloads. The response in the child protection area was funding for forty more positions in the 1993–94 financial year. It is ironic that the specialist positions of Child Protection Worker (CPW) were deleted from CSCs in 1987–88. CPWs worked with the teams, building the skill levels of staff and improving the quality of work. They have been replaced by area level Child Protection Specialists. The position now has a larger number of staff calling for their support and specialist input, while they have an audit–review role.

There was an attempt to juggle staff across the state in an effort to achieve 'equity' in resource allocation. The deckchairs were reshuffled.

Industrial action is still festering, as DOCS staff try to find some way of dealing with the situation. They feel quite powerless to cope with 50–90 per cent annual increases in workload. Some CSCs had more than half of the field staff on 'stress' leave during the 18 months to April 1995. The units where staff had high expectations of themselves in terms of client outcomes have suffered with the deterioration in quality of their work.

The department's insurer, the Government Insurance Office, has expressed concern at the escalation of claims for stress-related conditions, and can see very little change in the near future. The obligations of DOCS within the Workcover legislation are such that, to date, no claims for stress-related workers' compensation claims have been rejected, but the affected staff have been marginalised through informal questioning by managers at divisional and central levels. This perception is matched by a belief that the central office has grown once again. The trend to a central resurgence brings greater control at that level and more SES and highly graded positions.

Another casualty of the 1988 restructure was the department's library. The holdings were transferred to the University of Western Sydney, and much of the invaluable historical information, as well as the wealth of knowledge and information held by the library staff has simply gone. Many feel this reflects a strong anti-intellectual ethos, replacing knowledge, research and intellectual rigour with the cool pragmatism of the new managerial style. While the library existed there was a symbolically important centre of learning, and many staff used it for their own studies and to conduct research into the work of the department.

Conclusion

The clumsiness and cruelty which has been imposed on diligent staff in the New South Wales state welfare department is an indictment of managerialist ideology and practices. This chapter, written under an assumed name, provides information about trends that are largely hidden from public scrutiny. Without public debate, depression and powerlessness will persist. Articulation of humanitarian and professional alternatives is required to reverse what amounts to bullies playing with people's lives. Only then might state welfare be able to provide a public service that is unimpeded by the doctrinaire dogma of managerialism.

15.
Greed and Bullying

Stuart Rees

It is a dramatic commentary on the loss of business ethic that managers may exhibit greed and bullying with apparent impunity. In private and public sector organisations the greed of senior executives is apparent from salary disclosure, although the association between their rewards and the promotion of selfishness in society at large is seldom made explicit. Conversely, within apparently respectable organisations, bullying is largely hidden and may therefore be as difficult to talk about as domestic violence.

In Australia and overseas bullying seems to be the twin of greed. Modest rewards and sharing wealth are not on the managerialist agenda so it hardly matters that an accumulation of financial rewards for a few comes at the expense of the many. An ideology of managerialism — with its emphasis on doing more with less and appearing tough about the consequences — means that employee redundancy, low morale of those who remain, and dramatic increases in social and economic inequality can be condoned as an inevitable price to pay for the new managerial order.

This chapter illustrates the links between being greedy and being a bully and argues that such behaviour is an inevitable product of managerialist dogma.

Managerialism engenders bullying

The potential for bullying in the workplace has been heightened by several managerialist values and techniques: the fundamentalist claim that 'we know best', ridiculing the past, and mechanisms of control such as an intolerance of critics.

Fundamentalist assumptions in managerialism are that the language and values of a commercial marketplace provide goals for organisations and the means of attaining them. The dogma 'there is no alternative to the market' has become a motif for managers and a source of belief that public organisations should resemble private corporations. Within public sector organisations — in education, health and welfare — training programs are promoted to teach corporate language and behaviour and so mould the attitudes even of sceptics. The latest dogma, which has been swallowed without much public analysis and with little reference to human costs, is that competition will become a national panacea if it dominates the goals of public utilities (Hilmer 1993).

When the new managers arrive to convert an old organisation to managerialist values and language they like to disown the past, as though nothing happened before they arrived or, if it did, nothing good could be said about it. Corporatisation in universities has involved dispensing with those who knew how the old system worked and introducing staff from the world of business with little understanding of and little sympathy for the educational enterprise. For example, when policy regarding a university newspaper was to change, the executive officer in charge of that unit was reported to have explained to staff, 'We need someone from the outside to make a fresh start'. When the fresh-start manager arrived to explain new working arrangements, several staff reported his introductory remark: 'This place needs to be swept clean'. He subsequently explained his policy: 'Some jobs will have to go. All these jobs need to be redesigned. People will have to compete for them'.

A similar disowning of the past and raising of anxiety of remaining employees occurs when private organisations are to be licked into a new shape. When Bob Joss, a former vice-chairman of the American Wells Fargo bank, took charge of the New South Wales bank Westpac in February 1993, he quickly changed the top management and picked either Americans or staff who had spent much of their lives working in American banks. Of this radical changeover a former Westpac executive said: 'Westpac now has a very thick strata of management that has no connection, no loyalty, no overwhelming interest in the culture, or the heritage of what went on in the past' (Maley 1994). Another former Westpac executive complained that a past could be totally disowned: 'The thing that does annoy you is that an organisation which has a lot of positives is only seen from a negative angle' (Maley 1994).

A connotation that management means appearing strong and decisive gives a cue for managers to be seen to be in control, whether they are or not. They must not lose face even if, in moments of uncharacteristic humility, they might acknowledge to themselves that they do not know what they are doing.

The aura of management as neutral makes it difficult to expose techniques as a form of bullying. When such behaviour is challenged, the critics are told that they are merely the Luddites of inefficiency, always against change. The prescriptions of the new management are to be followed.

With a view to changing structures and abolishing old forms of autonomy, letters and memoranda are common weapons of assertiveness. Rebukes are explicit and control obvious. People can be directed, ordered and threatened. For example, in the spring of 1994 a senior administrator within the University of Sydney received a letter from the superior in his division. The letter contained the lines: 'Your response to Mr. B's call is unsatisfactory. You are hereby directed ...'. There was apparently no consultation, no discussion, no attempt to resolve conflict as colleagues. A military style prevailed. A one-dimensional issuing of a directive was regarded by the manager as the way to manage.

New management's use of such letters seems widespread. A senior physician in a Melbourne teaching hospital was informed by the chief executive of that hospital: 'I instruct you to attend the meeting on Tuesday. Let me remind you that failure to do so will be regarded as failure in your duty to the hospital'. The physician observed that: 'A familiar managerialist strategy is to regard anyone who opposes management as either crazy, a born troublemaker, or someone with dinosaur characteristics who is inherently opposed to change'.

Journalists in the university newspaper unit said that various means of overt control over critics had produced an atmosphere of fear and reluctant compliance. One staff member explained that: 'It was not that the new management disliked contrary points of view; they would not let people express them. They were hypersensitive to the point of being thin skinned'.

Some of the techniques used to sweep a place clean go beyond the discouragement of criticism. In the newspaper unit, threats were direct. Critics of the new management were asked to come to meetings to discuss voluntary retirement and to do so without representation. Nothing was put in writing so that any subsequent staff complaints could be regarded as untrue or an exaggeration. When staff consulted their union representatives they were reportedly advised: 'If you want to keep your jobs, say nothing'.

Orders, threats and an intolerance of critics produce atmospheres of fear and intimidation. When some bullying tactics are challenged, as in the newspaper unit, the behaviour being objected to was passed off as a 'breakdown in communication'. Similar tactics were experienced by staff of the New South Wales Department of Education when school education was subject to sweeping management rationalisation. An evaluation of conditions in the agency at that time concluded that:

> Within the higher echelons of the New South Wales Department of School Education there does not appear to exist a forum (free of retribution) for debate about the efficacy of recommendations from the Management Review. Indeed it is now public knowledge that senior executive staff in New South Wales state schools who are not seen to be embracing the Management Review are placing themselves outside the current expected and desired code of behaviour. (Retallick et al. 1990, p. 13)

In the London offices of the British Department of Education staff were moved sideways after they voiced criticism of market-oriented policies. A staff member who knew those who had been punished for voicing criticism said that: 'All those guys did was point out the problems with the planned reform of teacher training. They did their bloody jobs and got carpeted for it' (Hugill 1994).

Intolerance of criticism is not unusual in bureaucracies. Punishing critics by ignoring them, moving them sideways, pressuring them to leave an organisation is a sign of management by bullying (Martin et al. 1985). Beneath a camouflage of claims about consultation, what is less obvious is the promotion of only one point of view. Politicians and their managerial servants consult those whose views are similar to their own. The widespread and expensive use of management consultants to provide reviews gives an appearance of openness, but the general thrust of such reports is predictable, otherwise management could not risk such consultation.

On the use of outside consultants as a strategy to avoid hearing the advice of public servants, a senior British civil servant commented: 'We are not claiming we know best but we know how things work ... Too often they go to people who think like them, who come up with good ideas but have no idea how to implement them' (Hugill 1994).

When the new managerialism produced a distinct lowering of morale in the British Civil Service, the head of that service turned down a request from Labour and Tory MPs to send a questionnaire to all civil servants to enquire into their state of morale. Sir Robin Butler, the head of the civil service, caused some hilarity at a session of the Commons Select Committee when he told MPs that if they wanted to know about morale they should consult him.

Carmen: an impoverished life

Managerialist values and practices — such as insisting that this system is the only one, that the past should be derided and deviants controlled or removed — foster any potential to bully. In describing such attitudes some victims of managerialist practices have identified the human costs relative to particular incidents. The following illustration of bullying, which produced everyday experiences of fear and intimidation, charts the experience of one person over time.

Carmen is a 57-year-old woman who emigrated to Australia from South America in 1970. She was employed by a large financial institution for ten years and was highly proficient in her job. During a major cost-cutting exercise, a restructure and staff cuts were implemented. Management's apparent lack of understanding of the processes of change and therefore lack of effective planning, caused a dramatic drop in production and standards of processing. This created massive backlogs and extensive delays for clients of the organisation.

A culture of managerial credentialism and expectations that managers should employ the latest 'human resource technologies' as well as the imperatives of heroism and intolerance of failure meant that the facts needed to be disguised. Overworked and compromised by the cover-ups, Carmen spoke publicly. She was censured by her local management and threatened with discipline if she continued. She continued, and a campaign of vilification began: she was a troublemaker, malcontent, unable to cope with change. After months of harassment and when signs of stress threatened her health Carmen resigned.

Although Carmen was highly competent in her job, her skills and knowledge were developed over years and were specific to the organisation. Her age, heavily accented English, lack of transferable skills and a declining market for clerical skills meant that Carmen faced a period of long-term if not permanent unemployment.

Her increasing skills and promotions had allowed Carmen to set aside some money for her retirement and she had expected to continue such saving for several years to come. After she resigned and even when she qualified for unemployment benefit she still needed to supplement this income with her savings.

The cost to Carmen has been a protracted period of unemployment, the loss of most of her savings and a deterioration in her health. She has since gained a full-time position, but at a base-level clerical salary Carmen cannot save. She feels that she does not have enough time to gain the requisite skills which could provide access to higher paid positions. Not only has her standard of living fallen, she now faces impoverishment in her retirement.

Carmen acknowledges that the costs of these managerialist practices have not only been suffered by her. Other costs have included the stress on colleagues who also learned the consequences of speaking out; a continuation of cover-ups, increased feelings of powerlessness and decline in morale; the loss to the organisation of loyalty, knowledge and skills; a loss to the clients of the organisation through inordinate delays, low standards and higher than necessary financial costs.

There is an irony in the listing of this cost to the public. Under the influence of managerialist values and language, the organisation had proclaimed itself geared to 'efficiency' and oriented to 'customer service': another example of the false consciousness which managerialist claims engender. Bullying and intimidation are inevitable when profit and image are paramount, but much remains hidden because of the fears of recrimination.

The cultivation and encouragement of greed

Bullying does not necessarily involve direct physical contact. It has been identified in aggressive belittling of opponents and in demands for compliance reminiscent of 'prehistoric creatures, engaged in some form of ritualized male display' (Wynhausen 1995, p. 1). Such behaviour is fostered when a culture has been socialised into expecting abusive conduct from its leaders.

Such abuse is not only about people but concerns resources of all kinds: ideas, flora and fauna, the sea, the land and the environment generally (Birch 1993; Rosewarne 1993; Eckersley 1993). In policies to foster economic growth at all costs the environment has been regarded as an infinite resource to mine, pollute, exhaust, cut down and sell. Such treatment of the environment has been motivated by greed, and in human relationships the more familiar 'bullying' has been facilitated by huge differentials in income, wealth and power. In these respects greed is linked to those abusive kinds of dominance which are recognised as bullying. The one feeds on the other and vice versa.

It would be misleading to imply that bullying or greed is characteristic of individual behaviour unrelated to changed economic and social conditions and a culture of individualism. The essential point being highlighted is the extent to which commitment to fascist-style dogma engenders deviant behaviour. Deregulation of banks and financial institutions, of health care and postgraduate tertiary education has given a green light to greed. The ability of a university department to make money has become a key criterion for measuring success. Not surprisingly, schools of business management appear to lead the money-making stakes although, in Australia, their fee arrangements have been described as 'scandalous' (Scott 1994). At the University of New South Wales a part-time MBA degree costs $32 000. This-top-of-the-line product can be offered alongside various shorter courses in related areas, each course selling the idea that some form of management qualification will guarantee people's professional and financial futures. A Diploma in Total Quality Management at the University of Wollongong will cost $10 000, a Diploma in Sports Management at the University of Technology Sydney, is $7600 and — the irony surely

GREED AND BULLYING 203

does not escape the advertisers — a Diploma in Professional Ethics at the University of New South Wales 'will set a student back $7750'.

Deregulation and the accompanying rush to weigh the money-making potential of every venture is part of the ethos of economic rationalism. In Australia and across the globe this ethos has made a virtue of selfishness and ushered in massive increases in social and economic inequality (Brundtland 1990; Raskall 1993; Saunders 1990; Stilwell 1993). The think-tanks and governments which promoted these practices were playing to an appreciative audience of companies, entrepreneurs and bureaucrats with a particular kind of training (Pusey 1991) who had almost certainly had a hand in writing the script: 'the more you pay the better the performance'. This has become manifest in the myth of management worth and the rort of consultancy pay. More cynically, the high priests of economic rationalism have used the smokescreen of 'efficiency' to condone opportunistic greed.

The myth of management worth

A process of seizing as many rewards as possible and then justifying such conduct is dehumanising because it presupposes that the most worthy goal in life is to accumulate material rewards and surround them with status and the trappings of office. Such an outcome is promoted as the epitome of success. Inherent in such processes are assumptions about hierarchies of power which have been built on those commercially inspired values, that the more you pay the more efficient the performance and the better the control. In relation to these assumptions the new managerialism is interested not in truth but in performance, not in the quality of human relationships but in productivity of output, not in ideas and imagination but in financial gain.

Large private companies provide the cue for such a culture and the media seems happy to promote males with large salaries as exemplars of commerce. Even during a recession companies justify huge salary increases by reference to the familiar managerial imagery of having a strong man at the tiller to take them through tough times. A *Sydney Morning Herald* survey of the 1993–94 financial year showed an average 15 per cent increase in top pay given to executive directors, providing an average salary of $667 000 per year or almost $13 000 per week. This average conceals some astronomical rewards: the deputy chief executive of Fairfax taking home $1.8 million; Fosters' brewing chief receiving a 44 per cent rise to $1.35 million from $940 000 the year before; and TNT giving its chief executive a 27 per cent rise to more than $1 million (Mychasuk 1994).

A familiar defence of such salaries, that they are rewards for performance, turns out to be another fiction. Chief executive officers were obtaining substantial rises in pay even when profits were declining, and when profits to shareholders rose, the increases for executive officers were higher. Pay related to performance is not a plausible explanation. But what is?

Rewards paid to chief executives when they leave appear to dwarf even the rewards they had when in office. As soon as the word was around that laws on retirement payouts might be tightened, any idea of civic responsibility was dashed as long-serving directors ran off with their payouts: $5.4 million to Michael Nugent of Goldman Fielder; $3.4 million to Peter Wade of North Broken Hill; and $3.1 million to Stuart Hornery of Lend Lease. Even these payouts look modest by comparison with the $37 million benefits given to Coca-Cola Amatil executives: $19 million to Dean Wills; $10 million to Bill Gibson; and $8.2 million to John Priest. Wills was reported as saying that these payouts were not large by world standards (Weatherdon 1995).

These rewards are usually defended not so much by 'world standards' but by reference to remuneration which is common in the USA. Although very high salaries, like 'low taxes', is a fashion or dogma promoted as necessary, that still leaves unanswered the question of why public sector management should be expected to adopt the same values. Perhaps this is a naive question if financial rewards are assumed to influence performance.

But why are gross forms of greed associated with managerialism? Why not modest greed? Why not an acknowledgment that power and the perks of position coupled to an ample salary are sufficient rewards?

The self-serving practices of the marketplace have become global. Politicians and their advisers who want to give corporate trappings to public agencies and those who decide the rewards of the chief executives of newly privatised public utilities are apparently influenced by the assumption that 'the more you pay the better the ...'. For example, in Victoria the chief executive of Tabcorp received an $8 million salary package. That five-year package included a base annual salary of $675 000 a year, and an interest-free loan to buy $3 million Tabcorp shares worth more than $6 million and likely to pay more than $400 000 in dividends (Maganzanik & Green 1994). The agreement with the new chief of this public sector organisation, Ross Wilson, had also included a compensation package equivalent to the salary. Even the Victorian state Treasurer admitted in retrospect that it had been a mistake to approve such an excessive salary package.

An opportunity for greed occurs when public organisations produce hierarchies and imitate the packages and other perks which are regarded as commonplace in private industry. Organisations and basic-grade workers should become lean but chief executives fat. Opportunities for even greater greed occur when public utilities are privatised, and in Britain there has been public protest over the avarice of bosses.

In early 1995 it was revealed that the chairman of Britain's newly privatised National Electricity Grid, David Jefferies, had a package worth more than $4 million. Jefferies was perceived as merely joining other chiefs with their 'snouts in the trough' (Ellingsen 1995b). Sir Iain Vallance, chairman of the privatised British Telecom, received a $1.5 million per year salary; Ed Wallis, the chief of Power Gen, received $2.5 million of share options on top of his $750 000 salary; and Cedric Brown of British Gas was awarded a 75 per cent pay rise to more than $1 million.

In March 1995, in reaction to public revulsion at such pay deals, British Prime Minister John Major foreshadowed legislation to control — through a code of practice — the remuneration of directors, their bonuses and share options (Ellingsen 1995b).

The interrelationship between bullying and greed is apparent in the attitude of these men to other workers and in their justifications of their financial returns, but this avarice also takes place in the context of governments' sustained devaluing of public service and corresponding hero worship of entrepreneurs. At a time when junior doctors in Britain were receiving $26 000 a year and being refused a pay rise, Sir Iain Vallance said he would find it 'quite relaxing to be a junior doctor' (Ellingsen 1995b). Cedric Brown received his pay rise when he was simultaneously planning to sack 25 000 workers. At a time when the British Treasury refused a 2.9 per cent pay rise for 500 000 teachers Ed Wallis justified his tenfold increase with the observation, 'Yes I think I'm worth what I'm paid. Yes, of course I am' (Ellingsen 1995a). This is certainly not an atypical response. Such proudly proclaimed sentiments illustrate the extent of the loss of social conscience.

The rort of consultancy pay

Among senior managers the norms of private and public sector cultures have merged: produce efficiency drives and performance evaluations, send staff on training programs to learn the new language and give handsome rewards to people at the top. One aspect of this culture concerns the expectation that when public sector organisations must demonstrate efficiency, or in other ways address a problem they cannot solve, they bring in private management consultants.

The Public Sector Research Centre at the University of New South Wales does identify a value in consultancies, as in using a particular expertise and in opening up bureaucracies to outside influence. Nevertheless, in examinations of federal and state spending, certain trends are apparent: a. there has been a consistent and long-term upward trend in the reported number and aggregate cost of consultancies and some anecdotal evidence of an understating of reported spending; b. public reporting never includes evaluations as to whether the consultants' work was assessed positively.

Even in Australia, which is a low spender on a diminishing public sector (Esping Anderson 1990; Castles 1992), there has been no ceiling on the money available to pay for consultants. In 1988, when the management-oriented Greiner government came to power in New South Wales, that state witnessed a dramatic increase in the use of consultants. In the nine months from July 1988 to March 1989 the Office of Public Management 'extrapolated a figure of $150 m.' for management consultancy (Howard 1990, p. 7).

Reports show that Federal Government spending on consultants for the period 1988–89 to 1993–94 was $2.459 billion (Howard 1995). Leaving aside the Australian International Development Assistance Bureau (AIDAB) and the Department of Administrative Services, the increase in nominal spending by all Commonwealth departments over that period was 115.15 per cent, resulting in an average annual increase of 23.03 per cent (Howard 1995).

Although the costs of a public sector are strictly accountable to public scrutiny, a different set of values has been operating with regard to the costs of consultancies. The Commonwealth Public Service spent more than $180 million in 1993–94 to buy expertise from outside consultants, an increase of $15 million over the previous year. Regarding the quality and usefulness of the service given by such consultants, a newspaper editorial concluded that, 'there is no real way of knowing which consultancy has paid its way and which consultancy is rorting the Federal Government' (*SMH* 1995, p. 10).

Careful analyses of the use of management consultants has confronted issues such as who the consultants are, who gets the contracts and what is the difference between contracting out and consultancy (Howard 1990, 1993, 1994). The largest six to eight major global companies — such as Coopers and Lybrand, Price Waterhouse, Ernst and Young — obtain a disproportionately high share of the income available from consultancies, with the rest shared between small consultancy firms and self-employed individuals (Howard 1994). In terms of the spreading influence of managerialism, what is disturbing is that companies whose main expertise is in accounting now also claim expertise in policy evaluation, social planning, training programs and the delivery of welfare services.

This spreading influence, together with the increases in expenditure, the failure to identify whether consultants' work was useful, and the deskilling of internal employees, are some familiar problems associated with consultancies. Other issues concern the process by which consultancies are obtained and intimidation by representatives of some large companies.

Cronyism is a key means of obtaining contracts. Dr Grahame Dowling of the Australian Graduate School of Management told the *Financial Review* that: 'In consulting it's not what you know but who you know. Even if you're the best thing since sliced bread you won't get very far in consulting until you tap into the network' (Howard 1990, p. 10).

Politicians wanting to privatise government agencies, or the chiefs of bureaucracies who want to give their staff some corporate medicine, are in the habit of seeking management consultants. They already have these connections to a corporate world and like to cement such associations by awarding contracts. Being a patron is socially rewarding and ego reinforcing. In these circumstances — when privatisation or corporatisation is being considered — and for the duration of a contract, the management consultants are likely to become the new high priests who will not have to demonstrate the benefits of their presence or the value of their recommendations.

It has already been noted that although there are numerous management consultancy firms in Australia, a disproportionately high percentage of the contracts is awarded to the Big Six which are world-wide in their bases and influence. It is the fierce competition between these huge companies which appears to contribute to cutting corners and the use of bullying tactics. In the USA, Big Six management consultancy firms have been prosecuted for falsification of corporate accounts, the conducting of 'deficient audits and the active selling of tax evasion schemes' (Howard 1990 p. 17).

In Australia, Coopers and Lybrand and Arthur Andersen have been chastised by the New South Wales Supreme Court for 'inexplicable delays' in producing documents for the court. The Institute of Chartered Accountants concluded that creative accounting (cooking the books) was widespread, and they linked such practices to entrepreneurs Alan Bond, Christopher Skase and John Elliot whose companies were audited respectively by Arthur Andersen, Duesbury's and Price Waterhouse. Members of the Institute stated that they had been subject to 'harassment and aggro' during the course of their investigations (Howard 1990 p. 17).

It may be possible to identify the financial costs of such consultancies but the human costs are almost never immediately apparent, though the CSIRO scientists (see chapter 2) said that a first sign of trouble and a first feeling of losing control was the appointment of management consultants.

When interviewing some consultants it becomes apparent that if efficiency and doing more with less is the objective, human costs are not a consideration. There are other audiences to play to: jobs can be eliminated in the interests of shareholders and in the public sector costs can be cut to impress financial markets and to appeal to constituencies of voters. In 1994 a chief executive of an American multinational food manufacturing company took early retirement to become a management consultant for his previous employer. He explained his new job: 'I get very well paid for travelling the world and enabling companies to get rid of people'.

The human costs of greed are multiple. The humanness of those who accept such rewards, believing they are merited, is diminished. Costs endured by those subjected to managerialist practices include unemployment and associated poverty; part-time work and accompanying insecurity; stress, anxiety and loss of morale among employees; a persistent sense of powerlessness; and illnesses which may lead to premature death.

Greedy bullies may not ponder the practices to which they subscribe and the consequences of their behaviour. But once these are exposed there is a greater possibility for society to protest and to advocate corrective action.

References

Birch, C. 1993, *Regaining Compassion: For Humanity and Nature*, New South Wales University Press, Kensington.

Brundtland Report 1987, *Our Common Future*, Oxford University Press, Oxford.

Castles, F. 1992, 'Public expenditure and the culture of dependency; how much is too much?', in P. Vintila, J. Phillimore, & P. Newman (eds), *Markets, Morals and Manifestos*, Institute for Science & Technology Policy, Murdoch University, Perth.

'Consultants' costs grow' 1995, *Sydney Morning Herald*, editorial, 5 January, p. 10.

Eckersley, R. 1993, 'Rationalizing the environment: how much am I bid?', in S. Rees, G. Rodley & F. Stilwell (eds), *Beyond the Market*, Pluto Press, Sydney, ch. 17.

Ellingsen, P. 1995a, 'Free market greed clouds Major's human face', *Sydney Morning Herald*, 11 February, p. 21.

——1995b, 'Major calls a halt to boardroom pay grab', *Sydney Morning Herald*, 2 March, p. 11.

Esping Anderson, G. 1990, *The Three Worlds of Welfare Capitalism*, Polity Press, Oxford.

Hilmer, F. 1993, *Independent Committee of Inquiry Into Competition Policy in Australia, National Competition Policy*, AGPS, Canberra.

Howard, M. 1990, *The Use of Consultants by the Public Sector in Australia: Recent Evidence and Issues*, Public Sector Research Centre, University of New South Wales, Kensington.

——1993, 'Costs of consultants begin to emerge', *Directions in Government*, October, pp. 34–5.

——1994, 'Comet consultants and the money they make', *Directions in Government*, July, pp. 12–13.

——1995, *A Growth Industry? Use of Consultants by Commonwealth Departments, 1974–1994*, Public Sector Research Centre, University of New South Wales, Kensington.

Hugill, B. 1994, 'A civil service on its last legs', *Observer*, 29 May, p. 22.

Magazanick, M. & Green, S. 1994, 'Wilson package a "mistake"', *Sydney Morning Herald*, 9 September.
Maley, K. 1994, 'National identity may be cost of success', *Sydney Morning Herald*, 16 April, p. 35.
Martin, B. & Baker, C. (eds) 1986, *Intellectual Suppression*, Angus & Robertson, Sydney.
Mychasuk, E. 1994, 'It's open season for executive salaries', *Sydney Morning Herald*, 29 October.
Pusey, M. 1991, *Economic Rationalism in Canberra*, Cambridge University Press, Melbourne.
Raskall P. 1993, 'Widening income disparities in Australia', in S. Rees, G. Rodley & F. Stilwell (eds), *Beyond the Market*, Pluto Press, Sydney, ch. 3.
Retallick, J., Coombe, K. & Battersby, D. 1990, Schools renewal in New South Wales: legitimating the new managerialism, Paper delivered to the annual conference of the Australian Council for Educational Administration, Hobart.
Rosewarne, S. 1993, 'Selling the environment: a critique of market ecology', in S. Rees, G. Rodley & F. Stilwell (eds), *Beyond the Market*, Pluto Press, Sydney, ch. 4.
Saunders, P. 1990, *Income Inequality in Australia*, Lessons from the Luxemburg Income Study, Social Policy Research Centre–ESPG Income Distribution Seminar, Sydney.
Scott, M. 1994, 'Business studies fees "scandalous"', *Sydney Morning Herald*, 16 November.
Stilwell, F. 1993, *Economic Inequality*, Pluto Press, Sydney.
Wynhausen, E. 1995, 'A nation of bullies', *Weekend Australian*, 4–5 March, Weekend Review, pp. 1–2.

16.
The Cost of Efficiency

Karin Solondz

On returning to Australia from Europe in 1992, I remember the sensation of profound shock I experienced at the drastic changes which had occurred in my 'lucky country' in the space of the six short years of my absence. It seemed I had left a country of smiling, happy, friendly and creative people living in a modern western land and had returned to a Sydney of head-down, glum-faced workaholics and unemployed who were all apparently busily in search of the next dollar or the next job.

Apparently Australia was in the middle of a dreadful recession, the dollar had depreciated to one-third of its worth of a decade earlier, and the tycoons of the 1980s had 'disappeared overseas' with billions of dollars that many ordinary people were now sadly missing. The impression was of some disastrous mismanagement having occurred, which had robbed the country of much of its worth in a short period.

I heard rumours of financial institutions deregulation, of labour market deregulation, of the 'speculation' and 'excesses' of the 1980s; governments seemed to be racing against time to sell off profitable assets without consulting the shareholders. I heard the words 'levelling of the economic playing field' and wondered whether it meant Australians were now expecting to compete for a wage with the Third World and reduce their standard of living accordingly.

For the first time I heard those catchcries 'excellence' and 'efficiency' and, while on the surface they seemed desirable, something about their repetitiveness, tone and persistence did not seem congruent.

During the next two years I worked as a psychologist for the Employees Assistance Programme (EAP). The EAP is an organisation which subcontracts psychological services to big business and government departments. With the EAP I was involved in providing preventative and tertiary interventions for employees and organisations who, for organisational or personal reasons, were experiencing difficulties which impinged on work productivity. I also provided reports and suggestions to companies for related improvement in organisational practices. Where appropriate and possible, additional input such as organisational stress studies were also provided.

Business has boomed for EAPs due to the widespread privatisation and 'downsizing' of government departments, and the wholesale dismissal of employees in many large private companies. EAPs advertise themselves as providing counselling services and reducing stress-related workers' compensation claims. They recognise the interrelationship between stressful work situations and consequent disruptions of private life, as well as the interrelationship between certain organisational changes and reductions in productivity. Employees would come to counselling when large-scale deterioration in working conditions and work practices occurred in conjunction with dismissals which could destroy an individual's self-respect, long-term (work and private) relationships, and could result in stress-related disease such as work phobias or contemplation of suicide. Prominent in the complaints of employees was a feeling of betrayal. Those who could return to work were, more often than not, disillusioned and less productive.

Working for the EAP provided useful insights into the dynamics of a narrow or reductionist managerialist interpretation of concepts such as 'efficiency' and 'excellence'. These were being associated with the 'slash and burn' of an unquestioned 'change for change's sake' attitude. Traditional personnel management concepts such as staff morale, job security, career development, organisational direction and philosophy, professionalism, mutual trust, industrial democracy, low occupational stress and sound cooperative working relationships, which are factors known to contribute to productivity and efficiency, were placed to one side in the very name of efficiency and productivity! All logic seemed to have disappeared from Australia's economic institutions.

Productivity

While it is generally accepted that these factors impinge on productivity, the question of exactly how widespread changes to management practice have affected traditional personnel management concepts and productivity is seldom examined, despite managerialism's claims to rationality, 'accountability' and measurement. Managerialism attempts to supersede accepted knowledge in personnel practices without producing evidence of its superiority. It appears to exist alongside those concepts without challenging and overturning them, thereby creating the assumption of incorporation. This is a false assumption since managerialism's practice, as opposed to its rhetoric, destroys the human efficiencies created by respecting traditional principles.

Under managerialism, English-speaking western economies have turned these practices on end. Large corporations and governments have broken the long-established and fought-for social contract between employer and employee. Examples of de facto changes in the name of the managerialism rhetoric include a reductionist form of accountability (i.e. measurement equals greater managerial control); increases in job insecurity such as downsizing (shedding long-term employees en masse); the contracting in of expertise (externalising training costs and reducing internal career advancement); short-term employment contracts (termed 'consultancy', a further way of increasing control and reducing the power of the contracted employee); and enterprise bargaining (which has become the individual bargaining of the employee versus the corporate bargaining of the employer).

These changes reduced labour costs, increased profit and put pressure on employees to increase their piece-rate output. These developments have been claimed to increase productivity and efficiency.

The limitations

While short-term gains in company profit and redistribution of social product away from the employee and towards the employer have been made, there are natural human limitations to the methods of increasing productivity adopted by the managerialists; limitations made obvious by the virtual epidemic of occupational stress-related illness. (Staff at EAPs and health insurance officers have anecdotal evidence of a huge increase in occupational stress. Workcover statistics comparing 1991–92 and 1992–93 show an increase in mental illness and workers compensation claims, though the latter do not differentiate between various types of mental illness and stress.) Occupational stress represents only the tip of the iceberg in cost to the individual, her or his family, and the company. For each employee debilitated by occupational stress-related illnesses (both mental and physical), many cases of milder forms of distress are never reported and resultant productivity losses never 'measured'.

While there are thus limitations to the short-term gains of managerialism, the long-term losses are by contrast unlimited. This unlimited loss can be termed PIPL, or Potential Intellectual Product Lost.

PIPL is the sum total of the loss of all potential ideas contributed or 'transferred' by the employee to the employer. A low PIPL is a kind of 'goodwill' of employer–employee relations, and could be included in the company balance sheet. Unfortunately, PIPL, due to its unlimited nature, is not readily quantifiable. Perhaps this is the reason it has been excluded from managerialism's measurements of efficiency and productivity. PIPL is a term appreciated by 'clever' countries such as Japan and Germany since its principles are well established in their industrial relations policies. Despite, or because of, high labour costs and high levels of industrial and social security these countries have managed to maintain product excellence, cleverness, quality, and competitiveness.

Long-term, as opposed to short-term, productivity gains are more likely to be a result of low PIPL than the short-term and short-sighted policies of managerialists. This can be seen from a psychological as well as the common-sense perspective. Psychological studies show that the carrot is mightier than the stick (Bandura 1969) in reducing PIPL. It simply does not follow that a reduction in labour costs must produce long-term productivity gains regardless of its human consequences. Modern industry depends more on social stability, technology (human ideas), training (heavily government-subsidised), infrastructure and intensive capital, than it does on low labour costs. These in turn require the maintenance of an accepted social contract and consequent high transfers of intellectual product to employers. The destruction of social contracts is quickly followed by the destruction of the social system on which advanced society and industry depend. Where such destruction has happened, for example in South America, restrictions in capital investment soon follow.

Efficiency and the inquisition

The Inquisition was a period in history when arguments — patently illogical — were accepted as logical and factual, with the most dire of consequences. It was accepted that witches float. The perfect test for a witch was to throw someone into a river to see if she floated. Discovery of the flaw in the logic is only possible by looking at the broader picture, which reveals the contradictions in any narrow frame of reference. Any form of reductionism, as in managerialist definitions and applications of efficiency and productivity, carries inherent and inhuman dangers. However, people are generally more aware of flaws in the logic of other eras than of contradictions in the logic of their own time.

In modern efficiency, that which is efficient is defined as that which is measurable as efficient. Consequently, whatever is not measurable is not efficient and does not exist. Managerialism, which bears similarity to the Inquisition, never acknowledges that efficiency is defined in this way, it merely acts as if or assumes that this is the case.

The new procedures of many public and private organisations have the effect of stamping out professionals' resilience and opposing ideas from other sources. Efficiency procedures are often administered by a new breed of managers with a fetish for measurement and assessment.

Older-style managers fail to gain promotion because they lack the necessary prerequisites. Many are offered redundancy packages or leave of their own accord with a sense of defeat, disillusionment or both.

The organisational background to this new management recruitment is that change (a truly neutral term) needs to occur and efficiency needs to be improved. Efficiency and effectiveness similarly must be accounted for in real and measurable terms. Nothing 'airy fairy' (qualitative), is acceptable. Efficiency continues to be defined as that which is measurable.

This form of operation has real effects on the lives of many employees, on true efficiency, on professionalism, product quality, occupational stress and work relationships.

The inquisition

Any new dogma needs to prove its value. In order for managerialism to prove its efficiency, 'inefficiency' must be expelled. Thus, people with something new to offer in an ever more competitive labour market, particularly where they might be unsure of their own competencies, are under pressure to prove their efficiency by diverting attention away from themselves and proving the inefficiency of others. This can be morally justified as in the claim that 'the competent fulfilment of one's duties consists of closely monitoring via an "objective" measure the performance of other employees'. Of lower priority is the issue of whether the measurement criteria are a true measure of competency.

Efficiency criteria have been used arbitrarily to dismiss highly productive colleagues. Inefficiency as opposed to efficiency procedures are typically 'negotiated' by an employer with an employee. These highly unequal negotiators then jointly oversee the arbitrary efficiency criteria on which the competence of the employee is judged. The psychological effect of such procedures can be quite extreme, particularly since they are often based on coerced agreement, on arbitrary and mechanistic criteria, are known about by other employees, and place the employee under considerable stress for protracted periods. They have the effect of isolating the employee from colleagues and increasing the likelihood that he or she will make a mistake, adding further to the person's stress and distress. Once an employee begins to produce mistakes of real magnitude under this system, inefficiency is considered proven. The witch is a witch, the employee has become inefficient. Previously productive employees can be completely incapacitated by this method of improving efficiency. This form of systematic psychological terror can be repeated many times in a workplace by managers whose own competence in personnel management could be questioned.

The effect of these procedures on teamwork is even more destructive. Since employees are aware of the arbitrary nature of the procedure, and of the need to cut back on staff, they are also aware that anyone within a team could be the next to go. Criticism, questioning of the procedures, or siding with the 'victim' is avoided, and the team initially represents a closed and unified mind with the victim outside. Later, however, competition for the remaining positions increases and tension and division mount until the next victim to be expelled is found and attention is again successfully diverted away from the self. Staff morale is at a low ebb. Individualism and alternative views are not easily tolerated during periods of high job insecurity. Professionalism and quality are the first casualties of this lack of preparedness to discuss issues of importance in the workplace.

Managerialism and inefficiency

Time and money

Not only do the widespread efficiency measures require that the measurable nuts and bolts of material and intellectual production are counted minute by minute and hour by hour, they tolerate only directly productive work and disallow by implication such wasteful activities as sitting and thinking, talking to colleagues about new strategies, laughing and joking, looking up new trends in professional journals and so on. The reductions of these types of activities contain hidden costs in the loss of indirect but highly productive innovation and creativity. At the same time the cost of the measurement and collection of data soars in terms of time, money, staff, top-heavy management, paperwork and use of computers. Value for money in this endless collection of statistics of dubious scientific and managerial worth is not evaluated.

De-professionalisation

One of the most pervasive and damaging effects of managerialism has been on professionalism. Where professionals once determined work practices, management control has taken their place. The creation of generic positions, the decimation of professional values and status, and the reduction of training standards required for any given form of work, has led to debilitating working conditions. People ring a large institution and no one can give them correct and intelligent answers to their questions. People write letters to the public service and have to write four more until they recieve a reply. People buy new equipment and have to return it. They put something in for repair and bring it back three times.

The decimation of professional positions and status has been an aid in producing rapid change. Professional standards are normally highly resistant to quality reduction. For all the rhetoric of continual quality improvement it is continual quality degradation which has been most evident under managerialism.

The public broadcaster, the ABC, is a case in point. The standards of the broadcaster have arguably dropped due possibly to a number of concurrent factors. Among these are generic job classification and lack of support staff for journalists and broadcasters, so that instead of fulfilling specialised duties they are burdened with additional clerical duties. Training of new recruits from the private sector into the public broadcasting role is inadequate or lacking. Professional discussion of the contradictions between the ABC Charter as a public broadcaster and its new 'rating imperative' in conjunction with the role of broadcasting space is lacking. Professionals have been disempowered. High proportions of staff are contracted in and are on short-term contracts. Consequent lack of job security discourages professional discussion of contentious or controversial issues. Yet these are discussions which, for the sake of quality, must occur. There are systematically built-in conflicts of interest between permanent and contracted staff. Career opportunities for those who chose to stay on permanent contracts become restricted as 'experts' are brought in, and the opportunity to progress is lost. Experienced colleagues are devalued as the term 'generic' soon implies that anyone, no matter how incompletely trained, can fill many positions. Staff with vested interests in supporting the generic position and opposed to the professional position are brought in, and professionals lose their voice within the organisation. Standards drop. Resistance to 'change' is defeated. This scenario, repeated in many organisations Australia-wide, not only lowers work quality but reduces cooperation and teamwork among staff. Information is hoarded, not shared. Politics wins out in favour of productivity.

Job insecurity and inefficiency

In Germany employees are, after six months of employment in the private sector, as secure in their positions as are Australians in the public service. They can be dismissed only on certain grounds. This has the effect of making employees feel a part of the organisation and more responsible in their role. They cannot be dismissed on the whim of the employer, so they are more likely to discuss issues of import with each other and the employer. As a consequence, professional issues are not easily compromised and quality is maintained. In a win-win scenario the employee's ideas are more likely to transfer to the employer.

There have been situations in which psychological 'counsellors' have been requested to ask their clients who came to see them through an employer about a deep personal or work-related crisis, whether they would mind being videotaped during a therapy session! Not all counsellors saw the need to resist this request. The practice of using videos extended to management viewing psychologists performing their 'confidential' role. It became exceedingly difficult to resist this trend in the workplace. The subject of the use and abuse of video cameras in Australia and the erosion of human, even democratic, rights would make an interesting topic of its own.

It is not in the employer's own best interest to reduce the bargaining position of the employee to the point where the employee is not able to help ensure and contribute to the quality of the employer's own product. Industrial democracy and product quality are dependent on some balance of power between employee and employer. Any other path, in the era of ever more centralised economic power, leads to the gradual and insidious erosion of democratic rights. This trend can only be reflected in the thinking of future generations and in the acceptance of such erosion in the political system.

Occupational stress

Studies of occupational stress have investigated the amount of control an employee has over his or her working environment, the amount of work pressure and its relation to resources available (both personal and organisational) to do the job, as well as the clarity and consistency of occupational and supervisory goals (Andrew 1992). Peer relationships and job satisfaction, identification and involvement are other factors known to be related to the degree of occupational stress (Hennig 1984). Although management factors impinge on each of these, management is seldom specifically researched as a factor contributing to occupational stress. In the light of dramatic changes in management and organisational practices in Australia and the USA since the mid-1980s, and concurrent large increases in stress-related illness (Krusor & Blaker 1992) and their cost in lost efficiency, it is time to examine this question.

Control and peer relationships

Stress increases as control external to the employee increases, and as internal control — the amount of control the employee has over a situation — decreases (Andrew 1992; Hennig 1984). The reassertion of managerial control through painstaking efficiency procedures in conjunction with decreasing job security is therefore likely to increase occupational stress. In addition, employees must be socialised into justifiying closer control of their work.

Managerialism's effects on peer relationships and team cooperation have already been briefly examined. When team relationships deteriorate, occupational stress is known to increase (Lieberman 1982). Job satisfaction and identification are likely to decrease when employees are placed in competition with each other. In addition, it is exceedingly difficult for employees on temporary contracts to identify fully with a company which could discard them at any time. Job involvement is directly proportional to the level of control experienced by employees.

Clarity, consistency and resources

Change associated with de-professionalisation is instituted uncritically, with little resistance and without accountability. Slash-and-burn staff cuts have reduced the resources of remaining staff and increased workloads. The 35-hour week has effectively been abolished and the 48-hour week, without paid overtime, has taken its place. Workloads have increased; new diseases such as chronic fatigue syndrome have appeared. Work-related phobias and other psychological and physical illnesses have proliferated.

Partners in households where both are working are severely affected by stress (Krusor & Blaker 1992). But the population group at most risk are working mothers with very young children, a group which receives little support from employers and for which the erosion of real wages and increased mortgage rates has created a Catch 22 situation from which there is little escape. By contrast, many northern European countries provide up to one year's maternity leave at a comfortable level of existence.

Managerialism's unwritten personnel policy 'isms' contravene accepted wisdom. They act to reduce staff morale, job security, professionalism, and career development. They undermine mutual trust and the social contract between employee and employer. They reduce industrial democracy, destroy working relationships and increase occupational stress. In the last instance, they serve to undermine the stated aims of managerialism, especially the claims to accountability, improved efficiency, quality, cleverness and productivity.

References

Andrew, S. 1992, 'Steps for managing work stress', *Occupational Health Magazine*, May.
Bandura, A. 1969, *Principles of Behaviour Modification*, Holt, Rheinhart & Winston, New York.
Hennig, K. 1984, An investigative study of occupational strain in MICA officers of the Victorian Ambulance Service with particular emphasis on cognitive aspects, BA Hons thesis, La Trobe University, Melbourne.
Krusor, S. & Blakor, J. A. 1992, 'Family stress and employee productivity', *EAP Digest*, May–June.
Lieberman, N. 1982, 'The effects of social supports on response to stress', in L. Kutash, *Handbook of Stress and Anxiety*, Books on Demand, New York.

17.
Some Health Costs of Managerialism

Susan Britton

This interview that Stuart Rees conducted in March 1995 with Dr Susan Britton of the University of Sydney's University Health Service (which covers academic and non-academic staff needs) addresses the issue of whether illness is related to stress at work. Questions focus on managerial practices.

Illness related to work

SR: I understand you have some figures showing the profile of people who consult you and what proportion of symptoms presented have something to do with organisational pressures.

Britton: Yes, I have recorded the figures for the last four months of the consultations in which my final diagnosis is that the illness was institutionally induced. In 10 per cent of my booked patients my diagnosis was that of work-related illness. The ratio was seven non-academic staff to three academic staff. Sixty-five per cent of the patients were women, but I am a female doctor so that probably biases the figures.

SR: When people appear in this consulting room, what problems do they present which you subsequently think are related to work?

Britton: The commonest presenting symptom is profound fatigue. Usually the patients cannot identify the exact cause. They think it may be illness, so I go through all the possible causes, including stress. Once I ask about stress it becomes clear that changes in management structure have been a major contributing factor and it becomes apparent to the patients that stress is the cause of their excessive fatigue.

Some people present with anxiety, so they can more easily identify that the problem is related to work. For example, they dread entering the university grounds and even get palpitations on Monday mornings. Insomnia is common and people seek sleeping tablets. These are certainly not a solution, being potentially addictive. Dyspepsia, which is ulcers or acid feeling in the stomach region, is common. Headaches, jaw pain from teeth grinding — which is a stress symptom — neck and shoulder muscle tension and pain, and depression are the symptoms with which those people presented over that four-month period.

SR: What would make people fear coming into this university?

Britton: After some months or longer of chronic stress, people trying to solve the problem of too much work to do, or fear of losing their job, experience a background release of adrenalin that makes them very tense. During the weekend they have two days to try to unwind from that but by Sunday evening and particularly Monday morning the release of adrenalin is so preprogrammed that they can feel shaking, anxiety and palpitations just from the thought of coming to work.

SR: These are academics or non-academics?

Britton: The distribution of symptoms, I would say, is equal across both sexes and the academic and non-academic staff. Academic staff have become used to the fact that they are on contract work and may lose their job; those without security were first presenting to me years ago when contract work for academics became more common. I have been at the university for fourteen years. In the last two years I observe that the non-academic staff have become as stressed as the academic staff.

Explaining depression and treating work-related conditions

SR: Is the depression you refer to temporary or persistent?

Britton: I would only diagnose depression if it was persistent for at least weeks and people describe a feeling of dread when they wake up in the morning. I observe that the symptoms people present are rather like a grief reaction. They have been very loyal to the university, often working here for many years. They love the university and suddenly they perceive it as having betrayed them because they are now fearing for their job, or are involved in sacking other people or are left behind with enormous workloads and no guidelines about how to manage these demands. They receive no support or thanks for their efforts to manage these problems, so each of those groups wakes up feeling dread because they have lost control. It is a grief reaction. It is like the breakdown of a marriage or, for people who leave the university, a bit like a death. It sounds dramatic but that is what they present to me.

SR: I do not think it is dramatic. If you are saying that people are losing control and if you are implying that they feel rejected by an institution to which they have given a large part of their life, what is actually happening? Is the system a primary cause?

Britton: I would always try to understand where that individual is, what position in the system they have and to whom they are best to go to discuss their problems. I try to encourage people to discuss it within their department and try and find who might be approachable. Failing that, I would try to refer them to the counselling service because they are more skilful with counselling. I encourage people, if I believe the illness is work-related, to record it as workers' compensation but they are almost always anxious about doing that in the present climate for fear that they may be victimised for being stressed and for not coping. I am referring to people who have been here for twenty years and who have a history of success and satisfaction in their work. So, if people are willing to, I would try to encourage them to see Risk Management and seek mediation. Many patients are surprised that so many others suffer similarly. I think it would help if there was a forum for people in this position so people at the coalface could discuss strategies for action.

A dilemma: organisational problem, individual treatment?

SR: You are a medical practitioner and you are giving me a diagnosis of what is wrong with an organisation! You are confronting work-related conditions, so you are trying to unmask what is going on in an organisation that is dysfunctional for people's health.

Britton: If the diagnosis is work-induced illness, the treatment is not tablets, it is to look at the cause.

SR: I guess there is a temptation to treat problems as individual shortcomings?

Britton: The patient sees it as an individual shortcoming. I try to explain to them that I now see many people in this situation and that it really is, in this process and the particular style of change the university is going through, not their fault; it is a natural response to loss of control and lack of support.

SR: I am hearing about mis-match between an assessment that says the problem is located in the system but treatment remains focused on the individual: 'go for counselling' or 'go to Risk Management' or 'try mediation'.

Britton: Oh yes, that is true but I do not see that I am in a position to change the situation.

Changed working conditions

SR: Do you wish you were able to change the way the institution works? Do you sometimes get annoyed, angry, ashamed of what is going on?

Britton: I would like to be able to express this situation to upper management. We did ask a senior manager over for a meeting one day and expressed this problem to her, that we have such a high presentation with stress symptoms during these changes. She said it is inevitable and if people really cannot cope with the increased workload they should complain to their supervisor. So I pass this message on to every patient. But for some reason the patients fear doing this. When I first worked at the university, I did not come across that fear of management. People trusted that their complaints would be respected as genuine — that they just could not cope with the workload. Now they feel there is no flexibility. The individuals fear they are seen as failing, as they are in a competitive situation. For example, contract lecturers: if they do not work twice the hours and work twice as hard, someone else will get the permanent position — so fear preoccupies a lot of these patients.

SR: In terms of your deduction of what has been going on with patients, have you seen some of the excesses of managerial behaviour coming across as bullying?

Britton: My impression about management is that it is often displaced by two or three rungs from the people who are presenting to me with stress. So they do not see the level of stress that they induce a couple of rungs down the ladder. Somebody high in management decides we are going to cut costs in a particular way. There is no discussion with the people at the coalface who actually have to enact these cuts, even though these may not be the most efficient or the most relevant cuts, or even tenable ones. The people may just not be able to produce the work that is required.

For example, a biologist running a laboratory is now expected to run the department's computer system when the systems operator is lost and not replaced. He is told there is no money to employ help and he does not have the skill to cope when the system goes down. Another example involves the secretary of an academic department who is now expected to do all her duties, as well as accounts since the devolution of accounts to departments. Many patients describe the paperwork of interdepartmental billing, accounts within departments, as overwhelming.

There are individuals in the institution, managers who, I guess, the patients would see as bullying by nature. Yes, the manager has power and the worker is powerless and they may see that the manager makes no effort to understand the situation the worker is in, or respect their contribution, or thank them for anything they have done.

The response of medical practitioners

SR: You assess a certain percentage of people as having dis-ease related to conditions of work. What do you and your colleagues do apart from referring elsewhere? You speak to a senior manager who says 'it's inevitable'. Is this frustrating?

Britton: It is extremely frustrating to us. If any other new illness was affecting 10 per cent of our population there would be a major inquiry into it. It is very hard for us to address the actual cause except at an individual level. I do not know how else to do it.

SR: You mention stress-related symptoms included headaches, depression, anxiety, palpitations.

Britton: Yes, people present all those physical symptoms. I think another percentage of staff who suffer stress will be going directly to the counselling service. The institution sees that offering Risk Management and counselling is an adequate response. My experience is people are frightened of using the official system. I do not know how to address that.

Stress on practitioners

SR: How have these general trends affected you and your colleagues? Is the new managerial phenomenon, 'do more for less', making claims of 'new forms of efficiency' having an effect on you?

Britton: Well, we are an independent unit because we are not directly employed by the university. We have, I suppose, this attitude from Medicare. Medicare is pressing us for performance gains. All doctors are stressed. There are many reviews going on now about the level of responsibility we take, the pressure of numbers of people to see, the fact we are no longer well remunerated for it and that we are under threat of being sued much more than ever before. So we as doctors are also under stress. As a unit, this is, I think, very well run, with a lot of cohesiveness and support for each other and respect for each other's ability and that is what I do not see happening in some of the other departments. So, even in difficult times, people support and respect each other. Most people work because of the satisfaction of getting a job done. They feel rewarded by working as a team, rather than just for the money. Very few of my patients are really motivated by the money alone.

SR: Yes, just as an aside, I interviewed scientists from CSIRO. They said 'we used to go to work on weekends not because we were being paid but because we were not being paid'. Then, referring to management, they said that they would not understand that.

Britton: No. And many academics continue to work after retirement.

SR: So, we have a new management system, which has been marketed around the world, that we are all being subjected to. You see it — it appears in your consulting room — but are you saying we are powerless to do much about it?

Britton: I have just never thought about that, other than asking the senior manager to come over to try to discuss the problem with her. I am not aware of any other way, other than which political party I vote for.

SR: Yes, but the two major parties talk the same language. They both encourage competition and consumption, but respect for individuals and weightings of human costs seem to be neglected.

The issue of costs

SR: Could I just ask you a couple more questions about stress. We talked about things that the lay person understands as relatively unfortunate but not life-threatening, like depression and headaches.

Britton: Depression is life-threatening.

SR: Well, management might say it is inevitable; if you cannot stand the heat get out of the kitchen. But I have talked to middle managers in government departments who were made redundant, who developed cancers, and their doctors suggest that their condition was probably the result of work-related stress.

Britton: I think stress is recognised as suppressing the immune system and, therefore, permitting infection and cancers to occur. That would probably be over very many years and certainly not in the short timespan I am looking at.

SR: But how would you rate the overall costs of stress?

Britton: Enormous. The costs financially to the institution are considerable; I would say firstly to Medicare, not to the university, of course. But people quite often require time off. It is quite common to have someone who has had no sick leave at all in ten years, yet as a result of stress simply cannot function now. And there is usually a physical symptom that is the final straw, but they end up with time off work. The other cost to the university is that I perceive that the patients have lost their loyalty to the institution, and their willingness to work without pay, because they feel their work is not respected. It does depend on their situation, though. The contract academics work twice as hard and it is just dangerous to their health. Others have become very cynical about the university and say, well they will just do what they have to do and go home on time. So, the university has lost a lot of goodwill and also, I think, it loses creative input of people at all levels. For example, instead of cutbacks in the department, like Architecture, some people may be able to get funding from other institutions. But there is no effort to let them follow that up because they are too busy doing other duties, as staff reductions leave additional mundane work for those left.

SR: I like your point about creativity. If you are a scientist, or sculptor, or social scientist, or doctor it is unlikely that you will be creative under pressure to perform.

Britton: They are too busy surviving the day-to-day activities to have energy left for creativity. Creativity requires support from others and respect for what each does. It is not just the academics. Non-academic staff may see systems that could be better in their office, but channels of confident communication and trials of new ideas are suppressed. A common story is people inheriting responsibilities for which they are not trained and which they do not feel competent to carry out.

Systems or values?

SR: People say, well, you may criticise what we are doing but what is your alternative? You emphasise respect, trust, loyalty, wanting to work for the organisation without financial return. That presupposes enjoying being with one another, working with one another according to what I would call humanitarian values. As senior managers, what would we do, would we behave any differently?

Britton: I do not know. I do not have a problem with hierarchies or with people with at least loosely defined roles because, I think, that seems to make human communities work well. It seems to me, people see a need for a philosophy of systems. Most people are happy to work within the area of their expertise. So, I would not want to be the vice-chancellor. I do not support the 'collective' ideas of the 1970s. I was involved in a collective back then and it was too chaotic. I did not feel clear about what I was meant to be doing or what I was meant to be good at. And I did not think it was appropriate for the secretary to learn to do a pap smear. It is a nice idea but in practice it is just hopeless. So, I have no problem with a structure and defined roles.

SR: Maybe the institutional problem of the health of individuals in a modern organisation, like a university, derives from the overall stress under which the enterprise is operating. Could you comment on your experiences in relation to that perspective?

Britton: Working as a doctor in a large institution that is enacting major budget cuts, I have noticed a major new epidemic of work-induced stress and resultant physical symptoms. There is very significant anguish at a personal level in three groups of people: those leaving or losing jobs; those left behind with impossible workloads and duties for which they are not trained; and those who have to sack others. There the primary role for which they were first employed, that is, teaching and research or support of those who do that. They feel exhausted by workloads, frightened by lack of support and fear of job loss. These presentations remind me of studies I have read of work-related stress early in the twentieth century. It does surprise and shock me that I am seeing this as a doctor in the late twentieth century. I feel as helpless as I imagine the doctors did then.

If there are deemed to be necessary cuts in a budget, it would seem that those responsible for implementing these should also realise they are ultimately dealing with individual human beings who have just the same emotional needs and responses as themselves. The patients feel frightened, hurt and alone facing what they perceive as overwhelming loss of control. It could help if managers express humanity in attempting to communicate support and thanks to their staff in coping with the enormous demands now being placed on many of them. It is hard for the staff to see their job security and financial rewards fall while those of managers rise. There is a strong feeling that the 'administration' does not care, even preferring to get rid of staff who have worked loyally for the institution for years.

Transition

Transition

Parts I to IV present a stark account of the extent of managerial influence on society. A picture emerges of contrived policy yielding profound human costs and lasting damage to the social fabric. What is required is nothing less than a recovery of humanity. This would involve changes in emphases of the kind portrayed in figure 3 (a transformed version of figure 2). Three areas of significance for such an all-embracing transition are identified in order to indicate how a recovery of humanity might be effected — *ideology*, *work* and *money supply* — each being a major theme of chapters 1–17.

Ideological change would produce new intentions and policies, lead to a recovery of public sector status and diminish the perceived financial necessity to exploit domains of common wealth and common ownership, like the environment (figure 3). Motivation for and achievement of such outcomes is considered in part V, in relation to metaphors for humanity of work, play, social movement, common good and reflection (chapters 18–22, respectively).

Transforming ideology

Apparent from the preceding accounts is the profound influence of ideology, from orchestrated think-tank promotion to implemented policies in the areas of labour, education, health and welfare. This has been largely hidden from public view, with managerialism being presented as a politically benign process. By using a drive for greater efficiency and accountability as a smokescreen, controlling interests have

Figure 3: Emphases for Recovery of Humanity

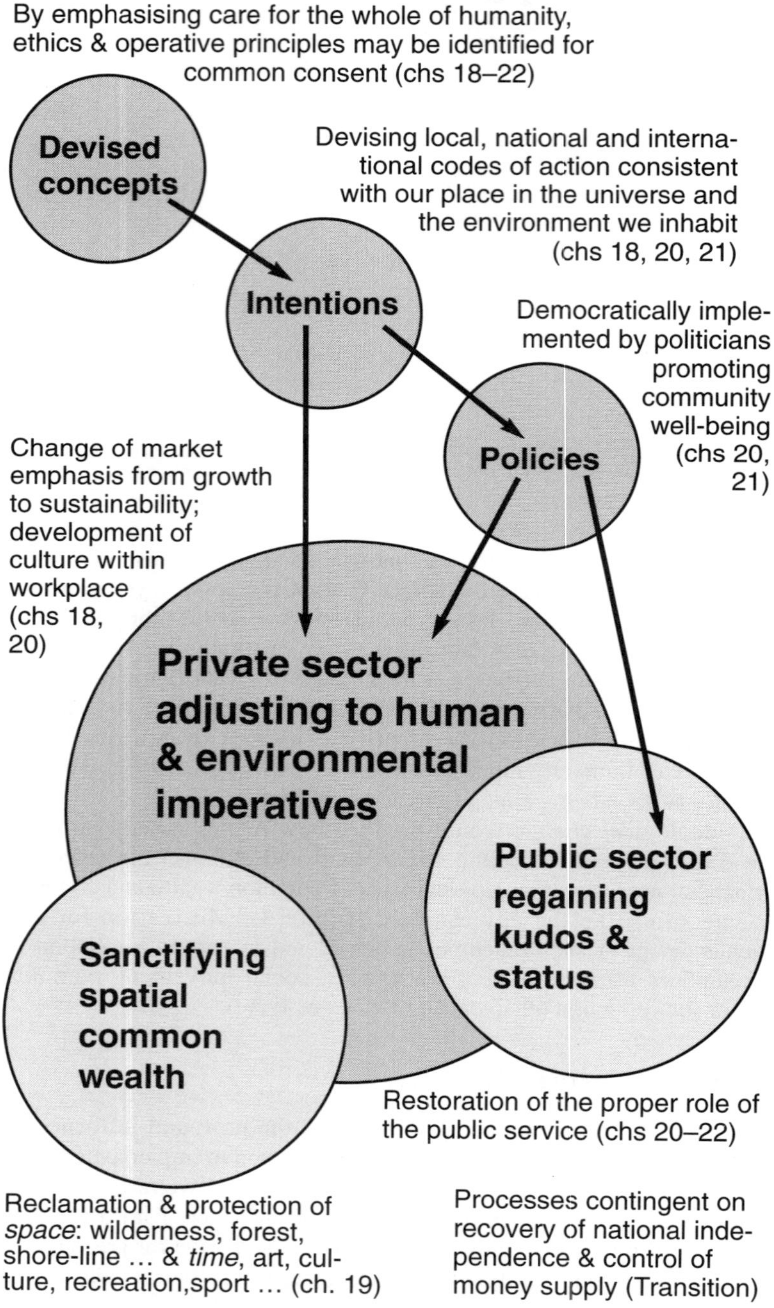

By emphasising care for the whole of humanity, ethics & operative principles may be identified for common consent (chs 18–22)

Devised concepts

Devising local, national and international codes of action consistent with our place in the universe and the environment we inhabit (chs 18, 20, 21)

Intentions

Democratically implemented by politicians promoting community well-being (chs 20, 21)

Policies

Change of market emphasis from growth to sustainability; development of culture within workplace (chs 18, 20)

Private sector adjusting to human & environmental imperatives

Public sector regaining kudos & status

Sanctifying spatial common wealth

Restoration of the proper role of the public service (chs 20–22)

Reclamation & protection of *space*: wilderness, forest, shore-line ... & *time*, art, culture, recreation, sport ... (ch. 19)

Processes contingent on recovery of national independence & control of money supply (Transition) been able to engineer social change on an unprecedented scale. Further, ideology lies behind the manner in which managerialism has been executed, through fraud and fiction, greed and bullying.

Managerialism is the bulldozer of market intent, clearing the ground for a takeover to rival even previous threats to humanity. Governments are both facilitating wholesale dismantling of the restraining influences of public sector bureaucracy and regulation, and systematically transferring public assets to the private sector. Through globalisation of economies, the door is now wide open for even greater exploitation of resources of all kinds. As Noam Chomsky in *Year 501, The Conquest Continues* has put it: 'In the current phase of intellectual corruption ... the economic doctrines preached by the rulers are instruments of power, intended for others, so that they can be more efficiently robbed and exploited ... '.

This book identifies the human costs of pursuing economic policies based solely on the profit motive. Even with the moderating influence of individuals of honour, the bottom line is always the pre-eminence of market forces. Every domain of human endeavour — cultural, sporting and scientific — is being sold to dominating financial interests. Apart from the immense injustices and hardships imposed on the 'losers' in this race to maximise profit and gain, society is losing its collective soul.

Society is becoming increasingly bereft of ways to counter this onslaught, as the reports on child welfare, community services and Victoria's government indicate. To date, no identifiable alternative to economic rationalism is in sight. The only significant response to modern financial practice is the expression of environmental concern. But the impact of this concern is largely thwarted by the strength of the countervailing influences of the market. Multinational companies have virtual carte blanche in many countries to exploit resources at huge expense to ecologies and social infrastructure.

Nonetheless, the environment remains a pivotal focal point because it is also almost the only remaining domain of democratic involvement for citizens. Governments have so profoundly and undemocratically deferred to market demands that democracy has effectively devolved to ecology. But concern for the environment could become a sufficiently potent philosophical imperative to switch political emphasis from doctrinaire worship of the market to stewardship of the concerns of humanity.

Prudent analysis of the immense impact of human activity on the biosphere should engender circumspection and restraint. It would be unwise to assume that current levels of 'growth' are benign.

Tim Flannery, in *The Future Eaters*, highlights the issue for the Australasian region. He comments, 'The problems of catering for continued growth in Australian cities seem almost insurmountable', quoting also A. D. Hope's lines from *Australia* (1995):

> And her five cities, like five teeming sores
> Each drains her: a vast robber state
> Where second-hand Europeans pullulate
> Timidly on the edge of alien shores.

But proponents of the market offer only one solution for national and international problems: 'growth'. From various standpoints the crucial issue is jobs. The market demands the cheapest possible labour to exploit any resource it has appropriated. Humanity desires work, but of a kind that is worthwhile and fulfilling.

Reassessing work

This book is largely about the place of work in people's lives. Work occupies a high proportion of our waking hours and it impinges in a major way on our health, social interactions and sense of well-being. In this regard, managerialism works well for a few but badly for most. A recurring theme of the book is that managerialism is exacting profound human costs from large sections of society. If pressed, its proponents would say that is the price we and the country have to pay in order to make our way in today's world. This certainly appears to be the case if the rhetoric about production and wages having to be internationally competitive is to be believed.

Before responding to that claim it is pertinent to identify features of work we value. Apart from personal satisfaction in making something or providing a service, equitable conditions, considerate colleagues and security of tenure are important. Likewise, having a sense of space within an organisation and an opportunity to express and pursue differences of outlook rate highly. Even a relaxed atmosphere allowing for chatter and gossip is of considerable value to many people facing difficulties elsewhere. These values may be encapsulated in the sentiment of ambience. But market emphases have robbed workers of this sense of spatial equanimity by rigorously controlling space and time in striving to maximise productive and financial gain.

Even techniques being developed to improve relationships and attitudes within organisations have the not-so-hidden agenda of increasing productivity. But where will this end with countless millions joining the international labour market? Will people for ever have to become increasingly more efficient? An associated dimension of current trends is the replacement of work by technology that is driven by the need for managers to reduce costs. Not only is long-term employment threatened but rounds of job-shedding and retraining have to be endured.

Privatisation of the public sector, using instruments of managerialism like outsourcing, has been facilitated by the development of myths about the public sector. The imposition of private sector criteria came in the wake of systematic vilification of the public sector as being 'inefficient', 'overstaffed' and 'wasteful'. What was not recognised was the hidden social value of the public sector. A certain level of slack in the system provided the less tangible benefits of social intercourse, as it did in the private sector. No matter what deficiencies may have existed, the public sector was a 'service' — the 'public service'.

The adoption of market-based practices has had a profound effect on the nature of public sector employment. Those left after 'downsizing' have to work under a range of new constraints — a reduction in funding (related to deregulation and unwillingness to increase taxes) being the primary one. Another crucial factor has been the denigration of the work of professionals and domination of their work by generic managers. This has been exacerbated by the underlying ideological sentiments of those imposing the changes. Attitudes to welfare payments and services have hardened considerably in many countries, enabling governments significantly to reduce funding in many welfare and social service areas. It has been doubly galling to professionals that these cuts helped to usher in a new class of highly paid managers to effect 'efficiency' gains.

Any change in employment will ultimately depend on a change of philosophical emphasis (Introduction, figure 1). Within the managerial context, regaining the role and kudos of the public sector could be a key factor (figure 3). For young people, in particular, traditional employment opportunities would become available again. With recovery of a wide range of positions, the ability to enter work in a more benign manner than possible at present, on-the-job training and the ethos of public service, significant social benefits could be realised.

The recovery of such elements of humanity are considered in part V within the context of metaphor and altered emphases (figure 3). In order to indicate the economic realism of making such a grand proposal as 'the recovery of humanity', a brief comment is needed on the issue of money supply.

Overcoming the illusion of shortage of money

The managerialist discourse about devising ways of being more efficient with money is invariably linked to supposed and indeed contrived notions of a shortage of money, necessitating the introduction of new accounting and monitoring processes. Ironically, though, managerialism is very loose with money when it comes to high-level salaries and consultancies.

Money supply, while crucial, is certainly not an insuperable problem. Governments have the ability to make zero or low-interest loans available for any enterprise. In Australia the Federal Government has powers under section 51 of the Constitution to use the Reserve Bank to issue interest-free or very low-interest credit (loans), as it has many times in the past. Until 1984 when the Federal Government accepted the Campbell Committee recommendation to fully deregulate all financial activities, the Reserve Bank offered 1 per cent loans to various spheres of government for brief periods to cover shortfalls in revenue. Deregulation of the financial system did the opposite of what it was touted to do. Rather than improving the lot of customers through increased competition, the big four Australian banks acted in unison to keep interest rates high and so earn very handsome profits.

The almost unknown, but far-reaching, factor is the fact that private banks are not only incorporated by the government to create credit for the entire economy, but can then lend it out at exorbitant interest rates. Instead of retaining the use of the Reserve Bank to issue credit for essential public works interest-free or for 1 per cent, the government yielded to those demanding deregulation, and governments around Australia now pay market interest of $18 billion annually on their public debts! It is no wonder that 'cuts' have become necessary. The contrived shortage of capital is an illusion, as earlier documented by Frances Milne in *Beyond the Market*. The situation may be readily reversed, given government will and determination to stand up to market dictates and to protect the rights of ordinary citizens. The case for money-supply reform is being cogently argued and promoted by the Sovereignty movement in Australia, the USA, Canada and New Zealand and by the social movement groups Economic Reform Australia and Reworking Australia.

If politicians decide to construct an impressive bridge or build a state-of-the-art frigate, money is readily found. Likewise, the proper demands of humanity may be readily funded, given political will. Consequently, the topics in Recovering Humanity concentrate on primary issues of philosophical and political necessity. But certain changes may be closer at hand than realised, as chapter 18 indicates.

Part V

Recovering Humanity

All One Race

Black tribe, yellow tribe, red, white or brown,
From where the sun jumps up to where it goes down,
Herrs and pukka-sahibs, demoiselles and squaws,
All one family, so why make wars?
They're not interested in brumby runs,
We don't hanker after Midnight Suns;
I'm for all humankind, not colour gibes;
I'm international, and never mind tribes.

Black, white or brown race, yellow race or red,
From the torrid equator to ice fields spread,
Monsieurs and senors, lubras and fraus,
All one family, so why family rows?
We're not interested in their igloos,
They're not mad about kangaroos;
I'm international, never mind place;
I'm for humanity, all one race.

Oodgeroo Noonucaal from Kath Walker, *My People* 1970

Equanimity

Whatever its variants of meat-cuisine, worship, divorce,
human order has at heart
an equanimity. Quite different from inertia, it's a place
where the churchman's not defensive, the indignant aren't on the
　　qui vive,
the loser has lost interest, the accountant is truant to remorse,
where the farmer has done enough struggling-to-survive
for one day, and the artist rests from theory —
where all are, in short, off the high comparative horse
of their identity.
Almost beneath notice, as attainable as gravity, it is
a continuous recovering moment. Pity the high madness
that misses it continually, ranging without rest between
assertion and unconsciousness,
the sort that makes hell seem a height of evolution.
Through the peace beneath effort
(even within effort: quiet air between the bars of our attention)
comes unpurchased lifelong plenishment;

Les Murray (from 'Equanimity' in the
New Oxford Book of Australian Verse 1987)

The Welder

Could have healed Ulster
or joined the Christians to the Shiites
with the same commitment he uses
to peer up the rusty rectum
of my station wagon

while in ungoggled pauses
he explains his forging
of Italian connections
to no-free lunch principles
and hears the complaints
from other casualties

then returns his gun and gaze
to white metal cooling to red
his oxyacetalene sign
to add a two-point-two offering
to seal the kinship lesson
burned into a repaired muffler
and my recall of welding
in unexpected places

Stuart Rees

```
A FAIRLY TYPICAL DISCUSSION
```

What profit a man if he gain the whole world but lose his soul....?

Well, we've done a few figures on that and you might be pleasantly surprised because it seems that there is QUITE a profit. Quite a NICE profit in fact...

And what would the profit be like if you lost, say, half your soul and gained only half the world?

Still very nice! It's a huge audience — a huge market and I'd like you to consider the following: I know a man who has only one sixteenth of his soul left and he's perfectly happy — perfectly happy!!

Leunig

Delight in Enlightenment

What joy to share this fertile earth with
painters, scientists & clowns,
with sculpting symbol-shapers, pithy
dancers' moods leapt up, wept down,
& social critics spinning 'oughts'
& song creators who revise
experience of sights, sounds, thoughts
through convolutions that surprise.

Henry S. Maas (from Tide Pools & Swoosh Holes 1988)

18.
Picturing Contemporary Management

Craig Bremner

Many of the models and patterns which have informed the development of Australia have been borrowed from practices enacted elsewhere. An immediate example is visible in the physical appearance of urban Australia, which is the direct result of a housing type whose origins describe a climate and geographical location other than Australia's. If this is hard to believe, look at heating and cooling costs.

There is nothing inherently wrong with borrowed models. For example, Japan's postwar success is attributed to borrowing selectively from existing patterns of other countries and then reworking them. Indeed, every culture has adapted patterns from another and in time made them their own. While there is nothing unusual about this practice, there are two risks.

The first risk with borrowed patterns is a little like pirating a copy of computer software — there is the program but no manual. In the same way the basic shape and function of the model might be easy to assimilate (or load onto the computer), but it lacks the handy hints, the advice and the cultural peculiarities which give the thing its character, thereby making it useable and, in particular, useable over time; that is, the model risks not fitting the needs. The second risk from borrowing models is visible in the example of Australia's built environment — constructing someone else's world while struggling to make sense of it here. In other words, the risk of not fitting into the pattern.

Australia's housing and the topography of the suburbs are not the only examples of borrowing models from other locations and cultures. Australia's political, economic, educational and industrial structures are direct reflections of models which have evolved elsewhere. The patterns of management used to guide the corporations in Australia, which complete these structures, were also generated elsewhere and, while there have been only two enduring models of organisation, Australia has borrowed and applied each of them with varying degrees of intensity. These two models have been integrated into the lives of Australians through two central metaphors.

The first and most dominant is that of the 'organisation as a machine'. This was proposed by the American Frederick Taylor at the turn of the century with the birth of the machine age, and set the pattern for the pursuit of efficiency throughout the twentieth century in both the commercial and domestic contexts. The second metaphor, advanced by systems theory much later into the century, is of the 'organisation as an organism' with a certain relationship with the business environment, other organisms and with itself (implying that the organisation has a wider set of relationships and reasons for existence other than just profit).

While there have been two models revealed through two metaphors, there has been a single image of corporate organisation. This is the image of the pyramid: the organisation as a hierarchy of distinct functions, or as a chain of command leading to the goal of profit.

Now that society has left the machine age and entered the 'information age' the most dominant medium of communication has become images. Therefore it comes as no surprise that a new 'image' has been projected as an organisational model. The image of the pyramid has been replaced by the image of a square with its interior divided by a grid. This image does not represent a new metaphor but prescribes literally the all-inclusive liturgy of Total Quality Management (TQM).

The TQM name combines an absolute proposition — totality (which is supposed to include every possibility), with a relative notion — quality (which is both ambiguous and complex), to the principles of organisation — management. In effect it is not a new management model but, as its image suggests, a pattern to be overlaid onto organisational practice. TQM prescribes a method which, when applied repeatedly, aims to produce the same measurable outcome. It is a proposal not unlike that put forward by Taylor. His metaphor of the machine as a model of efficiency that organisations should aim to repeat reappears in the TQM pattern. It prescribes a path to maximise the efficiency of repeated actions in response to the question: how does an organisation do what it does and how might it do it better? This is precisely the attraction of the machine in industrial production and the same analogy put forward by Taylor at the turn of the century.

The reality of late-industrial cultures — characterised by the shift from the pursuit of profit to the pursuit of BIG profit — has been the shift from the pursuit of efficiency to the pursuit of BIG efficiency. A visible result is not the dream of a leisure society whose working hours continually diminish, but a rise in working hours, the disappearance of countless full-time positions and the part replacement of these positions with casual or part-time work. This has changed the nature of the functional contract within industrial cultures where needs are satisfied in exchange for labour. It parallels the changed context of organisation from a situation where the actions of consumption and production appeared to be fixed and controllable patterns (ripe for manipulation by efficient management models), to a context where after fifty years of induced desire there exists appearance alone.

That much of the shape and image of the world has changed over the course of the twentieth century is evident to even the most reactionary spectator. The landscape in which actions may be repeated infinitely is no longer recognisable. The context of certainty, simplicity, objectivity and the logic of Taylor's era has been replaced with uncertainty, complexity, subjectivity and contingency. Still, the most popular current model for organisation is predicated on the assumption that an information-rich environment, which increasingly refuses to reveal itself with any definition, can be controlled. The popularity of this model comes from its capacity to paraphrase Taylor's metaphor of machine-like efficiency using new, apparently non-hierarchical, terminology under an apparently democratic image (thereby erasing the old hierarchical pyramid image but leaving the structure intact).

A dependence on the application of a seemingly absolute set of precepts (total?) on an entirely relative concept (quality, when it meant 'reliability' of materials) may have been useful in the machine age when the objective of production was simply a product. Taylorism, in its reconstituted form, TQM, has gained its currency in the information age because its emphasis on the repetition of 'how' suits the objective of the production of services. Ironically, for late-industrial production the necessity for not only more but also new 'stuff' is not addressed in the TQM pattern. The model does not propose a method to include the fundamental question 'what?'. Even more strange is that it does not include 'what next?'.

Perhaps this is not so strange given that people now live in an era where the objective of production is no longer goods nor even services. Now the objective of production is appearance. Society has entered the era of self-production. In a post-industrial society where the once 'scientific' method is now the ethics of 'complexity', the post-modern culture is a fragmented society of mass aesthetics satisfying its desires in a vivid display of mass taste (ironically, this is one end of the relative range of 'quality', the other end being value). What this means is that society has become one in which form is valued over content and in which look dominates character.

It is quite clear from this scenario that for these models of management for organisations there are no more enduring metaphors. The ambiguous frames of reference of both post-modern behaviour and post-industrial complexity have deprived managers of their steady relationship between order and disorder. However, there does exist a model for organisation which since the mid-1970s has not diminished in significance of the changes, nor the rate of change, nor the resulting immateriality of post-industrial society. In fact, it thrives on designing strategies to manage complex concepts, turning them into visible and consumable forms. This is the world of conceptual art where the manager is the artist.

That an 'organisation as a work of art' may even be considered as a metaphor is not such a challenge to the rational belief in organisational principles as it might initially appear to managers. Indeed, the relationship between corporations and art has been developing since the time of the Medici, when the practice of collecting art was established as a sign of the organisation's culture. Surprisingly, recognition of the existence of a corporate culture is a recent discovery. The metaphor of the 'organisation as an organism' brought with it the realisation that the internal management structure created its own life, and was dependent on the sharing of value systems, rules and codes of meaning. The awareness of this culture was not altogether confounding. It brought with it a sense of corporate individuality — the organisation's culture — that was then projected (marketed) via the images and artefacts of the corporation. The marketing areas of organisations invented the corporate imagery of the logo, print graphics, advertising, and so on. In effect all forms of corporate communication transmitted from organisations then had to conform to this aesthetic criteria. As a result of the creation of the artifice of organisations, managers have become increasingly involved in making purely aesthetic decisions, designing purely aesthetic strategies and relating the 'bottom line' to the visual lines of the organisation's image. This is precisely what the conceptual artist does.

Another common vehicle shared by management and conceptual art can be found on the information super-highway. The post-industrial organisation is now entirely dependent on extensive communication systems for its survival. But given that the majority of this information is universal (thereby available to everyone, everywhere, simultaneously) an organisation, which in response to the imperative of being up to date must remain at all times receptive to this common information, runs the risk of being created by the universal currency, trapping it in a position where it can only resemble its competitors. In order to differentiate themselves organisations have to abstract this universal information. The corporation must characterise this information in a particular way in order to distinguish its transmissions from those of its competitors. These transmissions must also attract the consumer because the existence of the consumer creates the service that is the post-industrial organisation's product. All this takes place in the aesthetic realm. Just as the products of the past have dematerialised, so too has the corporation. Where once organisations were visible through their products, corporations now exist as concepts which become actual through their ability to give visibility to their particular abstraction of the universal flow of information. These images of the organisation are created and their transmission guided under the watchful eye of an uncertain management attempting to find a familiar pattern to direct its actions.

Like the modern manager, the conceptual artist utilises extensive communication systems in the creation of the work. Extremely complex signs, symbols, images, text and varying forms of media are designed to include the viewer–consumer in sharing or completing, or consuming complex codes of meanings or services. Unlike the modern manager the conceptual artist does not seek familiar patterns but manages to make visible marks while playing with the appearance of appearances.

Here lies the key to the metaphor of the 'organisation as a work of art' (Carmagnola 1990, 1991).

- If organisations were to relinquish their dependence and emphasis on the model of rational, quantifiable planning they could discover the values of insight, intuition and symbolism which create a real meaning for the notion of 'style' (which has had no meaning as the cliché 'management style').
- The technical–rational machine of efficiency and its dependence on the traditional scientific model could be replaced with a new metaphor emphasising sensuous, aesthetic and 'artistic' aspects of corporate behaviour.
- In this scenario we cease to look at the manager as simply an agent of production, seeing instead the manager in the role of an interpreter of the signs and stories and creator of the images of the organisation to which they belong.
- This new paradigm for organisation creates the scenario where management activity can be seen as something distinct from the simple goal of economic performance. In its place an aesthetic and artistic dimension can relate management activity to the various complex scenarios that earlier codes, in their search for simplicity, failed to grasp.
- The new metaphor can give that desirable angle or twist to the whole of an organisation's behaviour. This could be the much sought-after differentiating factor in a sea of corporate sameness.

That managers and artists have been navigating the same territory may come as a surprise to both protagonists. The value in realising this commonality is twofold. The most obvious is that from the practices of conceptual artists management may learn the ability to *see* and *react* to the world-as-found, without relying on misleading data accumulated from past actions. The landscape is shifting too quickly for this old practice. Resulting from this, and less obvious, is the possibility that if organisations develop along this parallel path then, almost without trying, they might enter the cultural milieu (the real context of the 'market') which they shape and which in turn shapes them. Should this happen, then the violent struggle to fuel and satisfy desire will take on new measures and could ultimately be pacified without the feared loss of profit.

References

Carmagnola, F. 1990, 'Art as a metaphor for organisation', *Flash Art*, vol. 23, no. 153.

―― 1991, 'Art organisations and complexity', *Flash Art*, vol. 24, no. 159.

19.
Promoting the Sporting Ethic

Gordon Rodley

Sporting activity provides considerable individual and collective enjoyment: the excitement of contest, the creativity and skill it produces and the uncertainty of outcomes. Sport embodies a particular set of ethical imperatives, like 'fair play' and 'being a good sport'. It is said to 'build character' and it engenders corrective images, such as 'that's not cricket!'. Sport provides opportunities to test limits of endurance, display skill and experience the fun of social discourse and participation. But this time-honoured innocence is being eclipsed by an incursion of commercial and managerial interests. Sport has become yet another 'product' to be marketed and managed for financial gain.

These changes to sport are used to highlight broader features of market influence on people's lives and to indicate alternatives. Indeed, the recovery of sporting ideals is promoted as a metaphor for the wider recovery of humanity. Amateurism, 'an activity ... fueled by care and affection rather than by profit, and selfish, narrow specialization' (Said 1994), is identified as an appropriate ethical emphasis to advance for all spheres of human endeavour.

The winning streak

The underlying 'market' distortion of the sporting ethic centres on 'winning'. 'Being a good loser' has succumbed to 'winning at all costs' and 'winner takes all'. Of significance is the use of the sporting image of 'winning' by proponents of managerialism. Thus, George

Trumbull, the American executive imported to head AMP, 'brings with him an American management style — motivation, vigour and a highly competitive streak' (Knight 1994). 'It's all about partners, doers and winners', Trumbull, former gridiron player, says. 'I am very tough and very disciplined ...'

There is little concern about 'losers' in the world of finance. Unlike the level playing field of sport, the weak, the dispossessed and the disadvantaged lose out in the competitive world of the free market. When winning dominates the financial world it spawns conflict, impoverishment of the exploited and excessive use of natural resources. Growth and profits become paramount in the striving to beat each other for financial gain.

Commerce has found sport to be a winner. This has occurred with emphases on sophisticated equipment and promotional linkage to prominent codes. Sponsorship has become an unchallenged necessity, advertising ever-present, and corporate boxes a mandatory feature of spectator comforts. Current promotion of a Wallabies Top 100 club is described as a 'new concept in Rugby corporate hospitality'. The nexus between sport and commerce has become so profound that participatory play has been overtaken by managerial promotion of a marketable product.

The new ball game

The sporting scene exemplifies the market takeover of society, but also offers a model for recovery. Stilwell (1977) highlighted repercussions of the commercialisation of sport at an early stage, while Lawrence and Rowe (1986) provided a comprehensive account, from an Australian perspective, of the situation in the mid-1980s. In this assessment, sports journalists are cited to give an up-to-the-minute report on the continuing, tightly contested game. Commerce is forging ahead, gaining greater ground, while traditionalists struggle to 'hold the line' on sporting norms. Players breach rules in displaying the logo of a prominent maker of shoes. Sports officials counter by imposing fines (Australian cricketers in New Zealand, 1995) and providing no-logo caps (Australian Open, 1995). Elsewhere, reporters argue about principles of sport as a betting-on-cricket controversy flares. Meanwhile, mogul giants jostle for lucrative control of sporting codes, among hype of super-this and super-that. The play for gain is intense, with sport seemingly close to losing its essence. Sidelined from play, passive viewers watch professionals performing on cue. With vicarious delight people ogle their play, not noticing themselves being enmeshed by the 'market's' monetary agenda.

How is it that people have so readily given up the joy of play for viewing? In part, it is because they remain involved as they invariably support one competitor or team against another. People love to be on a winning side and that is what the marketeers depend on. Rather than playing into their hands we could regain the initiative by taking the game into ours. For the sake of self and humanity we need to be in the game, not on the sideline wishing for wins. When properly constituted, universal amateur sport engenders social goodness. It enhances conviviality, openness, generosity and cultural respect. Recovery of the sporting ethic could be a metaphor for a wider freeing of the human spirit from a preoccupation with monetary gain.

'Marketing' hype

As with other domains of human endeavour, the market has captured sporting codes for the inherent value these offer. Sport is simply another avenue for furthering financial interests. It is a goldmine, like so many features of human goodness, being coopted into market-based programs for making money. The market has become all-pervasive and all-invasive. Yesterday it took communications, today it wants water; nothing is sacrosanct, even our very selves, as indicated by Jerry Goodis, advertising manager for Benetton: 'in a sense what we are doing (in advertising) is wrapping up your emotions and selling them back to you'.

No one escapes the impact, certainly not top sporting personalities under immense pressures to promote as well as perform. Commercial takeover, as exemplified especially in the American baseball and basketball scene, has led to two major distortions of sport. Players push their rights with apparent impunity and supporters are marginalised. With the advent of very high salaries and idol status, players are disdaining sporting honour, commitment and sensitivity and becoming loutishly demanding. As Olsen (1995) has commented, 'what is happening as baseball's spring training camps opened this week [with top players not appearing] ... [is] ... all because a few hundred-millionaire athletes and their multimillion employers can't agree to play a kids' game'.

The TV fix

Television is the technological means by which the market plunders sport and changes social norms. Rather than playing a game, or observing it as a member of a crowd, involvement with sport for many is the doubly removed activity of watching it on a small screen. The dimensions of social interplay, the broad sweep of the ground, the feel of the air and the choice of view are reduced to flickering pixels on a light-emitting screen. Even with colour, close-up views and action replays the game has become a spectacle to observe rather than an activity to experience. No longer is it possible to respond intimately to the action. In a crowd people could shout. On the field people may influence outcomes. To the detriment of physical, cerebral and spiritual growth, passivity has replaced involvement.

Passivity has been compounded by commercialism. The sporting screen has become a vehicle for invading the mind with the titillating half-truths of advertising agencies. No longer can cricket be viewed for uninterrupted hours, punctuated only by the intermittent remarks of discreet commentators. Play comes sandwiched between commercial breaks, with overlays of sponsorship hype. This apparently acceptable format certainly pays, as demonstrated by one advertised car's dramatic sales during the 1994–95 Australian cricket season.

High sporting spectacle, once linked to people's passion for sport, offers advertisers a dream run. As TVNZ's new programming chief, Mike Lattin, has put it (McKewen 1995):

> Sport is now a driving force on television around the world. It's ... as important [a] prime time commodity as many of the top entertainment programmes ... in terms of economics, we make a lot more money by putting sport to air in prime time ... sponsors are very anxious to see their association with sport in prime time ... Sport is now a major daily event in people's lives ... I want to give fans a whole half hour of sport each night [at 10.30] ... People will hang in there for their nightly fix of sport.

Managerial game plan

With the invasion of sport by commerce has come the firm arm of managerialism. No longer can unpaid amateurs benignly run a sporting code. Experts who know the score and consultants' touting skill must be engaged to optimise financial gain. The game becomes subservient to commercial concern. An accompanying change in philosophy results, as illustrated by annual reports of the New Zealand Rugby Union for 1991 and 1993 (*Annual Report*, 1991, 1993). In 1991 the council stated:

> it is planned to review ... ways in which our rugby can be funded. In doing so it is intended that while we will maximise the commercial opportunities available we will also observe our strong philosophy that the proceeds from commercial activities must be used for the benefit of all rugby players at all levels of the game.

A different emphasis is discernible in 1993:

> unlike in previous years where sponsorship was a much looser arrangement ... contracts we have with sponsors are now very much business relationships ... From time to time there can be difficulties in that the rugby ethos of those involved in playing and

administering an amateur game can mean that stringent obligations of the business relationship may be overlooked.

The corresponding commercialisation of New Zealand cricket is even more explicit. In the annual report of New Zealand Cricket Inc. (1993–94) the chairman states: 'The operation of New Zealand cricket is now in three distinct units — Finance and Administration, Marketing and Promotion, and Cricket'.

Through such changes of emphasis, social and humanitarian dimensions are squeezed into the one-dimensional tunnel of monetary interest. While the influence is always measured and adaptable, there is little need for circumspection because of the insatiable global appetite for sport of any kind. So long as viewers continue to watch and crowds come by, the show goes on. Adverse influences are overlooked and may remain unrecognised.

Unsporting play

Sports writers are highlighting the adverse repercussions of the market takeover of sport:

> The people's game is in danger of being hijacked by business. A News Limited-run super league would be driven by profits. [T]hey (those old men who started the game ... with flint-hard faces and telling eyes ... railway porters and wharfies, noble jobs then as now ...) have been replaced by a new breed of administrator, infinitely more avaricious and less caring. (Masters 1995)

and: 'Rupert Murdoch has a history of paying whatever it takes to secure football broadcasting rights. Sport is part of the strategy for his global media empire ...' (Mychasuk 1995).

A central feature of market impact on sport is the close association developed with smoking and alcohol. While cigarette promotion has been extensive, this is gradually changing. For example, the New Zealand government has enforced a ban. But another connection remains strongly entrenched, 'that, sad, deadening nexus between booze and sport' (Wells 1994). In both Australia and New Zealand alcohol is vigorously promoted in association with sport, with advertising on the media occurring to blatant excess. Wells says: 'it is hard to picture winning Aussies these days without sponsors' beers in their mitts'. Wells looks to a time when it 'will be possible to bond without booze ... [and] ... cope without booze when the glory days [for sportspeople] are over'.

Then there is the major issue of spectator violence. Again a sports reporter comments on the conflict of interests:

> It has been argued recently that English football, corrupted by rampant commercialism and beset by evidence of sleaze, is lacking in

responsibility. Those in the game who feel no great obligation to society, those for whom profit is a god, should study closely the pictures of last night's violence [referring to the riot at the England v Ireland match in Dublin on 15 February 1995]. (Jones 1995)

The current global crisis in sport has been referred to as 'a sporting apocalypse' (Huxley 1995). 'Never before ... has the "beautiful idea" of sport — and the very notion of being a "good sport" — been more at risk. For that, blame the communications revolution as much as commercialism' (Huxley 1995).

All work and no play

While sport has become part of the market whole, by being coerced, the way the market manages workers affects sporting involvement. Its high demand on employee productivity and time diminishes the opportunity for leisure:

> In our determination to achieve faster economic growth and a rising standard of living, we must avoid the risk of creating an Australia that is richer — but not worth living in.
>
> We don't want to be a nation of workaholics, with all of us able to afford a yacht but not the time to sail it ... (Gittins 1994a)
>
> Australians are now among the hardest workers in the developed world [and] the trend towards more hours appears to be long-term rather than cyclical. (Verrender 1994)

The overriding emphasis of managerialism is greater worker output, as indicated by a preoccupation with 'efficiency'. Employees at all levels, including managers, are placed under considerable pressures to give more and more time to work.

Thus the appropriate recreation for many, tired after long hours of work, becomes watching sport on television or watching a match live. The nexus between demanding work and vicarious sport neatly satisfies the requirements of the captains of industry. Sport as entertainment has become a new 'opiate of the people'. In any situation driven by an overriding factor (in the modern world, the making of money) parallel and symbiotic features develop accordingly. Any breaking of the link between commerce and sport therefore involves a fundamental questioning of capitalism.

Promoting play

The requirement for a recovery of unimpeded play is nothing less than an about turn on capitalism. The market may be 'producing the goods' for some, but it is neither ecologically sustainable nor socially equitable. Directions for necessary change can only be briefly referred to here.

One concerns the overriding emphasis on 'growth', the catchcry that drives the commercial world and underlies reduced opportunities for cultural and sporting involvement. A recent reflection on this issue ('The fly in the ointment (growth) is the increasing insistence of our scientists that it can't go on much longer' (Gittins 1994b)) is prefaced by a significant admission: 'I try not to think about it, but every so often it worms back into my consciousness. What if our economy is going entirely in the wrong direction? What if the economics that I, among thousands of others, help to teach and preach is leading us to perdition?'. There is an urgent need for the disastrously self-defeating tactic of 'growth' to be replaced by a strategy of *sufficiency*. This would lead to lower levels of productive activity, less stress on the environment and less work and more play for all.

An accompanying tactic for 'play' would be sharing. Adele Horin (1994) identifies mollycoddling of the rich as a central issue ('the government has treated the top class with remarkable compassion and understanding') and suggests that 'sharing might be the right philosophy for the '90s'. Horin points out the sense of requiring the wealthy to share a little: 'Such wealth-sharing measures [outlined in the article] would hardly cramp their style, just curtail their ability to get even further ahead'. Sharing would enable the poor more readily to cope and to enjoy equality of play.

If a less frenetic approach to work and production can be achieved, it will be necessary to consider leisure more closely, as started to occur in the 1970s when it was assumed working hours would continue to decrease steadily. Sport is undoubtedly a key factor. But providing sporting opportunities is not a problem, as seen by the growth of facilities for retirees. In the cities many sporting facilities, such as tennis courts, are under-utilised. What may be required is a drive for much wider participation for the young to middle-age bracket. A review of sport in Australia (Vamplew & Stoddart 1994) provides information on the historical extent of the national involvement in sport.

The position of unemployed people is particularly critical with respect to sport. While time is available for play, viewing is more likely to be the psychologically preferred option. Sandra Coney (1995) has identified the conundrum in an article, 'Why young men are falling by the wayside':

> The downturn of the economy, the increased competitiveness of the job market, unemployment and the loss of apprenticeship schemes have removed work as a secure source of identity and pride for many young men. And the heroics surrounding sport, driven by increased commercialism, reinforce young men's feelings of being losers. They are intimidated by the elite sporting celebrities who are held up to them to admire.

In this case the 'play' to promote is work. Many reasonable and viable suggestions have been made for overcoming unemployment, including the premise of sharing work opportunities (e.g. Rees & Rodley 1993; Langmore & Quiggin 1994). The *dignity of work* is an absolute prerequisite for the game of life.

These sentiments for change are widely agreed, but people are caught in a political log-jam. With politicians enslaved by the market, hope for a way out is slim. The sell-out on human values has been profound. Recovery is likely to require a renewed appropriation of the ideals of humanity, but sudden change can be effected by creative political initiatives. While these are rare, Australasia has seen two significant examples: New Zealand going anti-nuclear, and implementation of Australia's High Court decision in favour of Aboriginal land rights. Both involved a measure of flair.

Regaining amateur flair

The challenge for change, while essentially related to excessive profit-making, requiring appropriate economics, also involves the vexed question of professionalism. Top sportspeople may be able to make substantial sums of money as professionals, but that is often at the long-term cost of permanent physical or psychological injury. The level of commitment required in training, travel and time is extreme. While high financial reward is certainly merited, other factors, besides physical health, such as education, must be considered in assessing the overall benefits of playing professional sport.

Is there a better way to combine high-level sporting involvement with an ability to retain a normal lifestyle, as in traditions of amateurism? An outcome of the Ben Johnson disqualification at the Seoul 1988 Olympics was a wide-ranging analysis of the role of sport in Canada. Subsequent proposals included one to 'develop strategies to raise the profile of amateur sports ... [and] ... to offset the dominance of professional sports ... mostly on television' (Wilcox 1994, pp. 365–75). A cynical response (Cox 1992) nonetheless illustrates the potential of such proposals: 'Imagine happy, united Canadians participating in sports, loving fair play ... disclaiming professional games on TV to watch well trained amateur athletes ... Seem a little idealistic? Naive? Yup'. Many top sportspeople could find enhanced sporting enjoyment as amateurs. Peter Roebuck (1994) has written about his greater enjoyment of playing amateur cricket after retiring from the professional game. Australian netball is a good model of a high-participation amateur game (Vamplew & Stoddart 1994, pp. 169–71).

Market domination of sport raises certain issues of principle for sportspeople. Endorsement of products, while lucrative, produces additional pressures to act in accord with sponsor demand. With a growing emphasis on winning at all costs, play has become dominated by an analytical scrutiny of factors which produce success. Opponents' play is video-analysed, psychological techniques are employed, and dietary and training techniques refined. While such developments undoubtedly enhance performance, these can destroy essential elements of sport, such as risk-taking, flair and inventiveness — hallmarks of the amateur. What is often left is a cautious professional determination not to lose.

A telling example of the influence of financial interests is the sacking at the end of 1994 (*SMH* 1994) of Ossie Ardiles, former soccer player of style, as manager of Tottenham Hotspur. Alan Sugar, founder of electronic giant Amstrad, had bought Tottenham Hotspur three years earlier. 'Sugar arrived on the scene, egged on by Rupert Murdoch, whose BSkyB satellite station was dependent on winning the rights for TV soccer. The Amstrad boss, a maker of satellite dishes, approached Tottenham as a businessman rather than a fan.' 'In the ensuing battle between the manager who dreamed of the beautiful game and the uncompromising businessman, there could be only one winner.' Ardiles was apparently more focused on scoring goals than ensuring Tottenham was not defeated. Various comments reveal his approach: 'I believe football is an art. It is not a science, not about a computer. Football is an art and a beautiful one if played properly', and 'Maybe I dream too much. I go for beauty. If you left it to me, I would play with a goalkeeper and 10 front players' (*SMH* 1994). But that would not guarantee financial success.

The amateur role has wider social significance. Edward Said (1994) has called for a universal retreat from the growth of professionalism towards recovery of amateur ideals. Society has gone too far by way of specialisation in all walks of life. Professionalism may appear to engender greater efficiency of operation, but life is a much more interlinked phenomenon, requiring innate knowledge derived from experiences of participation. People require wider views for creative play to displace this preoccupation with efficiency, managing outcomes and programming specialist skill. They have become less able to be flexible, creative and capable of acting with largesse and discretion. People require the David Campese rugby flair of seeing the whole unimpeded by time. Only then might they breach the market's apparently impenetrable wall of opposition to humanity and regain the pleasure of playing.

A sporting chance

Sport provides a metaphor for the recovery of humanity. It demonstrates the adverse repercussions of market encroachment into sacrosanct domains of human activity. And it provides in the amateur tradition a model for perceiving how people might circumvent such domination. Implicit in amateurism is the delight for all of being able to 'have a go'. To realise this we must reject market control and prescriptive managerialism. Let us protest against the commercialisation of sport and resist it in practical ways. Let us become amateurs again, free to invent improbable play that guarantees delight. We need no schema, neither promoter nor charismatic leader, just flair. The sporting ethic can be reclaimed.

The metaphor of sport encourages higher possibilities of emergent play; of overcoming apparently insurmountable odds. It has been fashionable to give free rein to baser instincts, believing these would be our souls' salvation. Let the market rule supreme, they preached, not seeing fault. It is time to bring false prophets crying 'Greed is Good' to heel and give humanity a chance to make the running. Who knows what better hope we may perceive once creative play finds space, cleared of managers? We may learn that fair play and level playing field mean equality of opportunity for all to play; equality to have basic needs for shelter, food, education and health met. Idealistic? Yes!

References

Coney, S. 1995, 'Why young men are falling by the wayside', *Sunday Star-Times* (NZ), 22 February.
Cox, B. 1992, 'A dose of athletic nationalism', *London Free Press*, 8 May.
Gittins, R. 1994a, 'How to be happy as well as rich', *Sydney Morning Herald*, Monday Comment, 28 November.
——1994b, 'When more is no longer sustainable', *Sydney Morning Herald*, 23 November.
Horin, A. 1994, 'Eat the rich? No, just get them to share', *Sydney Morning Herald*, 11 May.
Huxley, J. 1995, 'A sporting apocalypse', *Sydney Morning Herald*, 1 March.
Jones, K. 1995, 'Riot catapults England back into the dark days', *Sydney Morning Herald*, 17 February.
Knight, E. 1994, 'US executive to head AMP', *Sydney Morning Herald*, 5 May.
Langmore, J. & Quiggin, J. 1994, *Work for All*, Melbourne University Press, Melbourne.
Lawrence, G. & Rowe, D. 1986, *Power Play: Essays in the Sociology of Australian Sport*, Hale & Iremonger, Sydney.
McKewen, T. 1995, 'TV chief: I'll be good sport', *Sunday Star-Times* (NZ), 5 February.
Masters, R. 1995, 'Where profit will come before people', *Sydney Morning Herald*, 6 February.
Mychasuk, M. 1995, 'News bid is part of global TV push', *Sydney Morning Herald*, 6 February.
New Zealand Cricket Inc. 1993–94, *Annual Report*. p. 6.
New Zealand Rugby Union 1991, *Annual Report*, p. 6.
——1993, *Annual Report*, p. 15.

Olsen, L. 1995, 'Scab ball: game where players and bosses all strike out', *Sydney Morning Herald*, 24 February.
Roebuck, P. 1994, 'Amateur cricket offers fields of freedom', *Sydney Morning Herald*, 19 September.
Rees, S. & Rodley G. 1993, 'A proposal for the provision of "full" employment', in S. Rees, G. Rodley & F. Stilwell, *Beyond the Market*, Pluto Press, Sydney.
Said, E. W. 1994, *Representations of the Intellectual: The 1993 Reith Lectures*, Vintage, London.
Stilwell, F. 1977, 'Political economy of sport and pop music', *Journal of Australian Political Economy*, no. 1, p. 83.
Vamplew, W. & Stoddart, B. (eds) 1994, *Sport in Australia*, Cambridge University Press, Melbourne.
Verrender, I. 1994, 'Bludgers no more', *Sydney Morning Herald*, 1 October.
Wells, J. 1994, 'Boozing and losing — a hangover from another era', *Sydney Morning Herald*, 3 November.
'Why a visionary bit the dust' 1994, *Sydney Morning Herald*, report, 4 November.
Wilcox, R. C. (ed.) 1994, *Sport in the Global Village*, Fitness Information Technology Inc., Morgantown, WV.

20.
Reworking Australia

Frank Stilwell

The title of this chapter refers to humanitarian aspirations such as employment opportunities for all citizens. It draws attention to a social movement of that name which, since 1992, has been pressing for more progressive economic policies. It also suggests a broader project — the reconstruction of a nation that works better because its people do socially productive work. It is in developing this latter theme that the concerns which led to the formation of the Reworking Australia social movement can be best illustrated. This requires both a critique and the outline of a progressive alternative strategy for economic and social change.

The essential requirement is to build an alternative economics 'as if people mattered'. Developing this would indeed contribute to hope for humanity.

The fundamental problem with the prevailing corporate capitalist managerialism is that it treats people like conventional economic theory treats labour — as a factor of production — as a thing in the service of profits. This is ultimately self-defeating because, by denying their essential humanity, the economic system treats people in a manner to which they cannot ultimately lend allegiance. No economic, political or social system which systematically thwarts the aspirations of most of the people can be indefinitely sustained. The reaction to managerialism can be interpreted in this context as part of this reassertion of the goals of human emancipation, liberation and social progress.

Micro-managerialism — macro-managerialism

Managerialism confronts people daily in its diverse 'micro' forms: as more or less authoritarian practices in the workplace, in the access to social security benefits, in the health and education services, in the selective informational flows shaped by media conglomerates, and so forth. Managerialism also has its 'macro' or aggregate form. In part this can be regarded as the systemic aggregation of these various 'micro' elements. It is something more too. It is a particular political economic system, involving distinctive interests and values prescribing particular policies and proscribing other practices. It is a system of corporate capitalism which, despite its promises of greater economic efficiency and material well-being, is reducing economic security, generating economic inequality and fracturing social cohesion.

What is the essence of this macro-managerialism? Some would say it is just 'business as usual' for the capitalist system. Capitalism, from its inception, has been a system based on class relationships due to differential ownership of the means of production. Capital employs labour, not vice versa. The need for a dominant class to control the work force in order to produce an economic surplus is rooted in the normal functioning of this type of economy. Historically, such managerial techniques have emphasised Taylorism ('scientific management'), the use of machinery to control the place of work ('technical control') and diverse means of control via sticks and carrots embedded in promotions procedures and career structures ('bureaucratic control'). Contemporary experiments with different managerial forms adapted from Japan ('Toyotaism') are a variant of this theme. So too is the industrial relations and business school fad for human resources management. However, these techniques all serve the same macro-systemic goals — maximum profits relative to labour costs. That is what is meant by 'business as usual' for capitalism.

Can such an economic system create rewarding lives for the majority of the population? The positive view of the system is that because it is uniquely geared to capital accumulation it can be expected to feature a more or less continuous expansion of productive capacity and thus an increased flow of material goods and services. Satisfaction comes to consumers whether or not they are fulfilled as workers. No doubt the system has proved impressive in this respect — as a producer of a vast array of commodities. But the associated problems are manifold. Incomes (and therefore capacity to afford consumer goods) are highly inequitably distributed. Periodic recessions interrupt economic growth. Environmental constraints on growth are (or should be) biting harder. Most fundamentally, there is now growing recognition that people's principal sources of satisfaction — personal security, social recognition and interesting work — are often destroyed in the preoccupation with production and consumption (Lane 1991). Commodity fetishism proves ultimately unfulfilling.

There are also new elements in the system. Since the 1980s there has been substantial reorganisation of the capitalist economy worldwide. Technological change has opened up new production possibilities and information flows. The industrialisation of some hitherto poor Third World countries has caused a spatial rearrangement of many industries on a global scale. The commanding position enjoyed by multinational corporations and international financial institutions has given rise to an increased concentration of economic power. The collapse of the communist state alternative in the former USSR seems to have cleared away the main challenger to capitalist hegemony. New Right ideologies have flourished in these circumstances and led to important changes in the role of the state in many capitalist countries. The balance of power between capital and labour has tilted yet more firmly towards the former.

Contemporary managerialism can be interpreted in this context. It is not just 'business as usual' for capitalism, but a set of ideas and practices designed to integrate workers and citizens into contemporary global capitalist restructuring. In the process of habituating the victims of structural economic change into acceptance of its necessity and desirability, it legitimises an economic system characterised by increasing economic insecurity and economic inequality.

Insecurity and inequality

The trend towards growing unemployment is the most obvious manifestation of contemporary economic restructuring. This is not just a feature of periodic recessions; it has become a permanent feature of the economic landscape. Figure 4 shows the trend in Australia. By contrast with the consistently low unemployment rates in the 'long boom' of the 1950s and 1960s, the officially recorded unemployment levels since the 1970s have been climbing in a stepwise manner. Each recession takes unemployment to a higher peak, and the interim recoveries never get the level back to that which previously prevailed. Among the unemployed, the share of people who have been out of work for a year or more has been steadily rising, and in 1995 stood at approximately 40 per cent of the total unemployed.

This problem of long-term unemployment was the principal focus of the Federal Government's Working Nation package announced in May 1994. Only one year short of a half-century since the 1945 White Paper which embodied a previous Labor government's commitment to policies for full employment, this was a welcome initiative. However, the Keynesian focus on macroeconomic stimulus

Figure 4: Australia's Unemployment Rate (% of labour force)

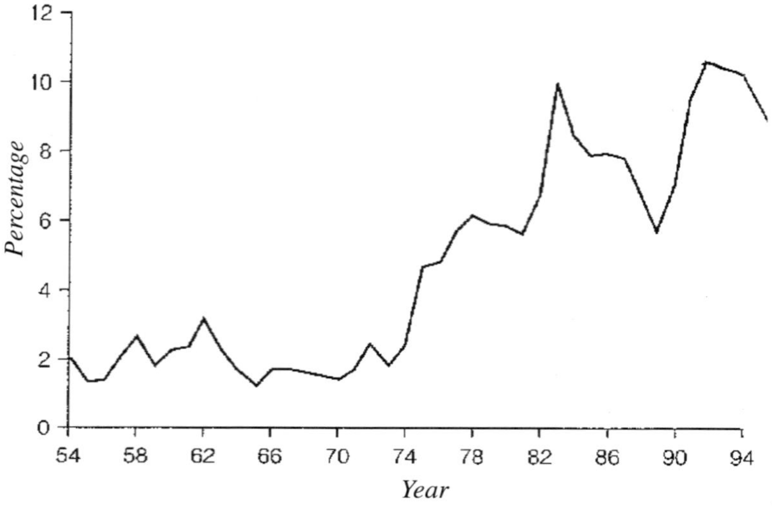

which characterised that previous policy stance is now replaced by 'fine tuning' of the labour market targeted at the long-term unemployed. That is the significance of the 'jobs compact' which promises a period of subsidised employment with the threat that benefits will be temporarily withdrawn from people who do not accept a 'reasonable' job offer. The underlying economic changes causing the unemployment in the first place are not tackled (Stilwell 1994b). Rather, the implicit assumption is that more rapid structural change is both necessary and welcome — hence the ongoing commitment to cuts in tariffs on imported goods and the further integration of the national economy into global capitalism.

Managerialism in this context means accommodation to structural changes arising from competition in the international marketplace. For many of the unemployed it means accommodation to a more-or-less permanently marginalised position.

Other aspects of growing economic insecurity impact on those who are employed. Here the most striking trend is the growth of contract, casual and part-time employment as manifestations of the push for a more 'flexible' work force. Some aspects of this flexibility have potential benefits for employees, in permitting people to integrate paid work with their domestic interests and responsibilities. But, in general, this flexibility better serves the interests of corporate profitability. The higher echelons of management are rewarded with ever higher salaries and the perquisites of office, while at the other extreme the workers in 'secondary labour markets' face increasing economic insecurity. The gulf is also revealed in the dispersion of working hours. Some people work very long hours, an official survey in 1995 showing that 20 per cent work over 49 hours per week, while others are denied any regular employment.

Like economic insecurity, economic inequality has been here for a long time. However, there is powerful evidence that it is now sharply increasing *(Economist* 1994; Raskall 1993; Stilwell 1994a). The mechanisms generating greater inequalities had previously been restrained by the defensive actions of trade unions and the partially redistributive policies of governments. These buffers are now less effective, themselves in danger of being swamped by the effects of structural economic change. The balance of power has tilted sharply towards capital and away from the organisations of labour and the state.

The phenomenon of the 'shrinking middle' in the income distribution is one obvious manifestation of the growing economic inequality. In Australia, as in other advanced capitalist countries like the USA and the UK, there has been a widening gulf between the rich and the poor. In part this is because of the disappearance of mid-income-range jobs, especially in manufacturing industries. In part, it is also the consequence of a general fall in the share of wages in the national income relative to incomes from profits, interest, rent and professional fees. There are major redistributions under way, with potentially very powerful consequences for social problems and social cohesion. The American situation, where the wealthy take refuge in walled, security-patrolled residential enclaves, leaving the streets to a marginalised underclass, is already a looming prospect for Australian cities. Structural economic change and the associated managerialism comes at a massive social cost.

Economics as if people mattered

Is there an alternative? The proponents of the 'conventional wisdom' in economics assert that there is not. Following the dictates of the market is both inevitable and desirable, subject to relatively minor qualifications. This is the claim of economic rationalism, the belief in the superiority of free-market forces over government intervention. The influence of this economic ideology in the Australian bureaucracy has been documented by Michael Pusey (1993). Its broader social influence is evident daily in the media, especially in the regular columns of economic and financial journalists. What is involved is a set of economic beliefs which has come to dominate debate about economic issues. Effectively, it negates debate, as illustrated by the absence of fundamental differences in the economic policies of the two major political parties.

However, alternative perspectives are possible. Economic rationalism has been subjected to various forms of critique, dealing with its shaky theoretical foundations, dubious ethical basis and its practical failures. Preceding chapters in this book have documented the deficiencies of the associated managerialist practices in many areas of society. It is possible to confront these prevailing orthodoxies with an 'economics as if people mattered'. This is not a new concept (see, for example, Schumacher 1973), but contemporary developments make its further development more urgent. The key element is to reorient economic thinking and economic policy so that they serve human needs.

Addressing the problems of economic insecurity and economic inequality must be the key aspect of this alternative approach. The concepts of nurturing, building and sharing thereby replace the 'cut and thrust' approach to economic policy issues.

Nurturing is the obvious place to start. Resource creation is more fundamental than resource allocation, the primary focus of conventional economic theory. The creation of human resources — as in putting child-care, health, education and work force training centre stage is essential to improved productivity. Similarly, nurturing new industries requires attention to the institutional processes needed for linking innovation and entrepreneurship, the establishment and growth of small and medium-sized businesses, and building cooperative industrial relations. Free-market competition on a level playing field is effective in weeding out inefficient industries, as seen as a result of tariff cuts in Australia, but it does little to foster the creation of new industries. The concept of nurturing provides an alternative starting point.

Building follows on. This requires a substantial role for the public sector in laying the foundations for a more balanced economic development. It requires planning and foresight rather than reaction to short-term market signals. The provision of infrastructure is one key element. This aspect of public expenditure needs to be recognised as capital spending, quite different in character from recurrent expenditure items, and a prerequisite for more balanced development. A second aspect of building involves the more systematic use of workers' savings in superannuation funds, variously estimated to rise to as much as $600 billion by the end of the 1990s. The establishment of a National Investment Fund could help to coordinate the disposition of superannuation funds and to ensure their productive use in developing Australian industries. A third aspect of building involves policies to develop 'green jobs' compatible with the often stated goal of ecologically sustainable development. There are plentiful opportunities here in areas such as energy-provision, recycling, waste management and transportation. Australian scientists are at the forefront of research in some of these fields, including solar energy, and there are good prospects for exports of more environmentally-sound products. The necessary structural changes need to be fostered through coordinated action — hence the need for positive initiatives rather than a passive reliance on market forces.

Sharing is the final element. Sharing of work is a means of taking advantage of technological change while ensuring that its benefits are dispersed throughout the work force. It can help overcome the irrationality and inhumanity of some being denied leisure because of their long working hours while others are denied effective leisure because they have no work. The mechanisms of sharing and the implications for levels of wage incomes are problematic issues to confront. So too is the relationship between sharing waged work and the social valuation of all work, including domestic work and other creative pursuits. The faltering steps towards a new means of evaluating gross national product, taking account of domestic work, leisure and the externalities associated with environmental degradation, puts these issues on the agenda. The point here is that this needs to be more than a measurement agenda, a new basis for national income accounting; it also needs to be an agenda for policy changes. A guaranteed minimum income scheme could provide an effective starting point. Over and above that, tax reform to link tax rates more effectively to 'ability to pay' is warranted, which means consideration of wealth taxes (for wealth in excess of, say, $1 million) inheritance taxes, and the termination of the system of full imputation which allows income from dividends to be effectively tax free.

These are merely a few illustrations of rethinking economic policy. They suffice to indicate how an approach to economic policy which emphasises nurturing, building and sharing cuts against the grain of conventional thinking. This alternative approach challenges the prevailing emphasis on rationalisation through competitive processes in the market and (dare one use the term?) 'incentivation'. But it makes more sense both within organisations and for the economy as a whole. Within organisations it emphasises these aspects of cooperation, which are conducive to a sense of well-being and high morale as well as improvements in productivity. Effective teamwork requires a belief that there will be fair shares in the outcome. This is precisely the opposite direction to the economic changes which are generating a growing gulf between the incomes of top executives, ordinary workers and a class of welfare recipients.

For the Australian economy as a whole, the policy approach advocated here means that, rather than competing in terms of cheapened labour and production costs in which Australia inevitably loses out to low-wage countries in the region, we become a world leader in a more qualitative sense. We show the rest of the world the advantages of balanced economic–social–environmental values. We build on those features of our current lifestyle in which we do indeed have an international 'comparative advantage' but which we are in danger of losing if trends persist. Australia can be an international exemplar of how to create a good society through 'economics as if people mattered'.

Is this really such a far-fetched ideal? There is no shortage of policy instruments for achieving changes towards a more egalitarian and self-reliant socioeconomic system. What is more fundamentally at issue is the political will. How to galvanise support around a more progressive economic alternative? How to effect political change? These remain the key questions for activists concerned to confront the twin ravages of economic rationalism and managerialism characterised by indifference to human costs and a preoccupation with narrowly defined economic criteria.

Reworking Australia

The foregoing concerns have been reflected in Reworking Australia. This social movement was formed in 1992, in the depths of economic recession, with unemployment in Australia running at over 11 per cent, the highest level since the Great Depression of the 1930s. It was never intended to be a political party. Rather, it set out to be a pressure group to focus on the social crisis of unemployment and to press for more progressive economic policies. It brought together individuals from various walks of life, including church groups, welfare groups, academics and community activists.

How can the impacts which a group like Reworking Australia can have ever be identified? Public meetings and rallies were held, petitions and submissions were sent to the Federal Government, some regional branches were set up, a little media coverage was achieved, and so on. Together with pressure from other interest groups, it may be claimed that some impact has been made. For example, for all its limitations as a new social charter, the government's Working Nation statement has given some extra attention to employment policy. But it is evident that there is no easy route to political influence. Recognising that, the Reworking Australia organisation decided to focus on a more long-term educational role in 1995.

Contemporary political conditions are complex. The major political parties are in broad agreement about economic policies, although differing significantly over methods and rates of change. There is as yet no substantial Left alternative, although the possibility of a progressive alliance, drawing on the New Zealand experience, is being discussed (Leach 1995). In general, it seems difficult for political parties nowadays to attract and sustain the interests of activists. But progressive activists are involved in many fields. Indeed, as Noam Chomsky emphasised in his lectures in Australia in 1995, there are numerous progressive groups worldwide, thinking globally and acting locally, addressing the full array of economic, social, cultural and environmental issues. There is a culture of resistance and an exploration of communitarian alternatives. It is in this context that Reworking Australia can be situated as a social movement.

Diverse groups will continue opposing economic rationalism and corporate managerialism. It is the failure of those contemporary economic and managerialist practices to harmonise with human needs which constitutes the source of radical challenge and of hope. The struggle continues ...

References

'Inequality: for richer, for poorer' 1994, *Economist*, 5 November.
Lane, R. 1991, *The Market Experience*, Cambridge University Press, Melbourne.
Leach, R. (ed.) 1995, *Alliance Politics: Beyond the Labour and Liberal Parties*, Catalyst Press, Sydney.
Pusey, M. 1993, *Economic Rationalism in Canberra*, Cambridge University Press, Melbourne.
Raskall, P. 1993, 'Widening income inequalities', in S. Rees, G. Rodley & F. Stilwell (eds), *Beyond the Market*, Pluto Press, Sydney.
Rees, S., Rodley, G. & Stilwell, F. (eds) 1993, *Beyond the Market*, Pluto Press, Sydney.
Schumacher, E. F. 1973, *Small is Beautiful*, Harper & Row, New York.
Stilwell, F. 1994a, *Economic Inequality*, Pluto Press, Sydney.
―― 1994b, 'Working Nation: from Green to White paper', *Journal of Australian Political Economy*, no. 33.

21.
Rediscovering the Common Good

Robert Simons

The basic premises of modern industrial society rest on a set of instrumental and market-oriented assumptions about human beings, what kind of universe we inhabit, and what is ultimately important to us. During the 1980s there have gradually been an increasing number of challenges to these premises by both humanitarian and religious faith visions of societies more respectful of human individuals and communities. A shared concern in most of the challenges is a long-term shift in value emphasis and priorities which, it is hoped, will bring about a transformation of industrial society comparable to the breadth of the transformation from medieval to modern society in Western Europe.

A long-term repositioning of economics in society, issuing out of a shift in basic beliefs and assumptions about what is good for, and needed by, humanity will involve many interrelated efforts to strive for the recognition of all people. This chapter focuses on the striving to ensure greater degrees of active and participative inclusion for diverse groups of people in all of society's most significant interactions. Accomplishing this goal necessitates an urgent shift from an instrumental understanding of what it means to develop as a human being — a managerialist understanding of workers — to a more appreciative recognition and inclusion of all people in the many ways in which they can contribute to the building of the common good.

Much of the vitality in western societies has been sustained by a strong and broad tradition of respect for every significant dimension which contributes to the experience of a full and healthy human life. Yet in the aftermath of the Industrial Revolution something has gone wrong. The richness of human consciousness has, in its institutionalised political and economic forms, been reduced to utilitarian perspectives in the service of technology. Technological mastery, guided by largely narrow economic values and an exploitative ethos, has become vulnerable to the priorities of unrestrained economic growth and an inadequately accountable managerialism.

Holistic human liberation has been usurped economically by large corporations and world financial institutions which have imposed their agendas on diverse countries in ways that are invasive and obstructive to a more broadly based community welfare. A more inclusive and participatory expression of political liberation has been stifled. Even the institution of democracy itself has been compromised by a set of budgetary goals which have proven to be insensitive to citizen concerns about the well-being of the planet and of future generations.

In responding to some of these problems, a more practical acknowledgment of the worth and diversity of human beings has to include not only their individual and communal dimensions, but also their maturation to political responsibility which builds on and consolidates the former. An argument can be made (Simons 1995) for a 'minority opinion' about the economic organisation of society which is expressive of both a Catholic Christian communitarian vision of the common good, and of economists who advocate a stronger degree of local economic management in the context of the global economy.

This approach places Christian doctrine in dialogue with economic theory and history from the bridging perspective of anthropology. It maintains that truly human communities, and the fully developed individuals who depend on them in order to realise their potential, could come about if local communities enhanced the social capital that fosters a higher degree of economic self-reliance. Also highlighted is the lack of a sufficiently developed anthropology within prevailing economic theories, this being one of the most radical and pernicious deficiencies leading to policies and structures which have been obscenely inattentive to the needs of human communities. Furthermore, those deficiencies have aggravated the non-recognition of minority cultures. Such a vision could only begin to become possible when economists from both capitalist and Marxist backgrounds agree to look with a greater critical thoroughness at the anthropological assumptions and beliefs from which their economic principles derived.

In relating the 'minority opinion' further to the theme of humanity specific principles can be taken from the political philosophy of Charles Taylor, principles which can underpin the economic organisation of society: *recognition* and *identity* considered together as interfacing processes mutually affecting one another, and the eventual possibility for *collective legitimation* which emerges when the prior principles have been satisfactorily realised (Taylor 1994, 1993,

1989a). The philosophical position of Charles Taylor on the implications of a politics of recognition for the economic organisation of society provides a way to incorporate significant dimensions of the contemporary political debate on the need to be recognised, included, and participative in society. It can also help in generating a viable vision towards which society can work for an economic organisation that can be life-giving for the common good. That is, Taylor's politics of recognition can contribute to a greater communal realisation of justice, more participatory involvement in the political processes, and a provisioning of goods and services which enable people from diverse human communities and cultures in the world to achieve their material, spiritual and creative potential more fully.

Recognition and identity

The task of discovering and following a development path towards a viable global future and sustainable global society presents what is probably one of humanity's greatest challenges at the end of the twentieth century. At the heart of a vision of economic organisation that can be life-giving for the common good is an unrelenting sensitivity to what humanity needs to reach its fullest and most holistic expression of development. This chapter shows how the mutually interrelated values of recognition and identity safeguard the universal need for individual and communal acknowledgment.

In the move towards an alternative future for the economic organisation of society, the values of recognition and identity constitute a prelude to the participatory activities of citizenship and production. People's identity, whether individual or communal, is partly shaped by recognition or its absence, or even by misrecognition. So, a person or a group of people or a subculture within society can suffer real distortion if people around them mirror back to them a demeaning or contemptible picture of themselves. Non-recognition or misrecognition can inflict harm, can be a form of oppression, imprisoning someone in a false, distorted and reduced mode of being. Due recognition, therefore, is not just a courtesy owed to people. It is a vital human need. Unfortunately, the various forms of social and economic excommunication brought on by the inequality created by much of present economic organisation deprives many people of this vital human need.

The transition into the modern period involved two changes that have highlighted a preoccupation with recognition and identity. The first was the collapse of social hierarchies, which used to be the basis for honour and respect. In contrast to this notion of honour there is the modern notion of dignity, used in a universalist and egalitarian sense — the inherent dignity of human beings or citizen dignity. The underlying premise here is that everyone shares in it (Berger 1983). This concept of dignity is part of a contemporary understanding of a democratic society. The importance of recognition, however, has been modified and intensified by the view of individual identity that emerged at the end of the eighteenth century, along with the related emphasis on 'authenticity', or being true to oneself and to one's particular way of being (Trilling 1969).

An emphasis on authenticity probably began in the eighteenth-century notion that human beings are endowed with a moral sense, an intuitive feeling for what is right and wrong. The origin for this position was the rejection of the view that knowing right or wrong was a matter of calculating consequences, in particular, those concerned with divine reward and punishment. The idea was that understanding right and wrong was not a matter of dry calculation, but was anchored in feelings (Taylor 1989a). Being in touch with moral feelings matters as a means to the end of acting rightly. This 'fact' is part of the massive subjective turn of modern culture, a new form of inwardness, in which people come to think of themselves as beings with inner depths. This 'fact' was eventually developed by Herder to proclaim that each person has an original way of being human, and that each person is his or her own measure (Taylor 1994).

While the ideal of authenticity undermines socially derived forms of identification as they took shape in hierarchical societies, and while it also affirms that identification is inwardly generated, the inward generation of identity is essentially dialogical. Identity is always in defined dialogue with, sometimes in struggle against, significant others. Even after some of these others are outgrown — parents, for instance — the conversation with them continues life-long (Mead 1934; Bakhtin 1984; Wretsch 1991). Thus, the contribution of significant others, even when it is provided at the beginning of life, continues indefinitely. The discovery of an identity means negotiating it through dialogue, partly overt, partly internal, with others. That is why the development of an ideal of inwardly generated identity gives a new importance to recognition. Personal identity crucially depends on dialogical relation with others.

Before the modern age, general recognition was built into the socially derived identity from social categories that everyone took for granted. In contrast, however, inwardly derived, personal, original identity does not enjoy this recognition *a priori*. It has to win it through exchange, and the attempt to do so can fail. What has come about with the modern age is not the need for recognition but the conditions in which the attempt to be recognised can fail. The importance of recognition in the public sphere requires people to work out a politics of equal recognition, one which emphasises the equal dignity of all people and brings about the equalisation of all rights and entitlements. In the socioeconomic sphere, for example, a politics of equal recognition concerns itself with the growing inequalities brought on by chronically unregulated operations of the market. In the political sphere, such a politics is directed towards such basic issues as the universal right to vote and to be elected to public office.

Ironically, the modern emphasis on equal recognition has also given rise to a politics of difference, that is, everyone should be recognised for his or her unique identity. With the politics of equal dignity, what is established is meant to be universally the same, an identical collection of rights and immunities. With the politics of difference, what people are asked to recognise is the unique identity of this individual or group, their distinctness from everyone else. In too many instances this distinctness has been ignored, glossed over, or assimilated to a dominant or majority identity. It has now become clearer, however, that the politics of difference grows organically out of the politics of universal dignity.

The politics of equal dignity is based on the idea that all humans are equally worthy of respect. It is underpinned by a notion of what in human beings commands respect. For Kant what commanded respect was the status of human beings as rational agents, capable of directing their lives through principles. Thus, universal human potential, a capacity that all humans share, is the crucial factor. This potential, rather than anything a person may have made of it, is what ensures that each person deserves respect. In the case of the politics of difference a universal potential is also at its basis, namely, the potential for forming and defining one's own identity, as an individual, and also as part of a culture. This potentiality must be respected equally in everyone. But in the intercultural context a stronger demand has arisen: that equal respect be accorded to well established cultures. Critics of European and white domination — as both oppressive and failing to appreciate other cultures — consider these depreciatory judgments factually mistaken and somehow morally wrong. The morality of equal recognition, then, extends beyond an acknowledgment of the equal value of all humans' potentiality, and comes to include the equal value of what they have made of this potential.

These 'equal dignity' and 'difference' modes of politics, both based on the notion of equal respect, can come into conflict. For one, the principle of equal respect requires that people are treated in a difference-blind fashion. The fundamental intuition that humans command this respect focuses on what is the same in all. For the other, there has to be a recognition and even fostering of particularity. The reproach the first makes to the second is just that it violates the principle of non-discrimination. The reproach the second makes to the first is that it negates identity by forcing people into a homogenous mould that is untrue to them. Then the minority or suppressed cultures are forced to take on an alien form. Consequently, the supposedly fair alien form. Consequently, the supposedly fair and difference-blind society is not only inhuman in its suppression of identities, but also, in a subtle and unconscious way, itself highly discriminatory.

The fairness of an emphasis on equal rights will be affected by whether or not a society opts for procedural or substantive commitments. Procedural commitments are those which choose to deal fairly and equally with all people, regardless of how they conceive their ends. Substantive commitments, in contrast, are directed towards agreed collective ends in life. As long as the rights of those who are not part of the majority in agreement are respected and safeguarded, it is not an impossible task to pursue collective objectives. In some senses, the problems do not in principle have to be greater than those encountered by any liberal society that has to combine liberty and equality, or prosperity and justice.

There is a form of the politics of equal respect, as enshrined in a liberalism of rights, that is inhospitable to difference, because it insists on a uniform application of the rules defining these rights without exception, and it is suspicious of collective goals. It cannot accommodate what the members of distinct societies really aspire to, which is survival. This is a collective goal which almost inevitably will call for some variations in the kinds of laws deemed permissible from one cultural context to another. Such a form of liberalism is guilty as charged by the proponents of the politics of difference.

Fortunately, however, there are other models of liberal society that call for the invariable defence of certain rights, for example of *habeas corpus*. But they distinguish these fundamental rights from the broad range of immunities and presumptions of uniform treatment that have sprung up in modern cultures giving a prominent place to judicial review. They are willing to weigh the importance of certain forms of uniform treatment against the importance of cultural survival, and opt sometimes in favour of the latter. They are thus in the end not procedural models of liberalism, but are grounded very much on judgments about what makes a good life, judgments in which the integrity of cultures has an important place. It seems more and more likely that as societies are turning out to be multicultural, in the sense of including more than one cultural community that wants to survive, the rigidities of procedural liberalism may rapidly become impractical in tomorrow's world.

One final challenge in the politics of recognition is the avoidance of two extreme attitudes towards multiculturalism: that of cultural superiority; and the demand that all cultures be accorded equal value. Unfortunately, the latter, in most instances, is little more than a disguised expression of the former. A demand for equally favourable judgments that is lacking in sufficient reflection on shared experiences and interaction is not only condescending but ethnocentric. It praises the other for being like us. Paradoxically, the peremptory demand for favourable judgments of worth has a homogenising outcome. For it implies that we already have the standards to make such judgments. The way beyond the extremes, the way towards real judgments of worth supposes a fused horizon of standards, a willingness to be open to comparative cultural study of the kind that displaces our original horizons.

If a politics of recognition is to bring about a stronger realisation of the values of recognition and identity, there will be a need for serious and widespread opportunities to interact and participate in those activities which are most pertinent to the realisation of the common good. The opportunities for interaction and participation, in turn, require a more broadly based perception on the parts of all peoples that political engagement is possible, needed and worthwhile. Unfortunately, that perception, because of a variety of levels of societal alienation — cultural, political and economic — is sorely lacking. Instead, major portions of societies put forth cynicism, apathy and an overall feeling of powerlessness as reasons not to become more politically involved. In the next section Habermas's theory of communicative action is used to identify ways in which the values of recognition and identity can be reinforced and strengthened, and so contribute to a future when the economic and political organisation of society might enjoy a much higher degree of legitimisation and vitality.

Reclaimed legitimation

Habermas (1988) has shown how the failure to acknowledge and include the breadth of human cultures and values in envisioning the economic organisation of society inevitably leads to the fragmentation of human communities and values. His analysis of the state of late capitalism alerts all peoples of good will to features of modern economic organisation which have to be redressed. His description of communities of communicative action demonstrates how people from diverse cultures and backgrounds can set about inserting the type of humanitarian values into economics which can begin to place the latter in the service of the former.

Habermas (1971) identifies three forms of knowing which can free people from constraining interests and also move them to greater degrees of liberation: empirical–analytical ways of knowing which provide technical control over a variety of scientific processes; historical–hermeneutic ways of knowing which help communities to gain the greatest possible consensus among participants of a particular tradition; and the knowing brought about by critical social science and philosophy which brings about even greater emancipation by releasing people from the rationalisations of uncritical thought in all three types of knowing.

Working from his own critical social science and philosophy Habermas suggests that the achievement of autonomy and responsibility becomes possible only in and through the structure of language. All language presupposes the communication of agreement on one point or another. Furthermore, the communication made possible by the use of language is preliminary to effective social action. With the latter outcome in mind, Habermas distinguishes between action oriented towards success and action oriented towards understanding.

Action oriented towards success, in which individuals or groups seek to accomplish specific ends, may be either instrumental or strategic. *Action oriented to achieving understanding* is only possible in intersubjective, open and free communication. There are three types: a. conversation, concerned with the attainment of truth, that is, with a group establishing that its utterances correspond to the external realities to which they claim to refer; b. intersubjective relations regulated by agreed norms, concerned with rightness, that is, with the correctness of the norms and assumptions which guide interpersonal interactions; c. expressive action, concerned with sincerity, that is, with a group's determining that the symbolic representations — both verbal and non-verbal — of its vision and inner self are expressive of truthfulness. Communicative action, a type of action oriented towards understanding, involves the continuing conversation of any human community about the direction and value of its actions.

When a breakdown occurs in communicative action, when there is a real or apparent rupture in the search for consensus, Habermas proposes dealing with the problem by an appeal to discourse ethics, the argumentation needed to respond to breakdowns in communication. It also aims at clarifying their causes, and restoring channels of communication. Habermas develops his discourse ethics by drawing the idea of communicative action into relation with his critique of the narrow instrumentality of late capitalism. Central to Habermas's critique is the distinction between 'lifeworld' and 'system'; respectively, substructure and superstructure.

Lifeworld refers to the shared meanings that make ordinary interaction possible. It includes social institutions, practices and norms, and also consists of the world of meanings into which people are born and in which they grow up. The lifeworld communicates the knowledge and norms that provide the background of the formation of the self and for the legitimation of society. In contrast, system refers to those administrative areas of modern society coordinated by money and power. Money and power coordinate human action in a way that differs considerably from action which takes place through communication.

Society is composed of both lifeworld and system. A successful society holds lifeworld and system in a unity in which the lifeworld has priority. For Habermas, modern capitalist societies are examples of pathological distortions of the equilibrium that should exist between lifeworld and system. In capitalist societies, systems are always threatening to instrumentalise the lifeworld. While Habermas believes that the division into lifeworld and system is one of the necessary stages in the development of society, he is also convinced that the lifeworld must be the place where the system is ultimately grounded. Unfortunately, throughout the world the power of established economic interests always short-circuits steps otherwise being taken to preserve the quality of life. The resultant transfer of the economy's problems into the lifeworld impinges on basic human freedoms.

Since the scale of the crises and pathologies is so immense, protest is no longer focused on demanding responses from the political system. In late-capitalist societies single-issue groups seek to defend the world and the human community from the influences of an unchecked system. They are united in their critique of growth, and focus either on the defence of class interests, or on opposition to tax reform, nuclear energy, pollution, or deprivation of privacy. Anxiety stirs up feelings of being overwhelmed by an international economic system which is largely beyond people's control. Habermas warns that the system will not solve the problems of the system. Only the exercise of human rationality in and through the communication community can be used to fight back against human loss of control over the system.

A society can regain legitimacy when the beliefs and attitudes of its members towards it include a willingness and a commitment to assume the disciplines and burdens which membership in the society entails. Legitimacy declines when this willingness dissipates. If that happens, then the society suffers a tangible malaise in, or breakdown of, social processes. Unfortunately, such a breakdown is already part of societies affected strongly by the operation of market economics and its attendant thrust towards managerialism.

One factor which especially contributes to the present legitimation crisis might be described as 'hypertrophy', that is, giving way to the economy's unlimited short-term economic growth goals. Hypertrophy also generates a number of fears that contemporary affirmations of freedom, equality, radical new beginnings, control over nature, and democratic self-rule will somehow be carried beyond feasible limits and will undo society. In that case, moderation or limitation alone is an inadequate response to the problem. Ironically, the very values of freedom, equality and technological control which, carried to an extreme, bring on hypertrophy, have to be rescued from the way they have been coopted by economic processes and restored in their integrity.

Freedom must develop into liberty, understood as a positive focus for communities and the individuals which depend on them; and technological control must be contextualised by a concern with nature and a holistic understanding of efficacy. Only then will equality become a more realistic possibility for greater numbers of people. Also, as part of the dynamic of rescue, it is indispensable that there also be a full retrieval of the understandings of the human good that have grown along with and underpinned the development of modern society (Habermas 1984, 1988).

Traditional moral views of the human good presumed that the fulfilment of ordinary needs involved with the production and reproduction of life provided the ground from which higher activities, such as contemplation and citizenship, became possible. While the first level of activity is good, it is the second level that gives life its higher significance. Modern moral views tended to reject the two tiers by assigning to the first level, nature — that is, the rational pursuit of ordinary life needs — a degree of nobility and honour. What defines proper human activity is a certain manner of going about meeting these needs in a sober, disciplined and rational way.

'Rationality' in the seventeenth century could be taken to sum up the properly human way of living. In the twentieth century rationality is defined less and less in terms of a vision of the true order of things and more and more in terms of instrumental reason. The rational pursuit of the needs of life crucially includes seeking them in an effective manner, that is, free individuals meet the demands of nature by aspiring to a higher degree of control over themselves and nature. Exercising the control that enables people fully to effect their purposes indicates an ability to pursue life's needs in a properly human way.

In modern society self-determining free agents are also the subject of rights. As free subjects, people are owed respect for their rights and have certain guaranteed freedoms. They must be able to choose and act, within limits, free from the arbitrary interference of others. Finally, modern free subjects have the ability to effect their purposes. Another name for this ability is 'efficacy'. Subjects without efficacy, unable to alter the world around them to their ends, would either be incapable of sustaining a modern identity or would be deeply humiliated in their identity.

Along with a sense of having equal rights, there are two other important features of people's status in society which have played a role in sustaining the modern identity. The first is their status as citizens, by which they collectively determine the course of social events. Only citizens are full persons capable of acting and making a name for themselves. The fact that people govern themselves is an extremely important part of their dignity as free subjects. A second dimension is that of production. As producers, in the broadest sense, people belong to a whole interconnected society of labour and technology which has immense efficacy in transforming nature. Insofar as people belong to this society, work in it, take part in it, contribute to it, they have a share in this efficacy. They can think of it as partly theirs, as a confirmation of themselves.

Modern subjects are not independent, atomistic agents. What western liberal societies need in order to overcome the one-sidedness of atomistic freedom lies in other facets of the modern identity itself. While the modern understandings of freedom and efficacy tend to undermine community, an emphasis on efficacy can also help to create contem-porary understandings of citizen dignity. The latter has sometimes been the basis of renewed community identification and solidarity. Towards this end the community dimensions of modern life, both family and state, can provide a type of therapeutic restraint on individualist atomism, which respects individual rights while doggedly keeping them in the context and service of the common good.

Liberal democratic societies presuppose a sense of citizen dignity based on citizens having a voice in deciding the common laws by which members live. Such societies also presuppose that their laws serve to unite a specific community. For unless there is a sense of a determinate community whose members experience a bond between them from this common allegiance, an identification with the common good cannot arise. Whereas in ancient republics these two conditions were naturally together, in modern liberal society they can come apart.

Inclusive participation: the hoped-for outcome

An adequate consideration of inclusive participation as a hoped-for outcome to a regained sense of societal legitimation means a reexamination of the views of individuals and society held by both liberals and communitarians (Taylor 1989a). A communitarian–participative perspective is considered to be better suited to bringing about the goal of regained legitimation than a liberal–rights oriented one. The differences between the atomistic–rights model and the communitarian–participatory model, however, can be seen to converge towards broader humanitarian principles on a number of levels. Such humanitarian principles, which highlight the convergences, may also be considered ontological. That is, they refer to terms which are accepted as definitive, and also provide a way of evaluating the societal outcomes of two otherwise contrasting starting points.

When people refer to 'liberals' and 'communitarians' they often assume that a given position on one of those camps commits them to a corresponding view on the other. If the taking of an ontological position is properly understood, however, it does not amount to advocating one position to the exclusion of the other. Rather, it structures a field of possibilities or options from which people may then move on to support one of those possibilities with some form of advocacy. Unfortunately, the failure to sustain an awareness of all of the possibilities leads to a confusion of issues which, in turn, contributes to a kind of eclipse of ontological thinking in social theory.

Since it is the ontological level at which important questions about the real choices open to people are faced, the eclipse is a real misfortune. So, for example, the ontological issues of recognition and identity as well as community have to be part of any debate on justice between liberals and communitarians. Those issues are highly relevant to questions of justice. The unfortunate consequence of not discussing them is to rely on an implicit and unexamined view of them. Unfortunately, in Anglo-Saxon philosophical culture, atomist prejudices predominate. The result is that an ontologically disinterested liberalism tends to be blind to the concerns of holism, along with other important questions and perspectives. There are a number of reasons for the blindness.

First of all, 'procedural' liberalism is very popular in the English-speaking world. It sees society as an association of individuals, each of whom has his or her conception of a good or worthwhile life and, correspondingly, his or her life plan. The function of society ought to be to facilitate these life plans, as much as possible, by following some principle of equality. Many writers seem to agree that the principle of equality or non-discrimination would be breached if society itself espoused one or other conception of the good life. Any view of society as a whole would be that of some citizens and not others. Thus, it is argued, a liberal society should not be founded on any particular notion of the good life. The ethic central to a liberal society is an ethic of individual rights, rather than common good. The crucial issue is that of procedures (hence the labelling of this brand of liberal theory as procedural), which denies the development of a socially endorsed conception of the good.

If a society is going to cohere freely and without submitting to a despotic form of control, then such coherence requires a willing identification with the *polis* on the part of the citizens, a sense that the political institutions in which they live are an expression of themselves. In such a context, laws reflect and entrench the dignity of individuals as citizens, and are also extensions of them. This is more than an apolitical attachment to a universal principle. Rather, the issue is the identification with others in a particular common enterprise.

Unfortunately, the growing power of atomist modes of thought in the last three centuries in the English-speaking world — modes of thought which have been reinforced and consolidated by the anthropology assumed in *homo economicus* — have worked against the practical realisation of solidarity in patriotic endeavours. Rather, political societies according to Hobbes, Locke, Bentham, or the twentieth-century commonsense that they have helped shape, are established by collections of individuals to obtain benefits — 'convergent goods' such as welfare provision and police protection — through common action that they could not secure individually. The action is collective, but the point of it remains individual.

Common goods as opposed to convergent goods reflect values not simply to individuals collectively, but to whole communities cohesively. Common goods presuppose and further foster a shared bond among individuals, a bond which Aristotle compared with friendship. Common goods, as opposed to convergent goods, presuppose established relations of shared identity and tangible bonds of community. Common goods also constitute the essential condition of a free, non-despotic society and government. Here, freedom is clearly citizen liberty, that is, the freedom for active participation in public affairs. Such participation means having a say in the decisions of the political domain which shape people's lives. Since participatory self-government is itself usually carried out in common actions, it is perhaps normal to see it as properly animated by shared identifications. Since people exercise freedom in communal actions, it may seem natural that they value it as a common good. So it could be said that republican solidarity underpins freedom because it provides the motivation for self-imposed discipline, or else that it is essential for a free regime because this calls on its members to do things that mere subjects can avoid.

In contrast to the common goods which underpin free republics, procedural liberalism does not offer a viable formula for free and participatory citizenship. Nonetheless, a procedural liberalist society can come together in the face of challenges such as multiculturalism, and high degrees of social and economic inequality, in order to bring about a more inclusive degree of recognition and citizen participation. In a viable holist, procedural, liberal society patriotism would have to involve more than converging moral principles. It would require a common allegiance to a particular historical community. Cherishing and sustaining this community has to be a common goal, and this is more than just consensus on the rule of right. It also entails sustaining a specific historical set of institutions and forms as a socially endorsed common end.

Within this context the further question can be posed: is it possible in a society marked by procedural liberalism, a society where large sectors of the populace are excluded from adequate exercise of participation in political processes, that cohesion might be experienced through a juridical process of redressing rights whenever they are violated as a result of being excluded? However this question might be answered, it is important not to fall into the trap of assuming that a liberal political option vitiates any possible degree of communitarian cooperation.

Unfortunately, liberal societies are not characterised by a highly developed sense of the common good. The influence of the excessively individualised anthropologies reflected in economic rationalism and its attendant managerialism have worked against such a possibility.

Nonetheless, with a set of humanitarian principles it is possible to imagine how communities might become more influenced by a strong sense of the common good. With such an influence it also becomes possible to imagine how societies might challenge managerialism and advocate the recovery of humanity. With the assistance of the anthropological principles of recognition and identity, and societal legitimation, a way of moving into the future becomes possible in which higher degrees of recognition may lead to greater participation in fulfilling socioeconomic responsibilities.

References

Bakhtin, M. M. 1984, *Problems of Dostoyevsky's Poetics* (trans. Caryl Emerson), University of Minnesota Press, Minneapolis.

Berger, Peter 1983, 'On the obsolescence of the concept of honour', in S. Hauerwas & A. MacIntyre (eds), *Revisions: Changing Perspectives in Moral Philosophy*, University of Notre Dame Press, Notre Dame, Ind.

Habermas, Jurgen 1971, *Knowledge and Human Interests*, Beacon Press, Boston.

—— 1988a, *Legitimation Crisis,* Polity Press & Basil Blackwell, Oxford.

—— 1988b, *The Theory of Communicative Action*, 2 vols, Beacon Press, Boston.

Mead, George Herbert 1934, *Mind, Self, and Society*, University of Chicago Press, Chicago.

Simons, Robert G. 1995, *Competing Gospels: Public Theology and Economic Theory*, E. J. Dwyer, Sydney.

Taylor, Charles 1989a, 'Cross-purposes: the liberal communitarian debate', in N. L. Rosenblum (ed.), *Liberalism and the Moral Life*, Harvard University Press, Cambridge, Mass.

—— 1989b, *Sources of the Self*, Harvard University Press, Cambridge, Mass.

—— 1993, 'Alternative futures: legitimacy, identity, and alienation in late twentieth century Canada', in G. Laforest (ed.), *Reconciling the Solitudes: Essays on Canadian Federalism and Nationalism*, McGill-Queen's University Press, Montreal & Kingston.

—— 1994, 'The politics of recognition', in A. Gutmann (ed.), *Multiculturalism: Examining the Politics of Recognition*, Princeton University Press, Princeton, NJ.

Trilling, Lionel 1969, *Sincerity and Authenticity*, Norton, New York.

Wretsch, James 1991, *Voices of the Mind*, Harvard University Press, Cambridge, Mass.

22.
Defining and Attaining Humanity

Stuart Rees

This chapter has four themes:

1. The indispensability of reflection, which exposes the consequences of managerialism and sets a rationale for humanitarian alternatives.

2. A justification for universal humanitarian goals and ways to achieve them, whether in bureaucracies or in international relations.

3. An explanation of why a vision of 'humanity' can influence social and economic policies and cues for the conduct of human relations.

4. An appraisal of how humanity might be expressed through diverse sources of inspiration: artists and scientists, novelists and poets, theologians and social workers, social and economic policy analysts, activists, and the membership of social movements.

Reflection and political literacy

In political circles, in bureaucracies and in the media, the dominance of economic rationalist precepts discourages dissent. Promotion of computer technology and the assumption that to achieve even greater productivity a 'clever country' must master machinery, also bolsters the managerialist message. To question these forces puts the questioner at risk of being labelled anti-progressive, unrealistic, insufficiently corporate, uncooperative or all of these.

Risks have to be taken to unmask ideologies which dominate and constrain debate. Without risk-taking, the capacity for reflection and shared communication would lie dormant and the only rationality would be the bad economics, poor human relations and rotten morality of the current economic and managerial fundamentalisms. A political literacy based on principles of empowerment (Solomon 1976; Rose & Black 1985; Rees 1991) would foster the potential for reflection and shared understandings, to not only expose the clumsy cruelties of the market mentality but also to develop confidence in humanitarian alternatives. This 'empowerment' refers to goals of equity and social justice and a working through interdependent stages, from awareness and shared understanding to dialogue and solidarity, and from there to the experience of taking action.

A capacity for reflection is inherent in any analysis of forces which affect each individual's notion of choice and the criteria to assess quality of life. Yet the assumption that all the world's peoples should worship growth for growth's sake, and that employees in health, welfare and educational bureaucracies should accept management's demands for conformity, stifles the capacity for reflection and leaves political literacy undeveloped.

All the authors in this book have contributed to political literacy. On the one hand they have shown how assumptions about the benefits of competition for material gain — a one-dimensional view of the exercise of power — are used to control the media, the organisation of sport and the policies which affect health and welfare, education and the arts, local government and civil liberties. On the other they have demonstrated that unless the values of generosity and collegiality, humour and humility, patience and persistence, courage and tolerance are advocated as virtues in society at large and in relationships at work, the human and environmental costs will continue to be horrendous. This argument has also been mounted with increasing urgency by philosophers and social theorists, by theologians and artists, by poets and political economists, by social workers and social policy analysts.

An analysis of 'the common good' (Daly & Cobb 1989) argues for economic policies to place priority on the well-being of 'the individual in community'. Scientist and theologian Charles Birch says that humanness can only be realised if individuals live in harmony with their environment, at one with the land and thereby with one another (Birch 1993). Ekins writes that a 'living economy' must enable all citizens to be treated and to see themselves as 'creative subjects' not 'efficient objects' (Ekins 1986).

The urgency of these arguments is also apparent in the work of Jurgen Habermas who saw reflection and communication as a lever for humanitarian principles to replace the 'iron cage' of capitalist values. Habermas hoped that one day:

> the pursuit of happiness might mean something different — for example, not accumulating material objects of which one disposes

privately, but bringing about social relations in which mutuality predominates and satisfaction does not mean triumph of one over the repressed needs of the other. (Habermas 1979)

In his appraisal of the visions and practicalities of Habermas's work, Michael Pusey summarises how economic preoccupations and associated marketing technology have replaced religious, community and cultural traditions as the reference points which influence the expression of goals and the solution of problems. Habermas offers an alternative political literacy: from communication-oriented success to communication-oriented understanding. This, he argues, provides a process of liberation because it moves beyond systems in which ideas are prepackaged and are expected to be swallowed uncritically, and focuses instead on the capacity for criticism, learning and mutual support inherent in day-to-day interaction. He makes a strong claim that:

> sanity, well-being, and the very identity of each individual ultimately depends on shared, or at least, reciprocally communicable, self understandings, upon 'ego defining structures', that join up your inner world with mine in such a way as to make mutual understanding, negotiation and relationships possible. (Pusey 1987, p. 100)

Organisations can be managed in such a way as to encourage a capacity for reflection, to enhance social and political awareness, to contribute to empowerment by fostering opportunities to learn. Bureaucracies as environments for learning has been a theme of several previous chapters, such as those on local government, urban planning, participation in sport, policies in tertiary education and the attainment of child welfare.

Reflection with a view to political literacy occurs when people realise the human costs of managerialism and then establish non-economic as well as economic criteria for evaluating well-being. But it would be inconsistent to reflect and communicate only on the destructive effects of managerialism. Reflection needs to range as widely as possible, to ponder examples of humanity and inhumanity. A principle of universal value and application needs to be unearthed and applied.

A search for universals

Pictures of inhumanity — accounts of massacres, ethnic cleansing, the cruelties of tribal conflicts and civil wars, violence in homes or on the streets — are the daily fare of the news media. It is easy to become dulled to such examples of inhumanity because people seldom find time to reflect on why they are appalled. If 'humanity' can be interpreted to mean far more than the opposite of inhumanity, that concept could deliver a new sense of philosophical, managerial and professional coherence which would have an application for human welfare in general — nationally and internationally.

A single act of violence, or a Rwanda-like massacre, is described as a crime against humanity, but the inherent moral principle in this gasp of shame is seldom addressed. Like the dictionary definitions — 'the nature peculiar to a human being', 'of human nature or attributes' — 'humanity' implies something to do with collective human welfare but is left without specific meaning, except perhaps as a term which is the opposite of the latest inhumanity.

Humanity is usually used unexceptionally but could refer to qualities of love, caring, communication to achieve understanding and to facilitate other forms of creativity. In the same vein, peace with justice means far more than merely an absence of war, and a non-violent society is not only without direct, observable violence but is also characterised by an absence of exploitation and other barriers to the realisation of human potential.

There are other reasons for wanting to define humanity. It has the potential to have a universal connotation, applicable to relationships in the home, on the streets, in the reconciliation between races, and as a guiding principle for preventing human cruelties, and for planning the long-term provision of humanitarian aid. The idea of humanity as a universal vision is compelling and contains guidelines for action which can easily be comprehended around the globe. This is especially the case in an age in which politicians and social theorists have suggested that individual freedom will be best served by giving up on a search for universals. For example, post-modernism has encouraged a view which says that nothing is certain, that principles of sovereignty entitle every group to establish their version of freedom and their accounts of what is paramount in life for them. In consequence, the idea of unifying principles, such as social justice, has been discredited.

At this point 'humanity' should be given a small warning label because it sounds anthropomorphic, having to do with human beings and by implication ignoring the environment, plants, animals and other living things. Yet the essential paradox of humanity is that concern for individuals cannot be attained by viewing human well-being as separate from respect for the environment. Confronting this paradox involves a perception of human well-being as derived from an interdependence of society, environment and an even wider universe.

It is no coincidence that the discrediting of the idea of universal principles is occurring at a time when intolerance and violence are rife and when management is encouraged to promote competition of all kinds as a solution for countries' fragile economies, or as the way for organisations to motivate their staff. There is a cost to such 'competition'. Advocating the idea that everything is possible, nothing is certain and each group is entitled to promote or defend its cause without too much regard for others, means giving up on ideas of connectedness and coherence.

Undue respect for marketplace competition as a guide to human conduct has contributed to a lack of spiritual and political coherence. Under the influence of dominant economic theory, every transaction between individuals is regarded as a commodity which only has bearing on the quality of life of others according to an economic price of exchange. If, as Margaret Thatcher argued, there is no such thing as society but only individuals bartering their way in a marketplace, even law, let alone custom, may be difficult to establish or enforce.

It is not being suggested that past eras of feudalism, benevolent despotism, communism, colonialism and imperialism always produced common benefits through the application of universal laws. Yet criticism of the shortcomings of those eras produced not a surrender in the efforts to redefine the role of the state in securing individual freedoms but rather a determination that only universal principles and standards, carefully reflected on and vigorously argued about, would eventually contribute to a common good. In the civil wars and revolutions of sixteenth- and seventeenth-century Europe this determination was apparent in the struggle to establish human rights before courts, and principles of civil liberty. In the decade following the Second World War, political will was evident in the social legislation which created a variety of welfare state regimes in North America, in Europe, in Australia and in New Zealand.

A corollary of the idea that no one knows any more or that no one can be certain, is that no one may care, except when provoked by pictures of the latest inhumanity. At which point a quick humanitarian response is made — perhaps a donation to an overseas aid organisation — before we settle back bemused and befuddled by the libertarian notion that even the idea of a nation–state is outmoded. That libertarianism presupposes a market in almost everything.

The question of whether competition and efficiency are antithetical to humanity is seldom posed, and for that reason the influence of economic rationalist and managerialist precepts has to be confronted. In addition to the sense of being helpless when faced with more evidence of human atrocities, there are other reasons for saying that the search to establish a universal meaning for humanity is urgent. These other reasons refer almost entirely to the dogma that the economy should dominate over society and that human relationships are merely a by-product of economic transactions. If cost-effectiveness is the criterion for judging the conduct of bureaucracies or the outcomes of relationships, a licence is given for a free trade in almost anything: arms, women and children, genetic engineering, business corporations, cultural artefacts or intellectual products.

At a time when the need to revive universal principles and unifying visions is urgent, cultures are being dominated by economic rationalist goals and by management techniques for achieving objectives. These goals and techniques have produced a view which says that on appearance modern societies are nothing more than a collection of strangers each pursuing their own interests under minimal constraints (MacIntyre 1989). Within institutions, such as universities or hospitals, the minimal constraint may also be the major one. Management creates the structures to talk cost-effectiveness and conduct exercises in performance evaluation. In this atmosphere efficiency becomes the means and the end. Instead of highlighting collegiality and care, an emphasis on efficiency demands that staff belong to separate administrative or business units whose responsibility is to compete and to be held accountable for the cost of doing so.

Yet the inhumanness within organisations and in policies which promote inequality and violence is disguised by disingenuous claims about equity. For example, government claims about justice are coupled to a promotion of the interests of those who least need any form of support. Since 1985 Australian governments have substantially cut the top marginal tax rate, subsidised the top class's superannuation, and cut the tax on share dividends.

An ideology of letting the market decide and being derisory about the role of the state produces societies without principle (Marquand 1988) and cultures in which human beings are counted as commodities (Esping-Andersen 1989). Given these trends, there is a need to confront the selfish egoism which uncritical respect for the market engenders. The managerialism which makes it difficult to speak of humanitarianism — of the interconnectedness of people, environment and universe — makes it even more imperative to do so.

Why 'humanity'?

Inherent in 'humanity' are values of 'community', of caring and sharing, of partnership and interdependence. There is a normative quality to humanity. There is not only an argument about the good but also about ways to influence choices as to what is good and ways to achieve the chosen objectives. Yet this interpretation of humanity is likely to provoke the response that other concepts can fulfil this need equally well. Why not rally around the ideals of social justice and spell out their implications for all peoples? Why not speak of the rights and obligations of citizenship, internationally as well as nationally? Why not revive commitments to universal services, not least because available evidence suggests that human needs are best met in societies whose governments spend generously on an infrastructure of public services (Esping-Andersen 1990; Doyal & Gough 1991)?

The case for spelling out a humanitarian vision for the future is not to dispute the value of those other principles. Each goes in tandem. But the tendency for people to say that they no longer know what is meant by justice, or that in the future no nation-state can afford any universal services, needs to be challenged.

Why might principles of humanity transcend a search for justice? The question of what is just often hinders, or at least postpones humanitarian responses to suffering. For example, countries keep refugees in closed camps for years while lawyers argue about the status of refugees. Instead of such automatic confinement, and agonising for ages over what is a fair and just solution for all refugees who might be in a similar predicament, a humanitarian response would be to allow new refugee arrivals out on parole in the community while their claims for asylum are investigated. Humanity elicits humanness. It has the potential to foster immediate and spontaneous responses to suffering. These claims do not demean a search for justice but they lend support to the argument that there are circumstances when humanity will come before justice (Campbell 1974).

The notion of humanity can address people's essential humanness. It can include perspectives which were not always part of the controversies surrounding the meaning of citizenship, universal services or even social justice. Debates about those latter concepts have often been confined to academic social policy and administrative circles. Intentionally or not, a process of exclusion operated.

For whatever reasons, references to humanity have not been conspicuous in policy debates. It might have been implied by some of the deliberations about the objectives of social policies but it has seldom been explicit, perhaps because it sounds like a notion that is too amorphous to be defined and too unexceptional to be attained. It might not have been regarded as 'wet' but it was hardly a concept which could influence the deliberations of the planners and evaluators of services. Yet it is probable that if the question were put, those with a direct responsibility for setting standards for the conduct of relationships and for the distribution of resources would not disagree that a society's well-being and an organisation's reputation should be measured in terms of the quality of life enjoyed respectively by all citizens and all employees.

Who are those other people whose thinking about humanity can be included in deliberations but who have not previously been part of the official debates about the means and ends of social policies? A brief answer to this question is to refer to all those groups and individuals whose creativity has contributed to their own and others' fulfilment. This could include relatively unknown citizens of whatever class or race: established residents, new migrants or indigenous peoples. They might be well-known citizens, artists, musicians or theologians. Each could bring a vitality to visions about humanity but their views are excluded from official deliberations. Poets, for example, produce visions for justice which have been found inspiring for centuries. In countries governed by authoritarian regimes, poets provide one of the few means of protest, the meaning of their lines appreciated by their readers and listeners but eluding those in positions of authority (Rees 1991, ch. 3; Harlow 1987).

Instead of confining questions about humanity to official or academic circles there are ways to widen the debate, as in discussing why a contribution to the arts is an essential prerequisite for civil relations and a civil society. Why should the arts be seen as central features of social and economic policies and not peripheral concerns? One answer involves an emphasis on the value of having the creativity of the arts and artists accessible to all peoples, of whatever income or social class (Cochrane 1993; Everitt 1994). Another way of widening the search for inspiration about the meaning of humanity is to ask what are some common characteristics of people who have been described as great humanitarians?

There are several reasons for posing this last question. There is the observation 'she or he was a great humanitarian', but the qualities inherent in that attractive description remain elusive. If those qualities are unmasked there are lessons to be learned. If their lives were so rewarding for those for whom and with whom they worked, it would be beneficial to build their values into social structures and services. Instead of seeing the traits of great humanitarians as merely the qualities of individuals, such sources of inspiration could be applied to general principles concerning the distribution of resources and the conduct of relationships.

Grasping the meaning of humanity is difficult if enquiries are confined within discipline boundaries. Artists and novelists (Llosa 1993) and great scientists who have made breakthroughs in understanding (Watson 1968; Crick 1994) have argued that creativity depends on a transcendence of disciplines. Humanitarians have seldom respected official boundaries. Their humanness was realised by appealing to other principles.

The study and attainment of humanity cannot be the preserve of any one discipline because groups like to protect their own interests and find it difficult to communicate across discipline boundaries. In their work *For the Common Good* (1989) Daly and Cobb argue against an idolatry of disciplines. Not only has the academic segregation of disciplines pitched one specialisation against another, it has obscured major questions about a common good or has ensured that such questions would not even be raised. In the 1930s Robert Lynd also put this point when he accused academics and politicians of ignoring the prospect of a holocaust made inevitable by fascism. They were, he said, lecturing on navigation while the ship was going down (Lynd 1964).

How can humanity be expressed?

In this discussion as to why 'humanity' should be resuscitated as a valuable universal principle, several clues emerge as to the meaning of humanity and how it might be expressed. It would cross discipline borders. It would contain guidelines for individual action on a day-to-day basis as well as a vision for those who effect the distribution of resources, whether in planning housing and urban environments, or in influencing other social and economic policies. Humanity implies a statement about quality of life. Any assessment of such quality should recognise an interdependence of environment, society and economy. To that trinity Vaclav Havel has argued for that touch of vision and humility which also recognises people's minute place in the universe (Havel 1994).

These guidelines produce an infinite number of possibilities, but in the search for expressions which can be moulded into principles, three topics will be addressed: the values and strategies which provide alternatives to market-oriented perspectives; the unity of environmental and human well-being; and the inspiration to be drawn from storytellers, poets and great humanitarians.

Alternatives to the market

A variety of scholars, from Polanyi to Titmuss, from Schumpeter to Etzioni, have identified the brutal consequences for societies if capitalist systems emphasise only the pursuit of well-being through unhindered economic growth and personal accumulation. Polanyi (1957) noted that capitalist society was conceivable only because it embedded social relationships in economic arrangements. Reference to the doyen of postwar British social policy, Richard Titmuss, concentrates mostly on the implications of his famous study of the international blood donor system. Whatever the subsequent evaluations of this study, Titmuss's essential message remains like a clarion call: that an objective of social policies is the dominance of altruism over egoism (Titmuss 1974).

In confronting the future of private enterprise Joseph Schumpeter (1975) observed that for two centuries economic liberalism may have produced growth but it had also contributed to moral confusion with serious social and political consequences such as large-scale unemployment, massive inequalities within and between countries, and only a residual or charitable concern for the vulnerable. In an analysis anchored around the notions of 'civility' and 'civil society' Etzioni wrote in his 1983 work, *An Immodest Agenda*:

> A society and its members require mutual civility for sheer survival. Unless the retreat to ego is overcome and community relations re-constituted, the level of conflict and frustrations will rise

and the limited energy channelled to shared concerns will make for an ineffectual 'can't do' society, continued deterioration and even, ultimately, the possibility of destruction. (Etzioni 1983, p. 185)

One alternative to the pursuit of individual interests has been labelled 'mutualisation', as when richer nations help poorer ones through international aid, or when work is shared between those in jobs and those who are unemployed. Such work-sharing is bolstered by that principle articulated by André Gorz that many should work less so that some may work. Programs to redistribute work as well as share existing work include the advocacy that it is socially just to pay a universal benefit allowance to a non-working population. Whether called mutualisation or, in a Papal Encyclical, 'subsidiarity' — powerful organisations and countries not arrogating to themselves activities that can be performed by smaller and less powerful countries and institutions — the essence of such proposals concentrates on sharing through redistribution, locally, nationally and internationally. In arguing that such sharing would be the means of regaining compassion, Charles Birch writes:

> The resolution of the problem of injustice requires a fundamental re-examination of the relationship between the one billion people, or 20 per cent of the world's population, who live in industrialized countries and who use 80 per cent of the world's resources and the majority of the world's population in poor countries who have to make do with 20 per cent of the world's resources. (Birch 1993, p. 113)

Unity of environmental, personal and social well-being

Although 'humanity' connotes 'to do with humans', the thesis promoted here is that human nature would be more likely to be consistent with civility than with acquisitiveness if it were seen as indivisible with environment. Indigenous peoples are living proof that personal identity and the land are inseparable, a point which those opposed to the principle of native title to land in Australia find so difficult to accept.

Charles Birch claims that human rights should be regarded as inseparable from the rights of all living things. In a warning against the use of technology to develop plants and animals and to gear them to a factory system of production, Daly and Cobb argue that human well-being is best served when individuals and communities are in balance with the seasons, living in respectful and complementary relationship to their environment, a point elaborated by eco-feminists who make the link between male-dominated relationships in society and the destruction of natural resources (Eckersley 1993). The mostly male violence in human relationships is mirrored in the plunder and destruction of the natural environment. If control and domination were seen as neither natural nor desirable, the machismo evident in managerialism would be regarded as a form of impotence. In which case the meaning of masculinity and leadership would also be redefined.

The thesis that it is biologically natural that men are aggressive and destructive has been confounded by the scholarship which shows that it is the shape of social relations, not the shape of genes, which is the effective cause of violence (Connell 1985). Whatever the school of thought, this issue has to be addressed. There is no automatic association between inhumanity and various forms of maleness and masculinity.

If a creative and non-destructive exercise of power is to be associated with principles of humanity, the norms for human conduct around the world should no longer be male norms. Masculinity can include those creative, caring and other non-violent features of femininity. If that redefinition holds, women's subservience to maleness would cease and all the obstacles to women's freedom of expression would be removed: as in the non-violent conduct of day-to-day relationships, in equitable access to social and economic resources, and in the structure of national and international legal systems.

Of story-tellers, poets and humanitarians

In any account of the virtues of caring and creativity insight can be gained from stories and storytellers, from poems and poetry. At the very least that enquiry will cross discipline boundaries and recall that the virtues identified in stories were not just accounts of individual characteristics. Those characteristics were linked to the values of a culture, whether in the political arrangements of a Greek city-state or in the customary laws of indigenous peoples.

Humanity presupposes a vision of certain virtues in the conduct of human relationships and in a social structure. Alasdair MacIntyre says that in heroic times the individuals regarded as worthy of stories were those who showed virtues which contributed not only to individual well-being but also to a civil order. He describes Greek, mediaeval and Renaissance cultures in which the chief means of moral education lay in the telling of stories. Each of those cultures produced stories from its own heroic times. In heroic societies there was an intimate connection between, on the one hand, the concept of courage and, on the other, the concepts of friendship, fate and death. Courage was important not simply as a quality of individuals but as the quality necessary to sustain a household and a community.

MacIntyre discusses the links between courage, friendship and their contributions to a civil society and to what constitutes 'the good life'. But already there is a separation of concepts which in heroic times was unimaginable. The notion 'contributes to' suggests a separation of personal traits and social well-being, a separation of individual characteristics from the values central to a society. Courage was an ingredient of friendship but also had meaning as a feature of citizenship and of the city-state. Friendship, company and a civil society were intertwined. In Sophocles' world, where so much was contestable, it was not contestable that friendship, companionship and citizenship were essential aspects of humanity (MacIntyre 1989).

Even a brief analysis of the traits attributed to great humanitarians suggests they have something in common with the heroic virtues discussed by MacIntyre, though with this important proviso. Characteristics of great humanitarians are depicted as separate from the dominant values which influence the conduct of economies. Those humanitarians — Edward (Weary) Dunlop, Fred Hollows and Sister Mary McKillop — are idolised precisely because they stand out as different from the essentially acquisitive, competitive and instrumentalist values which dominate economic and managerialist relationships.

What are some compelling characteristics of humanitarians? They were regarded as inspirational because they challenged conventional authority, whether it was Mary McKillop questioning a patriarchal Catholic Church and an uncaring state, or Weary Dunlop representing the interests of his fellow prisoners of war against their Japanese captors or Fred Hollows showing disdain for medical hierarchies, for bureaucratic rules and conventions. Bob Ellis says of Fred Hollows:

> All agreed on Hollows's foul mouth, bad temper, lack of basic organizational skills, impatience, political ferocity, unreconstructed Marxism, residual Christianity, pioneering zeal, primitive humanism, companionship with jailbirds and low life and poets, and intolerance of bureaucratic fools. (Ellis 1994, p. 25)

A second trait concerns their compassion and commitment to the powerless. Mary McKillop's vows of poverty were expressed through a fierce intelligence and considerable organisational skills. Both traits, the compassion and the organisational skills — which in her lengthy biography (Gardiner 1993) reads like political understanding — show her making a difference. Fred Hollows conceived it his role and responsibility to be outrageous, to make a difference, never to be held back by convention, by rules for proper conduct or even by the suffering associated with terminal illness. A virtual successor of Mary McKillop's, the Western Australian priest Edward Collick, who died in 1959, has also been regarded as demonstrating a powerful courage and compassion which made a difference. He worked with mining families and Aborigines in the Western Australian goldfields. The Archbishop of Perth wrote that, 'By contrast to those who sought an instant fortune, Collick gave all his material possessions to the poor and needy and died penniless in 1959 at the age of 91 years' (Hammond 1993).

There is a third virtue in these humanitarians which is the by-product of their courage and compassion. They gave inspirational leadership. Their concern for others (it would not be too lofty to say that it was a vision for all of humanity) transcended the materialist preoccupations of their age, let alone the demands for due respect for authority. In this regard they had much in common with the inspiration to be derived from poets, from Shelley to Henry Lawson, from Judith Wright to Maya Angelou. Shelley wrote that 'until the mind can love and admire, and trust and hope and endure ... reasoned principles are seeds cast into the highways of life which the unconscious passenger tramples into dust' (Reiman & Powers 1977).

Lawson too was a person of compassion and sensitivity. Of the challenge facing Australians 100 years ago he expressed himself against the soil and the weather and the evils of the capitalist system. 'Through humour', he said, 'ordinary people become articulate, enjoy self expression and the shock of self recognition'. In 1893 he was challenging:

> the curse of class distinctions from our shoulders shall be hurled,
> An' the sense of Human Kinship revolutionize the world;
> There'll be higher education for the toilin' starvin' clown,
> An' the rich an' educated shall be educated down,
> Then we all will meet amidships on this stout old earthly craft,
> an' there won't be any friction 'twixt the classes for-'n'-aft.

In the spirit of humanity, he goes on to say, when people work together there would not be any fore and aft (Lawson 1980).

The contemporary Australian poet Judith Wright champions the interdependence of individual and environmental well-being. She is both romantic observer and recorder of the Australian bush, and an advocate for non-violence as the means of expressing justice. On the keys to Australian identity she writes of an emphasis on duties to brothers and sisters, on basic equalities and on the importance of mutual trust which is the force which makes society cohere. As in her observations about a flame tree in a quarry, she conjures inspiration from the land:

> flesh of the world's delight
> the voice of the world's desire
> I drink you with my sight
> and I am filled with fire.
>
> (Wright 1971)

A similar sense of excitement and inspiration fills the black American poet Maya Angelou. Her autobiography, *I Know Why the*

Caged Bird Sings (Angelou 1993) is a story of courage and humour and of a developing artistic and spiritual confidence. From abject povery in rural and racist Arkansas she combined a career of mother, prostitute, dancer, singer, poet and prestigious academic. She has made a difference with the same scepticism for authority, compassion and courage which seems to characterise the great humanitarians. In a poem read at President Clinton's inauguration she called for an inclusiveness of all peoples, without which the humanness of any single person would be diminished. In that poem, 'On The Pulse Of The Morning', she managed to catalogue North American diversity, 'the gay, the straight, the preacher, / the privileged, the homeless, the teacher'.

An alternative to managerialism

Defining and attaining humanity is an enterprise which crosses cultures and discipline boundaries, which questions dominant economic values and assumptions about the meaning and the value of masculinity and looks for inspiration from diverse peoples, artists and cultures. Reflection on the central features of modern economic order, especially its individualism, acquisitiveness and elevation of the values of the market to a central social place, will show they are at variance with the principles of humanity.

In discussions at home, in the workplace and in political circles the opportunity exists to define human well-being and to apply numerous perspectives in doing so. The contribution of ecological and green perspectives provides that thread of coherence which says that human well-being and protection of the environment are indivisible. Feminist perspectives have unmasked the synonymous nature of machismo styles of management, of masculinity and violence. Controversies over the means and ends of empowerment have derived insight from the arts and humanities, from the social sciences, as well as from numerous kinds of literature, each related to the biographies of people as well as the lives of individuals.

Humanitarians' attempts to make a difference contrast with values committed not to community or society but to the market and to the ideology of managerialism. The conduct of such humanitarians is a challenge to develop a sense of hope, to avoid the fatalism that says that little can be done. In this respect values and beliefs can be analysed and the shortcomings of policies or the disempowering structures of bureaucracies can be criticised. The prospect of realising our own humanness and of attaining humanity is being hindered more by the values which lead to inequality and oppression than by the policies and structures which give credence to those values in the first place. Paul Wilding argues that 'the most troubling problems are the product of particular beliefs, attitudes, policies and inertia adopted by individuals, institutions and governments' (Wilding 1987).

The alternative values require a transfer of discourse from economic rationalism to social justice, together with the courage and skills to pursue goals of empowerment. Since even that exhortation may sound worn, the idea of humanity could emerge as a primary principle and vision to create a greater sense of hope and possibility. Previously given little attention in social policy circles and almost none in deliberations about conventional economics or in clichés about efficient management, humanity is not cluttered with controversies of different official definitions. It is multidisciplinary, multicultural and multinational. It can draw from infinite sources of inspiration and can breathe new life into everyday communication about a common good and ways to attain it.

References

Angelou, M. 1993, *I Know Why The Caged Bird Sings*, Bantam Books, New York.
Birch, C. 1993, *Regaining Compassion*, New South Wales University Press, Kensington.
Campbell, T. 1974, 'Humanity before justice', *British Journal of Political Science*, no. 4, pp. 1–16.
Cochrane, C. 1993, 'The purpose of public pictures', *Sydney Morning Herald*, 13 October.
Connell, B. 1985, 'Masculinity, violence and war', in P. Patton & R. Poole (eds), *War/Masculinity*, Intervention Publications, Sydney.
Crick, F. 1994, 'A mind's eye view', *The Times* (Magazine), 30 April, pp. 21–2.
Daly, H. & Cobb, J. 1989, *For The Common Good*, Beacon Press, Boston.
Doyal, L. & Gough, I. 1991, *A Theory of Human Need*, Macmillan, London.
Eckersley, R. 1993, 'Rationalizing the environment: how much am I bid?', in S. Rees, G. Rodley & F. Stilwell (eds), *Beyond the Market*, Pluto Press, Sydney.
Ekins, P. (ed.) 1986, *The Living Economy: A New Economics in the Making*, Routledge & Kegan Paul, New York.
Ellis, B. 1994, 'Eyes are the prize', *Sydney Morning Herald* (Good Weekend), 20 August, pp. 18–26.
Esping-Andersen, G. 1990, *The Three Worlds of Welfare Capitalism*, Polity Press, Oxford.
Etzioni, A. 1983, *An Immodest Agenda*, McGraw-Hill, New York.
Everitt, A. 1994, 'Lose the life support', *Guardian*, 23 May.
Gardiner, P. 1993, *An Extraordinary Australian: Mary Mackillop*, E. J. Dwyer, Sydney.
Habermas, J. 1979, *Communication and the Evolution of Society*, Beacon Press, Boston.
Hammond, J. 1993, 'Edward Collick', *Australian*, 2 June.

Harlow, B. 1987, *Resistance Literature*, Methuen, London.
Havel, V. 1994, 'The new measure of man', *New York Times*, 8 July.
Lawson, H. 1980, *Selected Poems of Henry Lawson*, Angus & Robertson, Sydney.
Llosa, M. 1993, 'The culture of the book', *Sydney Morning Herald*, 11 September.
Lynd, R. 1964, *Knowledge for What?*, Grove Press, New York.
MacIntyre, A. 1984, *After Virtue*, University of Notre Dame Press, Notre Dame.
Marquand, D. 1988, *The Unprincipled Society*, Fontana Press, London.
Polanyi, K. 1957, *The Great Transformation*, Beacon Press, Boston.
Pusey, M. 1987, *Jurgen Habermas*, Tavistock Publications, London.
Rees, S. 1991, *Achieving Power*, Allen & Unwin, Sydney.
Rees, S., Rodley, G. & Stilwell, F. (eds), *Beyond the Market*, Pluto Press, Sydney.
Reiman, D. & Powers, S. 1977, *Shelley's Poetry and Prose*, Norton, New York.
Rose, S. & Black, B. 1985, *Advocacy & Empowerment*, Routledge, London.
Schumpeter, J. 1975, 'The future of private enterprise in the face of modern socialistic tendencies', *History of Political Economy*, vol. 7, no. 3, pp. 294–98.
Solomon, B. 1976, *Black Empowerment*, Columbia, New York.
Titmuss, R. 1971, *The Gift Relationship*, Penguin, London.
Watson, J. 1970, *The Double Helix*, Penguin, London.
Wilding, P. 1987, 'Hope in our world', *The Way*, October, pp. 256–63.
Wright, J. 1971, *Collected Poems*, Angus & Robertson, Sydney.

Postscript

Significant hope for a recovery of humanity may be seen in people's expanding awareness of their place in the universe, discourse on national and international identity and, in Australia, a growing recognition of insights from indigenous people.

Concern for the planet, for the survival of species, and for human existence may engender a new language of humanitarian aspiration and action. Environmental awareness encompasses local and universal dimensions, while science is revealing further levels of interconnectedness. As Vaclav Havel, president of the Czech Republic, has argued, reflection on existence can elicit a deep sense of responsiveness:

> Politicians ... may reiterate a thousand times ... universal respect for human rights, but it will mean nothing as long as this imperative does not derive from the respect of the miracle of Being, the miracle of the universe, the miracle of nature, the miracle of our own existence.
>
> The only real hope of people today is probably a renewal of our certainty that we are rooted in the earth and, at the same time, the cosmos. This awareness endows us with the capacity for self-transcendence.

Only during the latter half of the twentieth century has humankind for the first time been able to 'see' the cosmic grandeur of space and the molecular detail of life. Matter has started to reflect on itself; 'In such a creature [as Humankind] matter has at last begun to contemplate itself', as biologist George Wald put it in his 1971 Massey Lectures. This pristine knowledge, gained from instruments dramatically extending our capacity to observe, is essentially the preserve of a privileged few. But as this understanding permeates a wider community it may engender a new sense of being, by grafting to growing environmental awareness a recognition of place in the cold expanse of space. As astronaut Michael Collins has commented:

> I really believe that if the political leaders of the world could see their planet from a distance of ... 100 000 miles, their outlook could be fundamentally changed ... [T]he planet we share unites us in a way far more basic and far more important than differences in skin colour or religion or economic system ... [I]f I could use only one word to describe Earth as seen from the moon, I would ignore both its size and colour and search for a more elemental quality, that of fragility.

And to this new sense of spatial place we should add the profound Einsteinian insight of the indissoluble linkage of time with space and matter. In *About Time* physicist Paul Davies has expressed a belief that 'we are approaching a pivotal moment in history, when our knowledge of time is about to take another great leap forward'. Such considerations stand in stark contrast to preoccupations with delineating peoples' space and time for the purpose of commercial gain.

As a uniquely young, mid-sized nation seeking to articulate an independent identity, Australia provides a vibrant milieu for a discourse on wider concerns. On the one hand, a necessity to come to terms with a harsh environment, consideration of constitutional change, the remarkable development of as wide a multicultural society as any in the world, and the desperate plight of indigenous peoples are formative factors. On the other, the community as a whole is being subjected to the debilitating stress of bipartisan implementation of inappropriate economic practice.

The wealth of current writing and cultural activity addressing these issues augurs well for the development of humanitarian emphases which may displace politicians' preoccupation with financial dogma. An optimistic perspective would forecast that the current widespread disaffection with political representatives (who favour business over the health of citizens) could translate into demands for the expression of a different set of values and associated policies.

Several authors have promoted the concept of Australia developing a unique identity. With light-heartedness and enthusiasm Australia could turn back the tide of economic rationalism to realise higher ideals to replace the one-dimensionality of monetary imperative. There is an opportunity to turn away from deference to powerful men intent on making money and instead applaud each other in our common habitation of a remarkable continent. The sentiment of wider reflection is a natural response to the evocative expanse of an outback landscape. It is congruent with an informing feel for place within the cosmos, as artist Lloyd Rees has commented: 'our lives are set between mundane details on the one hand and endless space on the other ... humanity will continue to ponder the mystery of its own existence ...'.

While recent arrivals argue the identity of Australia, its indigenous peoples stand, waiting in silence, out of sight, clutching a spatial history of profound dimension. Their land, considered by the British as *terra nullius*, groans from the burden of opportunistic rape and dispossession. These ground-of-being sounds of agony will have to be listened to.

Although this book is silent about their story, this is a silence which speaks. For couched in sentiments praising humanity are echoes of innate knowledge gleaned from millennia of time. The wisdom of circumspection, informed by traverse of a continental land, resonates with emphases of hope for humanity. In *The Road to Botany Bay*, writer Paul Carter, in identifying links to indigenous insight and intention, notes that we may come to appreciate: 'how it was possible for [them] to remain "intirely unmov'd" by the *Endeavour*, why they continued "attentive to their business" [and] why the "Idea of traffick" did not cross their minds'.

Moon Beams

Should I jump to the moon tonight
and be cradled in its ancient light,
the universe energies soothing my soul
as I look down to the planet below?

Would I shake my head in disbelief
weep out loud for the human race,
laugh at the path they choose to take
and see a change in Papatuanuku's fate?

Yes, I will jump to the moon tonight
and be cradled in its ancient light,
the energies of the universe will soothe my soul
as I peer down at the planet below.

No, I won't shake my head in disbelief,
I will not cry for the human race
or laugh at the path they choose to take
but I will weep for our earth mother's fate.

Would you jump to the moon tonight?

Vivienne Sinclair

Bibliography

Albin, S. 1992, *Bureau Shaping and Contracting Out: The Case of Australian Local Government*, Discussion Paper No. 29, ANU, Canberra.
Alford, J. & O'Neill, D. (eds) 1994, *The Contract State: Public Management in Kennett's Victoria*, Deakin University Press, Geelong.
Angelou, M. 1993, *I Know Why the Caged Bird Sings*, Bantam Books, New York.
Bartol, K. M. & Martin, D. C. 1991, *Management*, McGraw-Hill, New York.
Birch, C. 1993, *Regaining Compassion: For Humanity and Nature*, New South Wales University Press, Kensington.
Blyton, P. & Turnbull, P. 1994, *The Dynamics of Employee Relations*, Macmillan, London.
Bogdanich, W. 1991, *The Great White Lie*, Simon & Schuster, New York.
Boston, J. et al. (eds) 1991, *Reshaping the State: New Zealand's Bureaucratic Revolution*, Oxford University Press, Auckland.
Brundtland Report 1987, *Our Common Future*, Oxford University Press, Oxford.
Buchanan, J. & Callus, R. 1993, 'Equity and efficiency at work: the need for labour market regulation in Australia', *Journal of Industrial Relations*, vol. 35, no. 4, December.
Burnetta, R. & Dell'Aringa, C. (eds) 1990, *Labour Relations and Economic Performance*, Macmillan, London.
Callus, R., Morehead, A., Cully, M. & Buchanan, J. 1992, *Industrial Relations at Work: The Australian Workplace Industrial Relations Survey*, AGPS, Canberra.
Campbell, T. 1974, 'Humanity before justice', *British Journal of Political Science*, no. 4, pp. 1–16.
Carter, P. 1988, *The Road to Botany Bay*, Knopf, New York.
Carter, P. 1992, *Living in a New Country: History, Travelling and Language*, Faber, London.

Chomsky, N. 1989, *Necessary Illusion*, Pluto Press, London.
―― 1993, *The Year 501: The Conquest Continues*, Verso, London.
Chorney, H., Hotson, I. & Seccareccia, M. 1993, *The Deficit Made Me Do It*, Canadian Centre for Policy Alternatives, Ottawa.
Cockett, R. 1994, *Thinking the Unthinkable: Think-Tanks and the Economic Counter-Revolution*, Harper Collins, London.
Considine, M. 1988, 'The corporate management framework as administrative science: a critique', *Australian Journal of Public Administration*, vol. 47, no. 1, pp. 4–18.
Cooper, D. 1993, *Child Abuse Revisited*, Open University Press, Buckingham.
Coulter, J. (ed.) 1993, *Doing More With Less? Contracting Out and Efficiency in the Public Sector*, Public Sector Research Centre, University of New South Wales, Sydney.
Cousins, C. 1987, *Controlling Social Welfare: A Sociology of State Welfare Work and Organization*, Wheatsheaf, Sussex.
Curran, J., Gurivitch, M. & Wollacott, J. (eds) 1977, *Mass Communication and Society*, Edward Arnold, London.
Daly, H. & Cobb, J. 1989, *For the Common Good*, Beacon Press, Boston.
Dandeker, C. 1990, *Surveillance Power and Modernity*, St Martin, New York.
Davies, P. 1995, *About Time*, Viking, Middlesex.
Davis, A. & George, J. 1993, *States of Health*, Harper Educational, Sydney.
Davis, G., Weller, P. & Lewis, C. 1989, *Corporate Management in Australia*, Macmillan, Melbourne.
Dent, M. 1993, 'Professionalism, educated labour and the state: hospital medicine and the new managerialism', *Sociological Review*, May, pp. 244–73.
Doyal, L. & Gough, I. 1991, *A Theory of Human Need*, Macmillan, London.
Easton, B. H. (ed.) 1989, *The Making of Rogernomics*, Auckland University Press, Auckland.
Ekins, P. (ed.) 1986, *The Living Economy: A New Economics in the Making*, Routledge & Kegan Paul, New York.
Emy, H. 1993, *Remaking Australia: The State, the Market and Australia's Future*, Allen & Unwin, Sydney.
Esping-Anderson, G. 1990, *The Three Worlds of Welfare Capitalism*, Polity Press, Oxford.
Evatt Research Centre 1989, *State of Siege*, Pluto Press, Sydney.
―― 1990, *Breach of Contract*, Pluto Press, Sydney.
Fabricnat, M. & Burghardt, S. 1992, *The Welfare State Crisis and the Transformation of Social Service Work*, Armonck, New York.
Flannery, T. 1994, *The Future Eaters*, Reed Books, Chatswood, NSW.
Franklin, B. & Parton, N. (eds) 1991, *Social Work, the Media and Public Relations*, Routledge, London.
Gabe, J. et al. (eds) 1994, *Challenging Medicine*, Routledge, New York.
Galbraith, J. K. 1992, *The Culture of Contentment*, Houghton Mifflin, Boston.
Gardiner, P. 1993, *An Extraordinary Australian: Mary Mackillop*, E. J. Dwyer, Sydney.
Golden, M. & Pontusson, J. (eds) 1992, *Bargaining for Change — Union Politics in North America and Europe*, Cornell University Press, Ithaca, New York.
Gospel, H. 1992, *Markers, Firms and Management of Labour in Modern*

Britain, Cambridge University Press, Cambridge.
Gutmann, A. (ed.) 1994, *Multiculturalism: Examining the Politics of Recognition*, Princeton University Press, Princeton.
Habermas, J. 1971, *Knowledge and Human Interests*, Beacon Press, Boston.
—— 1988, *Legitimation Crisis*, Polity Press & Basil Blackwell, Oxford.
—— 1988, *The Theory of Communicative Action*, 2 vols, Beacon Press, Boston.
Hafferty, F. & McKinlay, J. (eds) 1993, *The Changing Medical Profession*, Oxford University Press, New York.
Ham, C. 1994, 'Reforming health services', *Social Policy and Administration*, vol. 28, pp. 293–8.
Hames, R. 1994, *The Management Myth: Exploring the Essence of Future Organizations*, Business & Professional Publishing, Chatswood, NSW.
Hayek, F. A. 1994, *The Road to Serfdom*, Routledge, London.
Headon, D., Hooton, J. & Horne, D. (eds) 1995, *Abundant Culture: Meaning and Significance in Everyday Australia*, Allen & Unwin, Sydney.
Head, B. & Walter, J. (eds) 1988, *Intellectual Movements and Australian Society*, Oxford University Press, Melbourne.
Headon, D., Hooton, J. & Home, D. (eds) 1995, *Abundant Culture: Meaning and Significance in Everyday Australia*, Allen & Unwin, Sydney.
Hilmer, F. 1993, *Independent Committee of Inquiry Into Competition Policy in Australia: National Competition Policy*, AGPS, Canberra.
Hoggett, P. 1991, 'A new management in the public sector?', *Policy and Politics*, no. 19, pp. 243–56.
Horne, D. 1989, *Ideas for a Nation*, Pan Books, Sydney.
Howard, M. 1990, *The Use of Consultants by the Public Sector in Australia: Recent Evidence and Issues*, Public Sector Research Centre, University of New South Wales, Kensington.
Howard, M. 1995, *A Growth Industry? Use of Consultants by Commonwealth Departments, 1974–1994*, Public Sector Research Centre, University of New South Wales, Kensington.
Howe, D. 1986, *Social Workers and Their Practice in Welfare Bureaucracies*, Gower, Aldershot.
Hudson, B. 1992, 'Quasi markets in health and social care in Britain', *Policy and Politics*, no. 20, pp. 131–42.
Jakubowicz, A., Goodall, H., Martin, J., Mitchell, T., Seneviratne, K. & Kendall, L. 1994, *Racism, Ethnicity and the Media*, Allen & Unwin, Sydney.
Jones, A. & May, J. 1992, *Working in Human Service Organizations*, Longman Cheshire, Melbourne.
Karger, H. J. 1986, 'The deskilling of social workers: an examination of the impact of the industrial model of production on the delivery of social services', *Journal of Sociology and Social Welfare*, no. 13, pp. 115–29.
Keating, M. 1990, 'Managing for results in the public interest', *Australian Journal of Public Administration*, vol. 49, no. 4, pp. 387–98.
Kelly, P. 1992, *The End of Certainty: The Story of the 1980s*, Allen & Unwin, Sydney.
Knudtson, P. & Suzuki, D. 1992, *Wisdom of the Elders*, Allen & Unwin, Sydney.
Lane, R. 1991, *The Market Experience*, Cambridge University Press,

Melbourne.
Langmore, J. & Quiggin, J. 1994, *Work For All*, Melbourne University Press, Melbourne.
Lawrence, G. & Rowe, D. 1986, *Power Play: Essays in the Sociology of Australian Sport*, Hale & Iremonger, Sydney.
Leach, R. (ed.) 1995, *Alliance Politics: Beyond the Labour and Liberal Parties*, Catalyst Press, Sydney.
Locke, R. 1989, *Management and Higher Education Since 1940*, Cambridge University Press, Cambridge.
Lupton, D. et al. 1991, 'Caveat emptor or blissful ignorance?', *Social Science and Medicine*, no. 33, pp. 559–68.
MacInnes, 1. 1987, *Thatcherism at Work*, Open University Press, Milton Keynes.
MacIntyre, A. 1984, *After Virtue: A Study in Moral Theory*, 2nd edn, University of Notre Dame Press, Notre Dame, Indiana.
MacKay, H. 1993, *Reinventing Australia: The Mind and Mood of Australia in the 90's*, Angus & Robertson, Sydney.
Marginson, S. 1993, *Education and Public Policy in Australia*, Cambridge University Press, Cambridge.
Marquand, D. 1988, *The Unprincipled Society*, Fontana Press, London.
Morgan, G. 1990, *Organizations in Society*, Macmillan, London.
Murnane, G. 1982, *Plains*, Norstrilia Press, Carlton, Vic.
Nettleton, S. & Harding, G. 1994, 'Protesting patients', *Sociology of Health and Illness*, vol. 16, no. 1, pp. 38–61.
Nile, R. (ed.) 1994, *Australian Civilisation*, Oxford University Press, Melbourne.
Osborne, D. & Gabler, E. 1992, *Reinventing Government*, Addison-Wesley, Reading, Mass.
Parton, N. 1991, *Governing the Family: Child Care, Child Protection and the State*, Macmillan, London.
Patton, P. & Poole, R. (eds) 1985, *War–Masculinity*, Intervention Publications, Sydney.
Pollitt, C. 1990, *Managerialism and the Public Services: The Anglo-American Experience*, Blackwell, Oxford.
——1993, *Managerialism and the Public Services: Cuts or Cultural Change in the 1990s?*, rev. edn, Blackwell, Oxford.
Pontusson, J. 1992, *The Limits of Social Democracy — Investment Politics and Sweden*, Cornell University Press, Ithaca, New York.
Pope, D. & Alston, L. (eds) 1989, *Australia's Greatest Asset: Human Resources in the Nineteenth and Twentieth Centuries*, Federation Press, Sydney.
Pusey, M. 1987, *Jurgen Habermas*, Tavistock Publications, London.
——1991, *Economic Rationalism in Canberra*, Cambridge University Press, Melbourne.
Rees, S. 1991, *Achieving Power*, Allen & Unwin, Sydney.
——1994, 'Economic rationalism, an ideology of exclusion', *Australian Journal of Social Issues*, vol. 29, no. 2.
Rees, S., Rodley, G. & Stilwell, F. (eds) 1993, *Beyond the Market: Alternatives to Economic Rationalism*, Pluto Press, Sydney.
Rose, N. 1989, *Governing the Soul: The Shaping of the Private Self*, RKP,

London.
Rosenblum, N. L. (ed.) 1989, *Liberalism and the Moral Life*, Harvard University Press, Cambridge, Mass.
Said, E. W. 1994, *Representations of the Intellectual: The 1993 Reith Lectures*, Vintage, London.
Sawer, M. (ed.) 1982, *Australia and the New Right*, Allen & Unwin, Sydney.
Schultz, J. (ed.) 1994, *Not Just Another Business*, Pluto Press, Sydney.
Schumacher, E. F. 1973, *Small is Beautiful*, Harper & Row, New York.
Self, P. 1990, 'Market ideology and good government', *Current Affairs Bulletin*, September, pp. 4–10.
——1993, *Government by the Market? The Politics of Public Choice*, Macmillan, London.
Senge, P. 1992, *The Fifth Discipline*, Random House, Sydney.
Simons, R. G. 1995, *Competing Gospels: Public Theology and Economic Theory*, E. J. Dwyer, Sydney.
Spicer, J., Trlin, A. & Walton, J. (eds) 1994, *Social Dimensions of Health and Disease: New Zealand Perspectives*, Dunmore Press, Palmerston North.
Stilwell, F. 1993, *Economic Inequality: Who Gets What in Australia*, Pluto Press, Sydney.
——1994, 'Working nation: from green to white paper', *Journal of Australian Political Economy*, no. 33, June.
Tacey, D. J. 1995, *Edge of the Sacred*, Harper Collins.
Taylor, C. 1989, *Sources of the Self*, Harvard University Press, Cambridge, Mass.
Turner, B. 1993, *Citizenship and Social Theory*, Sage, London.
Vamplew, W. & Stoddart, B. (eds) 1994, *Sport in Australia*, Cambridge University Press, Melbourne.
Vintila, P., Phillimore, J. & Newman, P. (eds) 1992, *Markets, Morals and Manifestos*, Institute for Science & Technology Policy, Murdoch University, Perth.
Weiss, C. 1977, *Using Social Science in Public Policy Making*, Lexington Books, Lexington, Mass.
Wretsch, J. 1991, *Voices of the Mind*, Harvard University Press, Cambridge, Mass.
Wright, C. 1995, *The Management of Labour: An Historical Analysis of Labour Management in Australian Industry*, Oxford University Press, Melbourne.
Wright, Mills C. 1956, *White Collar*, Oxford University Press, New York.

Contributors

Stephen Albin works as the Executive Project Officer at Manly Council, advising the general manager and mayor on economic and organisational issues. He is also an honorary research associate at the Australian Centre for Local Government Studies at the University of Canberra. As a consultant, Stephen has devised strategies for the national governments of Poland, Indonesia and Papua New Guinea regarding the development of local democracy.

Craig Bremner is a lecturer in the Faculty of Visual and Performing Arts at the University of Western Sydney, Nepean. He is also guest curator of architecture and design for the Museum of Contemporary Art, Sydney. He consults widely on design matters in Australia and Italy.

Wendy Bacon is an award-winning investigative journalist and a lawyer. She has been a social activist in the prison, anti-censorship, resident action and feminist movements, She is currently Director of the Australian Centre for Independent Journalism and an associate professor in journalism at the University of Technology, Sydney.

Susan Britton is a medical practitioner, mother and a colleague to university staff in several settings. In the eyes of staff associates and patients Susan has a reputation not only for high standards of clinical practice but also for addressing social trends — such as managerialism — and social justice issues. She has worked as a doctor in a major Australian university health service for the past fourteen years.

John Buchanan is currently Deputy Director of the Australian Centre for Industrial Relations Research at the University of Sydney. Previously he was director of policy research in the Commonwealth Department of Industrial Relations. His major research interests are management determinants of labour productivity and the role of the state in nurturing new forms of multi-employer coordination.

Meredith Burgmann was a senior lecturer in politics at Macquarie University until she entered the New South Wales Legislative Council as a Labor member in 1991. She was active in the anti-Vietnam, anti-apartheid and women's movements, and then in the trade union movement. She was the first woman president of the New South Wales Academics Union and her research interests are women's wages, equal pay and women's involvement in decision-making.

Alan Davis is a teacher and writer who maintains his commitment to students and to his professional discipline despite the erosion of resources in public sector institutions such as universities. As Associate Professor in the Department of Social Work and Social Policy at the University of Sydney he teaches sociology to undergraduates and postgraduates. Alan is the author and co-author of numerous reports, articles and books, including the best-selling *States of Health*.

Grant Duncan completed his PhD at Auckland University in 1989. He now lectures in the Department of Social Policy and Social Work at Massey University's Albany campus north of Auckland. His interests include public policy reform and social service management. He has published several articles on the reform of New Zealand's accident compensation scheme.

Brian Easton is a research economist and social statistician working on numerous aspects of New Zealand economic and social development. He is the Director of the Economic And Social Trust On New Zealand, a visiting senior lecturer in political studies at the University of Auckland, and an honorary lecturer in the Department of Community Health, Wellington Medical School.

Col Face has worked for more than ten years in the welfare sector, much of it with the Department of Community Services. Col started as a direct service worker after finishing a university degree and has worked with children and families in abuse and crisis situations. He has held a number of positions in policy and management in DOCS where he has witnessed and experienced at first hand regular and successive restructures since the mid-1980s.

Gary Hough is a senior lecturer in the Department of Social Work at the Royal Melbourne Institute of Technology where he coordinates the Master of Social Science (social policy, community development, community services management). He worked in public welfare for ten years before moving to social work education. His teaching and research interests are in community services organisation and management, and public welfare policy and practice. Gary was president of the Australian Association for Social Work and Welfare Education during 1993–94.

Jane Marceau is Professor of Public Policy at the Australian National University and has written extensively on what seems to some to be far too great a range of topics. When she decides to specialise it will probably be in a history of Catalan Romanesque churches. In the meantime Jane publishes on higher education, technology and industry policy, with an occasional visit to international business and Australia's place in the Asia-Pacific region.

Michael Muetzelfeldt teaches policy studies and political sociology at Deakin University, where he is Director of the Centre for Citizenship and Human Rights. His research is concerned with the effects on citizenship of the growing dominance of market and market-like processes in the public sphere.

Stuart Rees is Professor of Social Work and Director of the Centre for Peace and Conflict Studies, University of Sydney. His experience as a social worker in the courts and in community development in several countries highlighted the importance of interdisciplinary cooperation, whether in research, teaching or social action. His books include *A Brutal Game*, *Achieving Power*, *Verdicts on Social Work* and the co-edited *Beyond the Market*. His sentiments about social justice have also been expressed through poetry.

Gordon Rodley took early retirement from the Chemistry Department, University of Canterbury, New Zealand, in 1987. Since then, apart from a year at the Centre for Cellular and Molecular Biology, Hyderabad, India, he has been at the University of Sydney working at the Centre for Peace and Conflict Studies and pursuing scientific interests.

Mike Salvaris is Senior Research Fellow at the Centre for Urban and Social Research, Swinburne University of Technology, Melbourne. He is working on a three-year project with other universities to develop national benchmarks for citizenship and social rights in the context of constitutional reform. Mike was an adviser to the former Victorian Kirner Labor government.

Robert Simons received his doctorate in theology from the Catholic University of America and has been a visiting fellow at Harvard University for a research project on Christian systematic theology and economic theory. He has lectured at Flinders University of South Australia and Mary Immaculate Seminary, Allenstown, Pennsylvania. Robert is author of *Competing Gospels: Public Theology and Economic Theory*. His area of research is possible futures for the economic organisation of society.

Karin Solondz has a Master of Psychology and Bachelor of Behavioural Science. She has travelled extensively and worked professionally in Europe and Australia in the areas of clinical and organisational psychology. She has also been involved in environmental and socio-psychological research. Karin currently runs a private consultancy practice on the Central Coast near Sydney.

Frank Stilwell is Associate Professor of Economics at the University of Sydney. He has been a leading participant in the long struggle at that university for the teaching of political economy courses which challenge orthodox economic doctrines. He is the author of various books on political economy, the state and urban development, including *Economic Inequality* and *Reshaping Australia*. He is also Coordinating Editor of the *Journal of Australian Economy* and a founding member of the social movement, Reworking Australia.

Ted Wheelwright is an arts graduate of the University of St Andrews, Scotland, where he specialised in political economy, which he has been teaching and researching for over forty years in four continents. He believes economics must be demystified for ordinary people, as it is being used as an ideological weapon against them. Ted is a retired associate professor at the University of Sydney where he is now a Fellow of the Senate and Honorary Associate in Geography. He has served on government committees of inquiry and been a director of the Commonwealth Bank, consultant to the United Nations, and a Rockefeller fellow. He is the author, co-author, editor or co-editor of twenty-one books and numerous articles.

The Poets

Susan Bower is a young poet who has published in journals such as *Southerly, Artvoice, Tangent* and *Hermes*. She is completing a PhD in creative arts at Wollongong University.

Michael Brennan edits *Avernus*, a magazine for young poets. He is completing an honours degree in Australian literature at the University of Sydney.

Annette Falahey is a sociologist at the University of Sydney, specialising in media studies and sociological accounts of music. Annette is also a poet whose work has appeared in publications such as *Art Resistance*.

Henry S. Maas is the author of two books of poems, *Tide Pools & Swoosh Holes* and *Crests & Chasms*. He previously wrote or edited eight books of social research while teaching at the universities of Chicago, California at Berkeley, and British Columbia, where he now lives.

Les Murray lives in his native district of Bunyah on the New South Wales North Coast. His poetry has been praised widely throughout the English-speaking world.

Oodgeroo Noonucaal (also known as Kath Walker) was a poet well-known for depicting the predicament of Australian Aboriginals, for protesting against racism and for works such as the collection *My People*.

Vivienne Sinclair is a young poet from Christchurch, New Zealand, who derives inspiration from companions such as her dogs, and from the natural environment.

William Wordsworth was the late eighteenth-, early-nineteenth - century poet of the English Lakecal issues such as liberty, environmental protection and humanity. district who was also concerned with radical issues such as liberty, environmental protection and humanity.

Index

ABC 18, 77, 79, 150, 218
ACCI 57, 58
AMP 250
AWIRS 58–62
Aboriginal land rights 256
Academics Union of NSW 90
accountability 3, 151, 213
    cost displacement and 101–2
accounting firms 207–8
Adam Smith Club 33
Adam Smith Institute 33
Adams, G. 178
Adams, Phillip 18
advertising and the media 4, 70
    see also media
Age (newspaper) 150, 153, 158(n11)
aged care 100
air safety 20, 102
alcohol 253
Alexander, John 80
Alford, J. 165
alienation 277
All Across the Nation (Leunig) 53
All One Race (Oodgeroo) 239
alternatives 25–6
    see also humanity, recovery of
altruism 293
amateurism 249, 256–7
Amstrad 257

Angelou, Maya 297–8
Ansett 70
anthropology 272
anti-nuclear policy 256
anti-unionism 20, 32, 34, 149
    see also trade unions
Ardiles, Ossie 257
Arndt, H.W. 34
Arthur Andersen 208
Atlas Economic Research Foundation 33
atomist thought 282
Australia (Hope) 233–4
Australia at the Crossroads 34
Australian (newspaper) 69–70, 71, 76–7
Australian Broadcasting Corporation
    see ABC
Australian Business (magazine) 71
Australian Centre for Independent Journalism 72, 81
Australian Chamber of Commerce and Industry 57, 58
Australian Financial Review (newspaper) 207
Australian Human Resource Institute 58
Australian Institute for Public Policy 34
Australian National Audit Office 102, 104
Australian Workplace Industrial Relations Survey 58–62

Austrian School 31
authenticity 274
autonomy 278
aviation industry 70

BBC 77–8
BCA 57, 58
Babb, Jeffrey 34
balanced reporting 74
Baldwin, Peter 117
Barking at Thunder (Murray) 171
Battersby, D. 200
Baume, Peter 128
Baxter, Ken 98
benchmarking 126, 187
Benetton 251
best practice 126
Beyond the Market (Rees, Rodley & Stilwell) 6, 236
bioethics 131
Birch, Charles 286, 294
Black, Conrad 33
Black, Julie 77–9
Blandy, Richard 34
Bolger, Jim 42
Bongiorno, Bernard 149
Bonython, John 34
borrowed models 243–4
Bower, Susan 51, 109
Bowers, Peter 81
Brennan, Michael 11
British Broadcasting Corporation 78
British Gas 206
British Institute of Professionals, Managers and Specialists 21
British Telecom 206
Brown, Cedric 206
Builders' Labourers Federation 85
bullying 197–9
Burnham, J. 30
Business Council of Australia 57, 58
business magazines 71
Business Review Weekly (magazine) 71
Butler, Sir Robin 200

CSIRO 21–3, 208
Carauna, L. 69
career paths 63
Carers Association of Australia 100
Carlton, J.J. 34
Carmagnola, F. 247
Carmen (financial institution employee) 200–2

Carr, Bob 98
Carter, Paul 304
cartoons 6, 13, 14, 53–4, 100, 110, 152, 172, 191, 203, 242
case mix funding 100, 129, 147
Centre for Independent Studies 32, 33, 34
Centre for Policy Studies (British) 33
Centre for Policy Studies 34
Chiccio, Diana 78
child abuse 160–5, 173–6, 183
child protection 160–5, 173, 174
    mandatory reporting 175
Chipman, Lachlan 34
Chomsky, Noam 151–3, 233, 268
Chorover, S.L. 55
Christianity and economic theory 272
citizenship 145, 146, 280, 282, 290
civil rights
    see human rights
Clemengers advertising agency 80
Client Information System (DOCS) 188–90
Cobb, J. 286, 292, 294
Coca-Cola Amatil 205
Cockburn, Milton 81
Cockett, R. 30–3
Codd, Mike 95
Code of Conduct (CSIRO) 22
collectivism 87, 281, 282
    and legitimation 272
Collick, Edward 296
Collins, Michael 302
Commercial Services Group 102
commercialisation 41, 252
common goods 282
Commonwealth Scientific & Industrial Research Organisation 21–3, 208
communicative action 277–80
communitarianism 281–2
Community Services Dept (DOCS) (NSW) 7, 25, 183
    Chief Executive Officer 186
    information systems 187–90
    managerialism 184
    productivity savings 184–5
    restructuring 185–8
community services provision 142
    funding cuts in Victoria 146, 175–80
Community Services Victoria 178
competition 24, 198
Competition is Good (Wilcox) 14

competitive tendering 138
conceptual artists 246–8
Coney, Sandra 255–6
Connell, Bob 295
Connelly, Patrick 78
Consolidated Press 70, 80
consultants 19, 206–9
contingency theory 165, 179
Continuous Improvement (Saffron) 191
contract work 217, 219
contracting out 98, 104, 138–41, 234
    Victoria 95–6
control 22, 24, 61–2, 165, 198–9
    authoritarianism 148–51, 167
    Community Services Victoria 179
    contracting out and 140–1
    DOCS (NSW) 189–90
    peer relationships 218–19
    technical 262
convergent goods 282
Coombe, K. 200
Coopers and Lybrand 207, 208
corporate imagery 246
    and sport 250
corporatisation 16, 20, 23–4, 41, 127
    health sector in NZ 42
    universities 198
    see also public sector enterprises
cost displacement 98–101, 130
    accountability 101–2
    employees 103
cost effectiveness 3, 289
Costello, Peter 34
counselling services 223, 225
Cox, B. 256
creativity 257, 286, 291, 292
    and managerialism 226–7
    political 256
credit rating 155
cricket 250, 253
cronyism 207
Crossroads 34
Crown (Bower) 109
Crown Health Enterprises 42, 44–5, 46
cultural respect 275–6
culture management 17
Curran, J. 73–4, 77

Daily Telegraph (London newspaper) 33
Daily Telegraph (Sydney newspaper) 81
Daly, H. 286, 292, 294
Daniel, Greg 80
Davidson, Ken 153

Davies, Paul 302
Dayton, L. 21
decentralisation of authority 57, 59–61, 64, 126
decision-making 60, 63–4, 126
    structures 87
    trade unions 86–7
defensive medicine 122
    see also health care
Delahunty, Mary 150
Delight in Enlightenment (Maas) 242
demoralisation 4
Department of Community Services (NSW)
    see Community Services Dept
depression 222, 226
de-professionalisation 216–17
    see also professionalism
deregulation 16, 202, 204, 233
Diagnostic Related Groups 129, 130
difference 275, 276
dignity 275
Disability Act 1993 (NSW) 194
disability services 179, 183, 193
doctors, threats to dominance of 122, 128
Doonesbury (Trudeau) 100
Dowling, Grahame 207
downsizing 125, 184, 213, 235
Downward/Onward/Upward (Maas) 110
Ducker, John 86
Duesbury's 208
Dunlop, Edward (Weary) 296
Dusevic, Tom 33, 36

EAP 211–12
early childhood education funding 99–100
early discharge 129
Eastern Suburbs Newpapers 75
Eckersley, Robin 294–5
eco-feminism 294
economic growth 234, 255, 262
economic inequality 24, 145–6, 262, 265–6
    minimum income guarantee 267
economic policy
    see political economic policy
economic rationalism 15–16, 30, 112, 114, 127, 265–6, 285
    media and 71–2, 153
Economic Reform Australia 236
economic restructuring 264–5

and higher education 113
Economy, The (Leunig) 13
Economy Says, The (Leunig) 152
editorial policy 74–5
  see also media
education
  as production good 113
  equity 113
  goals 111–12
  intolerance of critics 200
  political economic policy 113–14
  Victoria 147, 151
  see also higher education
effectiveness 103–4, 112
efficiency 3, 16, 24, 96, 112, 245
  effectiveness 103–4
  measurability 214–15
  organisational cultures and 212
  quality and, in NZCYPS 163–4
  technical 96–8
    cost displacement and 98–9, 130
  social issues and 102
  see also inefficiency
    productivity
Ekins, P. 286
electricity distribution 43, 206
  Ellis, Bob 296
Employee Assistance Programme 211–12
empowerment 57, 59–60, 63–4, 286
enterprise bargaining 19, 213
  women and 88
enterprise size 62
environment
  abuse 202, 294–4, 302
  concern and the market 233, 262
environmentally sound products 266
equal pay 63
Equanimity (Murray) 240
Ernst and Young 207
Etzioni, A. 293–4
evaluation 118
Evans, Bob 43
Evans, Ray 34
Evatt Research Centre 98
executive salaries 29, 204
exhaustion 9–2

facilitators 57
Fairfax Community Newspapers 75
Fairly Typical Discussion, A (Leunig) 242
Falahey, Annette 52

Family Court 150
Financial Management System (DOCS) 190
Fisher, Anthony 32, 33, 34
Flannery, Tim 233
flexibility 95, 167, 264–5
  see also trade unions
football 76–7, 250, 252–4
For the Common Good (Daly & Cobb) 286, 292, 296
forms of knowing 277
Fosters' Brewing 204
Fourth Estate 73
Fraser, Malcolm 34, 35, 36, 98
Free Trade (Rees) 12
freedom of information 151
freedom of the press 72
Friedman, Milton 32, 33, 34
French manufacturing 64
Fusfield, D. 29
Future Eaters, The (Flannery) 233

GIO 195
Gaebler, T. 96
Galbraith, J.K. 30
Gardiner, P. 296
Geelong Council 150
generic managers 40–2, 44–5
generic reformers 43
German manufacturing 64
Gibson, Bill 205
Gittens, R. 254, 255
Glasman, Maurice 63–4
Goodis, Jerry 251
Goodman Fielder 205
Gorz, André 294
government accounting systems 42
Government Insurance Office 195
government spending 146
Greed (Wilcox) 203
greed 197, 202, 204–6, 209
green jobs 266
Greenpeace 80
Greiner, Nick 80, 184, 207

H.R. Nicholls Society 34
Habermas, Jurgen 72, 277–80, 286–7
Hammond, J. 296
Hannan Group 75
Harries, Owen 33
Harris, Ralph 32
Havel, Vaclav 293, 302
Hayek, F.A. 31–2, 33, 34, 35

Hayward, D. 153
health care
 Britain 20
 corporatisation of 42, 127–8
 economics 43
 organisation of 128–30
 threat to medical dominance 121–4, 128
health care costs 99, 100–1
 information systems 132
 managerial focus 124–7, 131–2, 133
 outcome measures 130–1
 underfunding 122
health reforms
 cost focus 133
 generic managers and reformers 43–7
 management and practitioners 131–2
 New Zealand 39, 42–3
 outcome measures 130–1
 threat to medical dominance 121–4, 128
health services managers 44
hierarchy 22, 46, 244, 273
 AWIRS 60, 61
Henderson, Gerard 33
Heritage Foundation 33
higher education
 economic restructuring and 113
 management theory and 117–18
 see also education
Hilmer, Fred 24, 198
Hobbes, Thomas 55
Hocking, Douglas 35
Hogan, Warren 34, 35
holism 272
Hollows, Fred 296
Hope, A.D. 233–4
Horin, Adele 255
Hornery, Stuart 205
hospitals 122–3, 147
household costs 100–1
Howe, D. 176
human costs 19–23, 166, 213–14, 217, 218, 226
 see also stress
human relations 17
human resources management 55, 56–8, 125, 262
 survey findings 58–62
human rights 149, 276, 289
humanitarians 296–8

humanity 25
 and the market 2
 defining 288
 expressing 292–3
 recovery 232, 286–7, 290–1, 301–4
 sport and the recovery of 255–8
Humanity (Wordsworth) 171
Huxley, J. 254
Hyde, John 34
Hymen, Richard 86

I Know Why the Caged Bird Sings (Angelou) 297–8
ICAC 101–2
ILO 149
identity and recognition 272–7, 280–2
ideology 4–5, 15, 265
 Kennett government 156–7
 transforming 231, 233–5
Immodest Agenda, An (Etzioni) 293–4
incentive structures 141
income distribution
 see economic inequality
Independent Commission Against Corruption 101–2
indigenous peoples 301, 303–4
individualisation of issues 57, 176
industrial democracy 63
industry development 266
Industry Task Force on Leadership and Management Skills 56
inefficiency measurement 215–18
 see also efficiency
information provision 91, 92, 246
information super-highway 246, 263
infrastructure 147, 155
 social 233
Ingersoll, V. 178
innovation and local government 137
inputs and outputs 97, 124–5
 Community Services Victoria 178–9
 education policy and 113–14
 NZCYPS 160, 162
Institute for Personnel Management 58
Institute of Chartered Accountants 208
Institute of Economic Affairs 32
Institute of Labour Studies 34
Institute of Public Affairs 33
International Labour Organisation 149
intolerance 3–4, 148–51, 198, 199–200
Intruder (Bower) 51
investment and employment 63

Jeffries, David 206
Jenkins, Elizabeth 21
job security 19, 264–6
    and inefficiency 217–18
job sharing 256, 267, 294
jobs compact 264
John Fairfax and Sons 71, 75, 204
Johnson, Ben 256
Jones, K. 254
Joreen (collective) 87
Joss, Bob 198 198
journalists 74–7

Kant, I. 275
Karpin Report 56, 103
Kasper, Wolfgang 35
Keating, Michael 97, 98
Keating, Paul 71
Kelly, Bert 34
Kelly, Paul 33, 34–6, 71
Kemp, C.D. 33
Kemp, David 35
Kemp, Rod 33
Kennett, Jeff 4, 95, 139, Ch 11
Kewley, T.H. 34
Keynes, J.M. 30–1
Knight, Elizabeth 250
Kramer, Leonie 33

Labor Council of NSW 86
labour management 55
    inefficiencies 56
    human resources approach 56–8
    survey findings 58–62
    worker involvement and 62–5
labour markets 62–3
Langer, Allan 77
language and autonomy 278
Larriera, Alice 131
Laski, Harold 31
Lattin, Mike 252
Lawrence, G. 250
Lawson, Henry 297
Leach, R. 268
leadership replication 89
legitimation 272, 279
Leunig, Michael 13, 53, 152, 242
Level Playing Field (Saffron) 14
Lewis, C. 98
liberalism 30, 282–3
liberation 272, 279, 287
lifeworld 278
    see also Habermas, Jurgen

Lilley, Roy 20
Lindsay, Greg 33, 34
local government 137
    community service provision 142
    Victoria 148–50
local taxes and contracting out 139
London School of Economics 31
Lynd, Robert 292

MBA courses 18–19, 24, 40, 202
MacIntyre, A. 24, 295, 296
McKewen, T. 252
McKillop, Mary 296
Maclellan, Robert 149
McMaster Laboratory 21
Maas, Henry S. 110, 242
machismo 89–91, 295, 298
macro managerialism 262
Major, John 206
male arenas 86–7
Maley, Karen 198
management 3
    attitude to people 261
    development of 16–17
    education policy and 114–19
    language 114–19, 125
    shareholder power and 30
    see also effectiveness
        efficiency
        public sector
Management By Objectives 125
management consultants 19, 124–6, 206–9
    CSIRO 21–2, 208
management education 18–19, 24, 40, 202
management fundamentalism 25
    bullying and 197–8
management philosophy 59, 61
management worth 204–6
managerial context 5
Mandate for Leadership (Heritage Foundation) 33
Marginson, Simon 119
market based economies
    and humanity 2, 261, 262, 289–90
    concentration of power 263
    destructiveness 3
    environment 233–4, 262
marketing 246, 253
Marsh, Ian 36
Master of Business Administration courses

see MBA courses
Maynard, Alan 43
Mayo, E. 17
media 19
    accountability 72–3
    and advertising 4, 70, 75–9
    economic rationalism 71–2
    ethics 76–7
    Olympic bid 79–81
    ownership and issues covered 69–70
    working class 73–4
Media, Entertainment and Arts Alliance 77
medical ethics 45
Medical Management Information Systems 132
mentoring 89, 90
mergers 40
Michels, Robert 86
micro managerialism 262
Milne, Frances 236
Mode (magazine) 78–9
Modern Work Practices (Saffron) 110
modernisation 16
Moir, Alan 6
Mont Pelérin Society 31–2
Moon Beams (Sinclair) 305
Moore, Des 33
moral education 295
morale 4, 23, 267
    British civil service 200
    DOCS (NSW) 193
    NZ health service 46
Morgan, Hugh 34
multiculturalism 276
multiskilling 125, 189
multi-tasking 125, 189
Murdoch, Rupert 33, 34, 70, 80, 253, 257
Murray, Les 6, 171, 240
mutualisation 294

NZCYPS
    key performance indicators 160
    quality assurance or control 161–3
Nash, Chris 72
national accounts 267
National Electricity Grid 206
National Institute of Labor Studies 20
National Investment Fund 266
National Provider Board 43
National Times (newspaper) 75
Necessary Illusions (Chomsky) 151–2

negotiating techniques 90
netball 256
networking 89, 90–1, 208
neutrality claims 17
New Zealand Children and Young Persons Service
    see NZCYPS
News Ltd 69–70, 71, 76, 80, 81, 253
News of the Day (Falahey) 52
Norma Rae (film) 90
North Broken Hill 205
North, Sam 80
Nugent, Michael 205
nurturing 266

O'Malley, P. 73
Office of the Public Advocate 100, 150
Ok Tedi 69, 71, 82-3
Olsen, L. 251
Olympic bid and the media 79–81
Oodgeroo Noonucaal 239
organisations
    culture within 164–5, 198, 212
    ethos 141–2, 287
    fragmentation 142–3, 179, 212
    male dominance in trade unions and political parties 85–93
    structures 244
    works of art 246–8
Osborne, D. 96
outsourcing
    see contracting out

PIPL 213–14
Packer, Kerry 70, 80
parents 176–7
participation 281–2
particularity 275
patient dumping 129–30
'pea' for the job 89
Peacock, Andrew 34
peer relationships and control mechanisms 218–19
performance indicators 97, 130, 150–1
    DOCS (NSW) 187
    Community Services Victoria 179
    NZCYPS 160–1
Peters, J. 17
Pharmaceutical Benefits Scheme 128
planning procedures 149, 150
play 254–8
poetry 6, 11–12, 51–2, 109–10, 171, 239–42, 305

and humanity 292, 297
Polanyi, Karl 293
police powers 148
policy making 112–13
political economic policy
 and education policy 113–19
 repositioning of 271
political literacy 286
Pollitt, C. 17, 167
Porter, Michael 34
positive thinking 17
post-modernism 288
Potential Intellectual Property Lost 213–14
power
 see control
Power Gen 206
powerlessness 4
 see also empowerment
Prescribed Benefits Schedule 129
Price Waterhouse 207, 208
Priest, John 205
privatisation 20, 42, 96, 234
 accountability 101–2, 151
 DOCS (NSW) 190, 192–3
 Victoria 146
problem manufacture 151–6
problem solving 142
productivity 44, 46, 58, 64, 212–13, 267
 see also efficiency
productivity savings 184–5
professionalism 74
 health system 122–3
 managerialism and 216–17
 see also de-professionalisation
progressive organisations 268–9
public choice theory 138, 166
public debt 153–5
public finance 235–6
Public Finance Act 1988 (NZ) 159
public sector 17–18, 20–1, 265
 denigration of 157, 235
 efficiency measures 96–104, 125, 233
 managerial role 124–7
 results emphasis 95–6, 125
 reform 166–7
  in New Zealand 41, 159–60
public sector enterprises 23, 41
 privatisation and accountability 101–2, 151
 see also corporatisation
Public Sector Research Centre 206

public sector spending 155
public servants 20–1
 cost displacement 103
 Victoria 150–1
Public Service Association 185
public sphere 72
public transport 20
Purvis, Barry 34
Pusey, Michael 114, 265, 287

Quadrant (magazine) 33, 35
quality assurance 161–3
Quality Circles 125
quality control 43, 161–3, 177, 179
quality management 117

Radcliffe, A. 20
Rand, Ayn 35
rates and contracting out 139
rationalisation 44
rationality 280
Ray, John J. 34
Rayner, Moira 149–50
recognition and identity 272–7, 280–2
Rees, Lloyd 304
Rees, Stuart 12, 241
resource creation 266
responsibility 278
Retallick, J. 200
Reworking Australia 236, 261, 268–9
right-wing think-tanks 4, 29–36, 204
Risk Management 223, 225
Road to Botany Bay (Carter) 304
Road to Serfdom (Hayek) 31
Roebuck, Peter 256
Rothbard, Murray 34
Rowe, D. 250
rugby league 76–7, 250, 253
rugby union 250, 252–3

SBS 79
Saffron, Vicki 6, 14, 54, 110, 172, 191
Said, Edward 249, 257
Sainsbury, Murray 34
Samuels, Peter 34
Sawer, Marian 33
scapegoating 176
Schumpeter, Joseph 293
scientific management
 see Taylorism
Self, Peter 157, 165
Senior Executive Service 183, 185, 186
7.30 Report (TV program) 150

Shack, Peter 34
shareholders and managers 30
sharing 255–6, 266, 267, 294
Shell Australia 35
Sheridan, Greg 32
short term contracts 217, 219
Simkin, C.G.F. 34
Simon, H. 17
Sinclair, Vivienne 305
skill formation 63
soccer 253
social contract and managerialism 213, 214
social justice 25, 290–1
social problems or individual cases 176, 177
social relations 295
social work culture and managerialism 164–5
Society for Austrian Economics 33
Society of Modest Members 34
solar energy 266
Solidarity (Polish union) 63–4
Soloski, J. 74
Sovereignty Movement 236
Special Broadcasting Service 79
spectator violence 253–4
speculative debt 155
Spirit of the Age (Brennan) 11
sport
  and managerialism 250–1
  and television 251–2, 256
  and the market 249, 253
  unemployed people and 255–6
sporting ideals 249
Stakeholder and Team (Saffron) 172
Standard and Poor 155
Star Hotel 86
State Coroner (Vic) 150
State Sector Act 1989 (NZ) 159, 166
state taxes 147
steering and rowing 96
Stilwell, Frank 250
Stockdale, Alan 156
Stone, John 34
Storey, J. 56–7
stress 21, 195, 213, 218, 219
  University of Sydney 221, 226–8
  see also human costs
Substitute Care Payment System (DOCS) 189
substitute care services 192
Sugar, Alan 257

superannuation 266
Superleague 76–7, 250, 253
sustainable development 266
Sydney Institute 33
Sydney Morning Herald (newspaper) 184
  CSIRO 21
  health costs 130–1
  management pay 204–6
  Olympic bid 80–1
  soccer 258
Symonds, Anne 93
Symons, Sandra 78–9
system and lifeworld 278–9
  see also Habermas, Jurgen
systems theory 17, 244

TNT 204
TVNZ 252
Tabcorp 205
Tawney, R.H. 31
tax reform 267
Taylor, Charles 272–7
Taylorism 17, 164, 244–5, 262
team approach 57, 267
  AWIRS 60, 61
  efficency criteria and 215–16, 218–19
technological change 263
Telecom New Zealand 43
telephones 89, 91
television and sport 251–2, 256
Thatcher, Margaret 32, 157, 289
Thinking the Unthinkable (Cockett) 30–3
think-tanks
  see right-wing think-tanks
Times (newspaper) 33
Titmuss, Richard 293
Toohey, Brian 71–2, 75
Total Quality Control (Saffron) 54
Total Quality Management 125, 126, 244–5
Tottenham Hotspur 257
toughness 16
Towers Perrin 193
Toyotaism 262
trade unions
  attacks on 20, 32, 34, 149
  Germany 64
  inflexibility claims 60–1
  male dominance and controls 85–93
  Poland 63–4

Trilling, L. 274
Troughton, Peter 43, 44
Trudeau, Garry 100
Trumbull, George 249–50
Tumbling Dice (Toohey) 71–2
Turner, B. 146
2BL (radio station) 25
Tyranny of Structurelessness (Joreen) 87

unemployment 19, 63, 147–8, 201, 263–4, 268
    green job creation 266
    sport and 255–6
universal values 17, 275–6, 288
university newspaper 198–9
University of Sydney 221–8
Unsworth, Barrie 86
Usher Report 192, 194

Vallance, Sir Ian 206
Veblen, T. 29
Verrender, I. 20, 254
Victorian Commission of Audit 103
Victorian Council of Social Service 146
vocational democracy 63
vocational training 63–5

Wade, Jan 158(n10)
Wade, Peter 205
Wald, George 302
Walker, Bob 156
Walker, Kath 239
Wallabies Top 100 club 250
Wallis, Ed 206
Walsh, Max 80
Waterman, R. 17
Weber, Max 166
Weiss, Carol 112, 116
Welder, The (Rees) 241
welfare rationing 174
    and child abuse 177
welfare workers 173–4
    managerialism and 178
    quality control 177, 179–80

Weller, P. 97
Wells Fargo Bank 198
Wells, J. 253
Westpac 198
whistle blowing 46
Whitlam, Gough 113
Wilcox, Cathy 14
Wilcox, R.C. 256
Wilding, Paul 298–9
Wills, Dean 205
Wilson, P.D. 46
Wilson, Ross 205
winning 249–50
women
    cost displacement 100–1
    establishing confidence 87–8
    exhaustion 91–2
    political parties and trade unions 86–93
    ten commandments for 92–3
    women's magazines and advertising 77–9
Wordsworth, William 6, 171
work reassessment 234–5
work-related illness 221–8
worker control 63
    see also control
Worker's Party 33
workforce segmentation 62
working class press 73–4
working hours 19, 20, 103, 189, 194–5, 213, 221–2, 245
    work sharing and 267, 294
Working Nation 263–4, 268
workloads
    see working hours
workplace organisation 58–63
Wright Mills, C. 30
Wright, Judith 297

Year 501, The Conquest Continues (Chomsky) 233
youth homelessness 147